SUCCESS
A Search for Values

AUDREY J. ROTH
MIAMI-DADE
JUNIOR COLLEGE

HOLT, RINEHART AND WINSTON, INC.
New York   Chicago   San Francisco
Atlanta   Dallas   Montreal   Toronto

For David and Sharon
because they helped so much.
May they always have success.

Copyright © 1969 by Holt, Rinehart and Winston, Inc.
All Rights Reserved
Library of Congress Catalog Card Number: 72-75925
SBN: 03-076500-5
Printed in the United States of America
1 2 3 4 5 6 7 8 9

TO THE TEACHER

This volume contains works from many media. Several different eras and cultures are represented. There are examples of fiction and nonfiction, of prose and poetry—and of pictures. The myriad of forms are bound together because all are but facets of a single idea—**success**.

Many of the words in this book will be unfamiliar to its readers. But which words are new to which people is difficult to forecast. Therefore, no vocabulary lists appear, no marginal comments or footnotes give the meaning of words which can be found in a standard dictionary.

A practical way of learning unfamiliar words is to underline them during reading. After finishing the selection, each new word can be looked up and its definition written above the word or in the margin. Making a separate list for later study is an additional aid. Or, the instructor may suggest other methods of vocabulary development that will make reading easier and more pleasurable.

Three kinds of activities that will enhance student appreciation appear after most selections in the book. In the exercise section in the back of the book they are grouped under the headings "For Understanding," "For Discussion," and "For Writing."

The items headed "For Understanding" have to do specifically with reading comprehension. However, there is no attempt to ask the kind of questions which check on whether or not a student has done assigned reading. Instead, the questions in this section concentrate on calling attention to the principal ideas and to the language or writing style of each selection.

The questions are as specific as possible. Instead of asking for "some ways you know this story was not written recently," the wording is: "List four clues in the story that show Harry did not live within the past two or three years." And page numbers are routinely requested for reference.

Each section headed "For Discussion" consists of questions or topics chosen to provoke conversation. Through them, a student can explore how he feels and what he thinks. Principally, they are topics designed to lead a student to form his own value system, especially with regard to concepts of "success." These sections might, therefore, be the focus of classroom activity.

Under the heading "For Writing" are composition suggestions that afford students the opportunity to write their own ideas on a variety of

v

vi   *To the Teacher*

topics related to the readings—always without recourse to research or other reading. The subjects selected are within the ability level of the students and should appeal to their interests. They also provide an opportunity to write in all the traditional rhetorical forms.

The advantage of immediate answers to questions on understanding a selection is obvious. Therefore, space is provided for the answers to each question.

There is also writing space in the units designed for discussion and theme writing. Taking the time and making the effort to write down notes discourages thoughtless or fruitless discussion and superficial or repetitive writing. Thus, for each discussion topic a method of approach is offered by giving the student a place to jot down basic ideas to use in his discussion; the notes also require a marshalling of thoughts. With the theme topics, too, space to write in note form the kind of information each essay ought to include will help both students and teachers.

By reading the notations students write in response to discussion and composition topics, teachers can check student preparation and progress at a glance. And often the writing done as preparation for these topics can be a valuable diagnostic tool.

Films can be an extremely useful adjunct in any search for values and their use will make this book a true multi-media presentation. Like the materials on these pages, they can become the bases of both discussion and writing. As an aid to choosing appropriate short and feature-length films, there is a list of movies which further illustrate the many forms success may take.

Miami, Florida   A. R.
January 1969

TO THE STUDENT

A student about to graduate from school goes to the placement office for help in finding a job. His interests and qualifications give him a choice:

JOB A: trainee in a large company with the prospect of a rising salary as he advances in the hierarchy, provided he fits into the "corporate image"

or

JOB B: worker in an urban ghetto area at the same starting salary but with little hope for increases and no real guarantee that the goal of his work can be completely attained

Which job should the graduate choose?

His selection will be dictated to a great extent by his values—by those principles which govern his behavior and give direction to his life.

The values a person chooses to live by are very personal. Two people may be subject to the same forces of custom, attitudes of friends and family, economic and social pressures. But in the end, choices are made by an individual because of his own special combination of experiences and ideas and beliefs.

The meaning of "success," for example, depends upon the values of the person defining the word. If it means having material possessions or social status to the graduate in the example above, perhaps he would choose the corporation job. If it means the chance to make contact with individuals and work with them meaningfully, perhaps he would choose to work in the ghetto.

One way to arrive at a personal code of beliefs, or values, is to examine the choices that are open and how other people have acted, and then to make a personal decision. Reading, looking, thinking, listening—these are the ways to discover what is available before deciding what has worth or merit to you, personally.

This volume examines the many aspects of only one value: success. Its purpose is to help an individual in his search for meaning and attitude toward this single concern.

vii

viii   *To the Student*

To that end, this book is divided into three sections. The first provides examples of traditional "success stories," the ideals that have, in the past, been held up as goals to achieve. Many of them are still valid goals, to be sure; some of them may no longer be considered worth attaining because of changing times and circumstances.

The second section of this book offers examples of successes achieved by group action. In time, they range from the conquest of Mexico to the conquest of space. In subject, they vary from science to personal relations.

Finally, section three offers a variety of personal touch-stones for success exemplified (as in the other sections) by story, poem, cartoon, essay, speech, and advertisement. They were selected for what they could say about—and to—individuals, as well as for the method of communication. To people more likely to read newspapers than philosophy books, to listen to music rather than orations, and to talk about ads instead of ideas, what appears in the familiar forms (including the films listed near the end of this book) is more meaningful than what is strange. We may not believe, for instance, that using the right mouthwash will help us find the right marriage mate, but we all know that such a method is widely publicized as the route to that goal—the way to individual success.

Some of the people, acts, and ideas in these three sections you will believe commendable. Some you will not. Which falls into each category is personal, open to discussion and examination, and probably not final. But from the diverse genre and media represented in this book will come, hopefully, the individual choice and private commitment which forms a personal set of values regarding success.

Miami, Florida   A. R.
January 1969

CONTENTS

TO THE TEACHER	v
TO THE STUDENT	vii

PART I *TRADITIONAL SUCCESS STORIES*

Introduction	3
How We Feel about Our Money (questionnaires)	
MAX GUNTHER	4
Montage of Success Stories	9
$500,000 Thaws Peggy's Icy Outlook	10
Exercise, page 213	
Harry	
WILLIAM SAROYAN	11
Exercise, page 219	
Businessman Who Can't Fail (cartoon)	
JEAN-JACQUES SEMPÉ	18
The Ruler of the Queen's Navee	
WILLIAM S. GILBERT	22
Exercise, page 227	
You Got to Be a Hero	
ROBERT CRICHTON	24
Exercise, page 233	
Boy with balloon (cartoon)	
WARREN MILLER	30
Success Rushed Up to Pat Palmer	
MARTIN ABRAMSON	31
Exercise, page 241	
Richest of the American Rich	
TIME	34
Strength in 77 Seconds (advertisement)	35
The Personal Rolls-Royce—$19,600 (advertisement)	36
Moon Cooperated for Greenes' Party	
HELEN WELLS	38
Eight Days to Foreclosure and Family Strikes Silver	39
Exercise, page 247	
Man on Globe (cartoon)	
MORT GERBERG	40

ix

x   *Contents*

If at First You Don't Succeed . . . Skip It
    MIKE ROYKO   41
        Exercise, page 251
Anne Marie and Steven
    NEWSWEEK   43
How Savitri Retrieved Her Husband from Death
    trans. OROON GHOSH   45
        Exercise, page 255
Richard Cory
    EDWIN ARLINGTON ROBINSON   49
        Exercise, page 261
Ozymandias
    PERCY BYSSHE SHELLEY   50
Ozymandias Revisited
    MORRIS BISHOP   51
        Exercise, page 265

PART II *GROUP SUCCESS*

Introduction   55

Most successful suit sale (cartoon)
    SID HOFF   57
The Overshoe
    MIKHAIL ZOSHCHENKO, trans. SIDNEY MONAS   58
        Exercise, page 269
Robot at M.I.T. Builds Towers Out of Toy Blocks
    ROBERT REINHOLD   61
        Exercise, page 273
How Plays Shape Up on Great White Way   63
Tactical Missiles: A Report from General Dynamics   64
(advertisement)
        Exercise, page 277
As U.S. Speeds Up the Space Race
    U.S. NEWS AND WORLD REPORT   66
        Exercise, page 283
Historic Voices from Space (dialogue)
    U.S. NEWS AND WORLD REPORT   67
*How a U.S. Astronaut "Walked" from Hawaii to Florida in
20 Minutes*
    U.S. NEWS AND WORLD REPORT   68
from *THE BERNAL DIAZ CHRONICLES*
    trans. ALBERT IDELL   70
        Exercise, page 289
from *"Underwater Bonanza"* in *PIECES OF EIGHT*
    KIP WAGNER as told to L. B. TAYLOR, JR.   75
        Exercise, page 295

Contents   xi

from *The Mouse That Roared*
    LEONARD WIBBERLEY   80
        Exercise, page 299
from *Through History with J. Wesley Smith* (cartoon)
    BURR SHAFER   84
Making Park Promise Good   85
        Exercise, page 305
from *"Where We Are Going"* in
    WHERE DO WE GO FROM HERE: CHAOS OR COMMUNITY?
    MARTIN LUTHER KING, JR.   86
        Exercise, page 307

PART III   *INDIVIDUAL SUCCESS*

Introduction   91
Peanuts (cartoon)
    CHARLES SCHULZ   92
Kindly Unhitch That Star, Buddy
    OGDEN NASH   93
        Exercise, page 311
Grandmother, 62, Runs 100 Miles for a T-Shirt   94
Policeman in Brooklyn Lassoes Zebra in Bay   95
The Ghost Horse
    CHIEF BUFFALO CHILD LONG LANCE   96
        Exercise, page 315
The Ego Trap
    LEONARD SCHECTER   104
The Notorious Jumping Frog of Calaveras County
    MARK TWAIN   105
        Exercise, page 319
18-Foot Leap Wins Frog-Jumping Title   111
Elopement (cartoon)
    MORDILLO   112
A Sure Way to Succeed from
    THE MIDRASH   113
The Passionate Shepherd to His Love
    CHRISTOPHER MARLOWE   114
The Nymph's Reply to the Shepherd
    SIR WALTER RALEIGH   115
        Exercise, page 323
Cleopatra's Joke on Marc Anthony: 40 B.C.
    PLUTARCH   116
"... and of course you all remember ...." (cartoon)
    CHARLES RODRIGUES   117
Miniver Cheevy
    EDWIN ARLINGTON ROBINSON   118
        Exercise, page 327

xii   *Contents*

Davy, the Dicer
    SIR THOMAS MORE   120
The Way Up to Heaven
    ROALD DAHL
        Exercise, page 331   121
The Verger
    W. SOMERSET MAUGHAM   133
        Exercise, page 337
from *Men Who Manage*
    MELVILLE DALTON   140
        Exercise, page 342
Japanese Child Eats Nails After Viewing Stunt on TV   143
Academy of Sciences Chooses 50 Members and 10
Associates   144
The First Great Woman Scientist—And Much More
    SUSAN RAVEN   146
        Exercise, page 347
from *"The Wrath of Achilles" in*
THE ILIAD OF HOMER
    trans. I. A. RICHARDS   159
        Exercise, page 353
Studies for Guernica   163
Guernica
    PABLO PICASSO   165
from *The Real Black Power*
    TIME   166
        Exercise, page 359
from *Fidel Castro Speaks*
    trans. PAUL E. SIGMUND   168
        Exercise, page 363
The Wonderful Dog Suit
    DONALD HALL   171
        Exercise, page 367
A Bachelor at 16
    TIME   173
        Exercise, page 371
from *PYGMALION,* Act III
    GEORGE BERNARD SHAW   175
        Exercise, page 375
The Day the Mouse Roared   (advertisement)   180
Chapter 2 of *The Pearl*
    JOHN STEINBECK   181
        Exercise, page 379
Existence
    GUADALUPE DE SAAVEDRA   186
        Exercise, page 385

Contents   xiii

from *DON QUIXOTE OF LA MANCHA*
    by MIGUEL DE CERVANTES, trans. WALTER STARKIE   187
      Exercise, page 287
Success is something you can't leave a son
(advertisement)   191
from *The Explainers* (cartoon)
    JULES FEIFFER   192
      Exercise, page 393
When She Lost Pounds, Fat Friends Left at Same Time
    ANN LANDERS   194
Tongue Twisters
    ARNOLD ARNOLD   195
Dream Variation
    LANGSTON HUGHES   196
James Brown Sells His Soul
    MEL ZIEGLER   197
      Exercise, page 397
Nehru Speaks to Mourning Millions
    NEHRU   204
      Exercise, page 401
"The odd thing about assassins . . . ." (cartoon)
    BILL MAULDIN   206
from *"I Have a Dream"*
    MARTIN LUTHER KING, JR.   207
      Exercise, page 405
I May, I Might, I Must
    MARIANNE MOORE   209

EXERCISES   211

APPENDIXES   409

    Biographical Notes   411
    Using Films   419
      Short Films   420
      Full-Length Films   422

INDEX   425

ALTERNATE CONTENTS BY GENRE

PLAYS

from *PYGMALION*
GEORGE BERNARD SHAW 175

POEMS

The Ruler of the Queen's Navee
WILLIAM S. GILBERT 22
Richard Cory
EDWIN ARLINGTON ROBINSON 49
Ozymandias
PERCY BYSSHE SHELLEY 50
Ozymandias Revisited
MORRIS BISHOP 51
Kindly Unhitch that Star, Buddy
OGDEN NASH 93
The Passionate Shepherd to His Love
CHRISTOPHER MARLOWE 114
The Nymph's Reply to the Shepherd
SIR WALTER RALEIGH 115
Miniver Cheevy
EDWIN ARLINGTON ROBINSON 118
Davy, the Dicer
SIR THOMAS MORE 120
Existence
GUADALUPE DE SAAVEDRA 186
Dream Variation
LANGSTON HUGHES 196
I May, I Might, I Must
MARIANNE MOORE 209

SPEECHES

Fidel Castro Speaks
trans. PAUL E. SIGMUND 168

Alternate Contents by Genre xv

Nehru Speaks to Mourning Millions
    NEHRU 204
from *I Have a Dream*
    MARTIN LUTHER KING, JR. 207

SHORT STORIES

Harry
    WILLIAM SAROYAN 11
How Savitri Retrieved Her Husband from Death
    trans. OROON GHOSH 45
The Overshoe
    MIKHAIL ZOSHCHENKO 58
The Notorious Jumping Frog of Calaveras County
    MARK TWAIN 105
The Way Up to Heaven
    ROALD DAHL 121
The Verger
    W. SOMERSET MAUGHAM 133
The Wonderful Dog Suit
    DONALD HALL 171

FROM LONGER FICTION

from *THE MOUSE THAT ROARED*
    LEONARD WIBBERLEY 80
from *THE ILIAD OF HOMER*
    trans. I. A. RICHARDS 159
from *THE PEARL*
    JOHN STEINBECK 181
from *DON QUIXOTE OF LA MANCHA*
    trans. WALTER STARKIE 187

NONFICTION (ESSAYS)

You Got to Be a Hero
    ROBERT CRICHTON 24
Success Rushed Up to Pat Palmer
    MARTIN ABRAMSON 31
If At First You Don't Succeed . . . Skip It
    MIKE ROYKO 41
The Ghost Horse
    CHIEF BUFFALO CHILD LONG LANCE 96
The First Great Woman Scientist—And Much More
    SUSAN RAVEN 146
James Brown Sells His Soul
    MEL ZIEGLER 197

xvi   *Alternate Contents by Genre*

FROM LONGER NONFICTION

from *THE BERNAL DIAZ CHRONICLES*
    trans. ALBERT IDELL   70
from *PIECES OF EIGHT*
    KIP WAGNER as told to L. B. TAYLOR, JR.   75
from *WHERE DO WE GO FROM HERE: CHAOS OR
COMMUNITY?*
    MARTIN LUTHER KING, JR.   86
from *MEN WHO MANAGE*
    MELVILLE DALTON   140

NEWS STORIES

$500,000 Thaws Peggy's Icy Outlook   10
Eight Days to Foreclosure and Family Strikes Silver   39
Anne Marie and Steven
    NEWSWEEK   43
Robot at M.I.T. Builds Towers Out of Toy Blocks
    ROBERT REINHOLD   61
As U.S. Speeds Up the Space Race
    U.S. NEWS AND WORLD REPORT   66
Historic Voices from Space
    U.S. NEWS AND WORLD REPORT   67
*How a U.S. Astronaut "Walked" from Hawaii to Florida in
20 Minutes*
    U.S. NEWS AND WORLD REPORT   68
Making Park Promise Good   85
18-Foot Leap Wins Frog-Jumping Title   111
from *The Real Black Power*
    TIME   166
A Bachelor at 16
    TIME   173

OTHER NONFICTION

How We Feel About Our Money
    MAX GUNTHER   4
Moon Cooperated for Greenes' Party
    HELEN WELLS   38
When She Lost Pounds, Fat Friends Left at Same Time
    ANN LANDERS   194

ADVERTISEMENTS

Strength in 77 Seconds   35
The Personal Rolls-Royce—$19,600   36

Alternate Contents by Genre   xvii

Tactical Missiles: A Report from General Dynamics   64
The Day the Mouse Roared   180
Success is something you can't leave a son   191

CARTOONS

Businessman Who Can't Fail
    JEAN-JACQUES SEMPÉ   18
Boy With Balloon
    WARREN MILLER   30
Man on Globe
    MORT GERBERG   40
"Most successful suit sale . . ."
    SID HOFF   57
from *THROUGH HISTORY WITH J. WESLEY SMITH*
    BURR SHAFER   84
Peanuts
    CHARLES SCHULZ   92
Elopement
    MORDILLO   112
". . . and of course you all remember . . ."
    CHARLES RODRIGUES   117
from *THE EXPLAINERS*
    JULES FEIFFER   192
"The odd thing about assassins . . ."
    BILL MAULDIN   206

PAINTING

Guernica
    PICASSO   (mural and 4 studies)   163

LISTS, FILLERS, QUOTATIONS

ALTERNATE CONTENTS
BY RHETORICAL FORM

PERSUASION

The Personal Rolls-Royce   (advertisement)   36
from *WHERE DO WE GO FROM HERE: CHAOS OR COMMUNITY?*
      MARTIN LUTHER KING, JR.   86
Fidel Castro Speaks
      trans. PAUL E. SIGMUND   168
from *DON QUIXOTE OF LA MANCHA*
      by MIGUEL DE CERVANTES, trans. WALTER STARKIE   187
Success is something you can't leave a son   (advertisement)   191
Nehru Speaks to Mourning Millions   204
from *"I Have a Dream"*
      MARTIN LUTHER KING, JR.   207

PERSONAL DESCRIPTION

Success Rushed Up to Pat Palmer
      MARTIN ABRAMSON   31
If at First You Don't Succeed . . . Skip It
      MIKE ROYKO   41
The Real Black Power
      TIME   166
A Bachelor at 16
      TIME   173
James Brown Sells His Soul
      MEL ZIEGLER   197

DESCRIPTION

You Got to Be a Hero   24
The Personal Rolls-Royce   (advertisement)   36
Moon Cooperated for Greenes' Party   38
Tactical Missiles: A Report from General Dynamics
(advertisement)   64
from *THE BERNAL DIAZ CHRONICLES*
      trans. ALBERT IDELL   70

Alternate Contents by Rhetorical Form   xix

from *PIECES OF EIGHT*
 KIP WAGNER as told to L. B. TAYLOR, JR. 75
The First Great Woman Scientist — And Much More
 SUSAN RAVEN 146
from *THE PEARL*
 JOHN STEINBECK 181

HUMOR

If at First You Don't Succeed . . . Skip It
 MIKE ROYKO 44
The Overshoe
 MIKHAIL ZOSHCHENKO, trans. SIDNEY MONAS 58
from *THE MOUSE THAT ROARED*
 LEONARD WIBBERLEY 80
The Notorious Jumping Frog of Calaveras County
 MARK TWAIN 105

NARRATIVE

Harry
 WILLIAM SAROYAN 11
How Savitri Retrieved Her Husband from Death
 trans. OROON GHOSH 45
The Overshoe
 MIKHAIL ZOSHCHENKO 58
from *THE BERNAL DIAZ CHRONICLES*
 trans. ALBERT IDELL 70
from *PIECES OF EIGHT*
 KIP WAGNER as told to L. B. TAYLOR, JR. 75
from *THE MOUSE THAT ROARED*
 LEONARD WIBBERLEY 80
The Notorious Jumping Frog of Calaveras County
 MARK TWAIN 105
A Sure Way to Succeed
 THE MIDRASH 113
Cleopatra's Joke on Marc Anthony: 40 B.C. 116
The Way Up to Heaven
 ROALD DAHL 121
The Verger
 W. SOMERSET MAUGHAM 133
from *THE ILIAD OF HOMER*
 trans. I. A. RICHARDS 159
The Wonderful Dog Suit
 DONALD HALL 171
from *THE PEARL*
 JOHN STEINBECK 181

xx   *Alternate Contents by Rhetorical Form*

EXPOSITION

$500,000 Thaws Peggy's Icy Outlook	10
You Got to Be a Hero	
ROBERT CRICHTON	24
Success Rushed Up to Pat Palmer	
MARTIN ABRAMSON	31
Eight Days to Foreclosure and Family Strikes Silver	39
Anne Marie and Steven	
NEWSWEEK	43
Robot at M.I.T. Builds Towers Out of Toy Blocks	
ROBERT REINHOLD	61
Tactical Missiles: A Report from General Dynamics	
(advertisement)	64
As U.S. Speeds Up the Space Race	
U.S. NEWS AND WORLD REPORT	66
How a U.S. Astronaut "Walked" from Hawaii to Florida in	
20 minutes	
U.S. NEWS AND WORLD REPORT	68
from WHERE DO WE GO FROM HERE: CHAOS OR COMMUNITY?	
MARTIN LUTHER KING, JR.	86
The Ghost Horse	
CHIEF BUFFALO CHILD LONG LANCE	96
18-Foot Leap Wins Frog-Jumping Title	111
The First Great Woman Scientist . . . And Much More	
SUSAN RAVEN	146
from DON QUIXOTE OF LA MANCHA	
by MIGUEL DE CERVANTES, trans. WALTER STARKIE	187

PART 1

*Traditional
Success Stories*

3
91

Introduction

What is the standard by which we measure success? Is it a Cadillac? A passing report card? A wedding announcement? A big bank balance? Perhaps these are just the symbols of success rather than the quality itself.

Ask a millionaire to define success for you. Ask a public official, a professor, a farmer, a ditch digger, a friend. Ask yourself. The chances are that each person will give you a different definition—or a different set of symbols.

Success means achieving a goal, fulfilling an ideal. But whose goal? The goals—and symbols of those goals—used to be rather well defined in our society: they were money or social status, preferably both, and they were materialistic.

Horatio Alger was a national hero. As a novelist's creation, this boy who rose from rags to riches by hard work and "right" living, became an example for all boys to imitate. His moral uprightness helped, but only in order for him to achieve the riches.

Girls could always follow the example of Cinderella and *her* rise from the fireplace of her harsh stepmother's house to the throne room of the castle. Handsome princes (and fairy godmothers) have always been in somewhat short supply, so the acceptable substitute has become marrying the boss's son.

Individuals achieved these successes. And generally they did so by themselves.

"Of course," we murmur, "there were more chances in 'those days.'"

The cowboy could swagger down the dusty frontier street; his only responsibilities were to keep his horse well fed and his manliness unquestioned. If anybody threatened either, his trusty six-shooter settled the argument.

The man with an idea for a business could get right to work: no lawyers to incorporate him or accountants to keep him in the clear with the government, no unions to contend with and no syndicates to compete with.

These success stories are all too familiar; we have been brought up with them on TV and in the movies. Many people have never questioned such traditional goals or sought to understand their purposes. They have been there. The fashion has been to believe that such goals, and their evidence of success, are desirable.

3

4   *Success: A Search for Values*

There are many such representations of these traditional kinds of success evidenced in this section by fiction and non-fiction, ads and essays, stories and poems. They include such subjects as sports, business, society, love, political power, and, of course, money. Most are spectacular. And most emphasize the materialism which has long been the mode of American life.

Some of these examples of success you will agree with. You will decide that they are what you yourself would like to achieve. Others, you will determine, are not at all what you want. But after reading this section you will at least know what some of the choices are, and you will be more knowledgeable when it comes to eventually choosing the values you want to live by.

How We Feel
*about Our Money**

Max Gunther

On a street of clean but aging apartment houses in Boston, Robert J. Gill sat in the Saturday-morning sunshine and contemplated his future. Gill, a young man in his 20's, had been buttonholed by a lady polltaker from Roper Research Associates. They were talking about money. "Would you like to be wealthy?" she asked.

"Of course," he replied, grinning. His tone suggested that he thought the question silly.

"Do you expect to be wealthy?"

He looked serious. "Expect to? I'm *planning* to."

The United States is an interesting country, and this is an interesting time to be living in it. Never before in world history has a nation been so affluent that its ordinary citizens could coolly plan for wealth. To become rich used to be an idle dream —and, in many parts of the world, still is. It used to be the subject of fairy tales. Now, quite suddenly, the fairy tale has become real. . . .

---

* Reprinted from Max Gunther, "How We Feel about Our Money," *Saturday Evening Post*, December 30, 1967, by permission of the author. Reprinted with permission of *The Saturday Evening Post* © 1967 The Curtis Publishing Company.

Traditional Success Stories   5

TO GET RICH FAST...

For a million dollars, would you:

	yes	no
• leave your family permanently?	☐	☐
• give up your American citizenship?	☐	☐
• marry someone you didn't love?	☐	☐
• give up all your friends permanently?	☐	☐
• take off your clothes in public?	☐	☐
• serve a year's jail term on a framed charge?	☐	☐
• take a dangerous job in which you had a 1-in-10 chance of losing your life?	☐	☐
• become a beggar for a year?	☐	☐

Of the people polled, 1% would leave their families, 4% would yield citizenship, 10% would marry lovelessly, 11% would give up friends, 12% would undress, 13% would go to jail, 14% would take the risky job. But 21% would beg.

Reprinted with permission of *The Saturday Evening Post.* © 1967 The Curtis Publishing Company, and with permission of the author. Artwork © Richard Erdoes.

Success: A Search for Values

1. If you saw a penny lying on the street, would you pick it up?

   yes ☐ no ☐

2. If someone gave you a $20 bill, and it later turned out to be counterfeit, would you:

   turn it in? ☐   spend it? ☐

3. Do you think quite a lot of people, or very few, cheat on their income tax?

   a lot ☐   a few ☐

4. If you were working at a job where you knew that one of your co-workers whom you liked was taking small sums of money from your employer, would you:

   say nothing about it? ☐
   tell the person to stop? ☐
   tell your employer? ☐
   tell the police? ☐

5. Do you feel you are paid what you're worth, or less, or more?

   paid right ☐   paid less ☐   paid more ☐

6. Do you live about as comfortably as your parents did when they were your age, or less comfortably, or more?

   same ☐   less ☐   more ☐

7. Do you expect to get a raise every year or two?

   yes ☐   no ☐

8. What is the highest yearly salary that anyone should be allowed to get in this country?

   $_____

Traditional Success Stories 7

9. If you were working for a company that was having a difficult time financially, and everyone was asked to take a 10 percent pay cut, would you take the cut or quit?
take cut ☐   quit ☐

10. If you had to choose between these two kinds of jobs, which would you pick:
one that was satisfying and paid a modest income? ☐
one that you didn't like but that paid a high income? ☐

11. If someone gave you $2,500 tax-free and said you could triple it at the toss of a coin or lose it all, would you take the chance?
yes ☐   no ☐

12. If your whole income suddenly stopped, could you live for six months just the way you are living now if you used your savings, investments and ready cash?
yes ☐   no ☐

13. If you had to choose between supporting your elderly parents in a rest home and sending your children to college, which would you choose?
parents in rest home? ☐
children to college? ☐

14. Would you like to be wealthy?
yes ☐   no ☐

15. Do you ever expect to be wealthy?
yes ☐   no ☐

How people coast-to-coast answered the questions

1. Only 9% wouldn't pick up the cent; 2% couldn't decide. **2**. 86% would turn in the counterfeit bill—or say they would. **3**. More men than women— 61% to 45%—suspect there is a lot of tax cheating. **4**. While no one at all would report the company thief to the cops, only 13% would keep mum: 15% of us would tattle to the boss, and 67% would scold the thief. **5**. Almost half of us feel underpaid; 3% feel overpaid. **6**. Three fourths feel they live better than Dad did. **7**. And three fourths expect that raise. **8**. 73% insisted there be *no* limit on pay, but 4% felt $20,000 should be tops. **9**. Fewer of the rich (16%) would quit than would people in general (21%). **10**. Only 15% would take the nasty, high-paying job. **11**. Just one quarter of us would try to triple the $2,500, but 42% of the wealthy would. **12**. 46% of us could last six months on savings, etc.; 66% of the poorest group couldn't. **13**. A majority (and more women than men) would send the kids to college instead of the old folks to a home. **14**. 56% would like to be wealthy. **15**. But just 12% actually expect to be, and another 1% announced they already are.

Traditional Success Stories 9

"Baseball Standings": Reprinted by permission of the *Miami* (Florida) *Herald*. "Pop Records": Copyright © by Pop Scene Service. Reprinted from the Pop Scene Service by permission of Bell-McClure Syndicate. "2,800 High School Students": © 1968 by The New York Times Company. Reprinted by permission. "Montreal Ices Eastern Crown," "Horse Race Results," and "Greyhound Results": Reprinted by permission of the *Miami* (Florida) *Herald*. "Alltime Bestsellers": Reprinted from *Seventy Years of Best Sellers* by Alice Payne Hackett, by permission of R. R. Bowker Company.

Success: A Search for Values

ON PROFESSIONAL SKATING CAREER

$500,000 THAWS
PEGGY'S ICY OUTLOOK*

GRENOBLE, France — (AP) — Glamorous Peggy Fleming, the new Olympic figure skating queen, will sign a $500,000 contract to skate with the Ice Follies, The Associated Press learned Saturday night.

The follies, bidding against two other world famous professional ice shows, have made the slender 19-year-old beauty from Colorado Springs an offer that is almost impossible for her to refuse.

Under the arrangement, she will perform only in the major cities. She will still have time to follow her desired pursuits — possible marriage, return to Colorado College for a degree and a later career as a kindergarten school teacher.

Both Peggy and her widowed mother, Mrs. Albert Fleming, have steadfastly denied any consideration of a professional career for one of America's foremost feminine sports personalities.

"I only want to win the Olympic Gold Medal," Peggy said repeatedly to questions of her future intentions.

Recently, after taking a big lead in the Olympic competition, she gave a hint that her eyes might be on a temporary fling at show business. "A girl my age can do many things," she said.

* **Reprinted from Associated Press Newsfeatures.**

Her mother said, "I want Peggy to finish college. Her father would have wanted it. We aren't interested in a professional career for her."

Traditionally, Olympic figure skating queens take on the aura of movie and theater celebrities.

Sonja Henie made a fortune after her Olympic triumphs. Tenley Albright, the Bostonian who won in 1956, spurned rich offers to become a prominent doctor. Carol Heiss, the champion in 1960, took a fling at television spectaculars but quit to become a housewife.

Peggy is an unusual commodity — strikingly beautiful, talented and with a nice personality that is almost electric.

She is 5 feet 4 inches and weighs 110 pounds — a svelte, graceful girl who spins, jumps and pirouettes over the ice like a talented ballerina.

With raven hair which she wears in a high bun and eyes that are a mixture of blue and green, she has a classical beauty.

Every time she takes to the rink, an excitement sweeps through the stadium and people press to rails to watch her in action. Even her competitors stop to look and marvel. There's hardly a sound as she whirls through her routine.

It is the mark of a queen.

[SEE EXERCISE ON PAGE 213]

Traditional Success Stories   11

> *Some people seem to have a "golden touch." Whatever they do turns out right. They can submit a report on sugar production that rates an A; they can take an annoying "ping" out of a car motor almost by looking at it.*
>
> *Harry's "golden touch" has to do with making money. He is, therefore, in many ways a personification of the American tradition (sometimes also called a myth) that anyone can "make good"—that is, make money—by ingenuity and perseverance.*

*Harry**

William Saroyan

This boy was a worldbeater. Everything he touched turned to money, and at the age of fourteen he had over six hundred dollars in the Valley Bank, money he had made by himself. He was born to sell things. At eight or nine he was ringing door bells and showing housewives beautiful colored pictures of Jesus Christ and other holy people—from the Novelty Manufacturing Company, Toledo, Ohio—fifteen cents each, four for a half dollar. "Lady," he was saying at that early age, "this is Jesus. Look. Isn't it a pretty picture? And only fifteen cents. This is Paul, I think. Maybe Moses. You know. From the Bible."

He had all the houses in the foreign district full of these pictures, and many of the houses still have them, so you can see that he exerted a pretty good influence, after all.

After a while he went around getting subscriptions for *True Stories Magazine*. He would stand on a front porch and open a copy of the magazine, showing pictures. "Here is a lady," he would say, "who married a man thirty years older than her, and then fell in love with the man's sixteen-year-old son. Lady, what would *you* have done in such a fix? Read what this lady did. All true stories, fifteen of them every month. Romance, mystery, passion, violent lust, everything from A to Z. Also editorials on dreams. They explain what your dreams mean, if you are going

---

* From *After 30 Years: The Daring Young Man on the Flying Trapeze*, copyright, 1934, 1962, by William Saroyan. Reprinted by permission of Harcourt, Brace & World, Inc.

12   *Success: A Search for Values*

on a voyage, if money is coming to you, who you are going to marry, all true meanings, scientific. Also beauty secrets, how to look young all the time."

In less than two months he had over sixty married women reading the magazine. Maybe he wasn't responsible, but after a while a lot of unconventional things began to happen. One or two wives had secret love affairs with other men and were found out by their husbands, who beat them or kicked them out of their houses, and a half dozen women began to send away for eye-lash beautifiers, bath salts, cold creams and things of that sort. The whole foreign neighborhood was getting to be slightly immoral. All the ladies began to rouge their lips and powder their faces and wear silk stockings and tight sweaters.

When he was a little older, Harry began to buy used cars, Fords, Maxwells, Saxons, Chevrolets and other small cars. He used to buy them a half dozen at a time in order to get them cheap, fifteen or twenty dollars each. He would have them slightly repaired, he would paint them red or blue or some other bright color, and he would sell them to high school boys for three and four times as much as he had paid for them. He filled the town with red and blue and green used automobiles, and the whole countryside was full of them, high school boys taking their girls to the country at night and on Sunday afternoons, and anybody knows what that means. In a way, it was a pretty good thing for the boys, only a lot of them had to get married a long time before they had found jobs for themselves, and a number of other things happened, only worse. Two or three girls had babies and didn't know who the other parent was, because two or three fellows with used cars had been involved. In a haphazard way, though, a lot of girls got husbands for themselves.

Harry himself was too busy to fool around with girls. All he wanted was to keep on making money. By the time he was seventeen he had earned a small fortune, and he looked to be one of the best-dressed young men in town. He got his suits wholesale because he wouldn't think of letting anyone make a profit on him. It was his business to make the profits. If a suit was marked twenty-seven fifty, Harry would offer the merchant twelve dollars.

"Don't tell *me*," he would say. "I know what these rags cost. At twelve dollars you will be making a clean profit of two dollars and fifty cents, and that's enough for anybody. You can take it or leave it."

He generally got the suit for fifteen dollars, alterations included. He would argue an hour about the alterations. If the coat

Traditional Success Stories 13

was a perfect fit and the merchant told him so, Harry would think he was being taken for a sucker, so he would insist that the sleeves were too long or that the shoulders were too loose. The only reason merchants tolerated him at all was that he had the reputation of being well-dressed, and to sell him a suit was to get a lot of good free advertising. It would bring a lot of other young fellows to the store, fellows who would buy suits at regular prices.

Otherwise, Harry was a nuisance. Not only that, the moment he made a purchase he would begin to talk about reciprocity, how it was the basis of American business, and he would begin to sell the merchant earthquake insurance or a brand new Studebaker. And most of the time he would succeed. All sorts of business people bought earthquake insurance just to stop Harry talking. He chiseled and he took for granted chiseling in others, so he always quoted chisel-proof prices, and then came down to the regular prices. It made his customers feel good. It pleased them to think that they had put one over on Harry, but he always had a quiet laugh to himself.

One year the whole San Joaquin valley was nearly ruined by a severe frost that all but wiped out a great crop of grapes and oranges. Harry got into his Studebaker and drove into the country. Frost-bitten oranges were absolutely worthless because the Board of Health wouldn't allow them to be marketed, but Harry had an idea. He went out to the orange groves, and looked at the trees loaded with fruit that was now worthless. He talked to the farmers and told them how sorry he was.

Then he said:

"But maybe I can help you out a little. I can use your frost-bitten oranges . . . for hog and cattle feed. Hogs don't care if an orange is frost-bitten, and the juice is good for them the same way it's good for people . . . vitamins. You don't have to do anything. I'll have the oranges picked and hauled away, and I'll give you a check for twenty-five dollars, spot cash."

That year he sent over twenty truck loads of frost-bitten oranges to Los Angeles for the orange-juice stands, and he cleaned up another small fortune.

Everyone said he could turn anything into money. He could figure a way of making money out of anything. When the rest of the world was down in the mouth, Harry was on his toes, working on the Los Angeles angle of disposing of bad oranges.

He never bothered about having an office. The whole town was his office, and whenever he wanted to sit down, he would go up to the eighth floor of Cory Building and sit in M. Peters'

14 *Success: A Search for Values*

office, and chew the rag with the attorney. He would talk along casually, but all the time he would be finding out about contracts, and how to make people come through with money, and how to attach property, and so on. A lot of people were in debt to him, and he meant to get his money.

He had sold electric refrigerators, vacuum cleaners, radios, and a lot of other modern things to people who couldn't afford to buy them, and he had sold these things simply by talking about them, and by showing catalogue pictures of them. The customer had to pay freight and everything else. All Harry did was talk and sell. If a man couldn't pay cash for a radio, Harry would get five dollars down and a note for the balance, and if the man couldn't make his payments, Harry would attach the man's home, or his vineyard, or his automobile, or his horse, or anything else the man owned. And the amazing thing was that no one ever criticized him for his business methods. He was very smooth about attaching a man's property, and he would calmly explain that it was the usual procedure, according to law. What was right was right.

No one could figure out what Harry wanted with so much money. He already had money in the bank, a big car, and he wasn't interested in girls; so what was he saving up all the money for? A few of his customers sometimes asked him, and Harry would look confused a moment, as if he himself didn't know, and then he would come out and say:

"I want to get hold of a half million dollars so I can retire."

It was pretty funny, Harry thinking of retiring at eighteen. He had left high school in his first year because he hadn't liked the idea of sitting in a class room listening to a lot of nonsense about starting from the bottom and working up, and so on, and ever since he had been on the go, figuring out ways to make money.

Sometimes people would ask him what he intended to do after he retired, and Harry would look puzzled again, and finally he would say, "Oh, I guess I'll take a trip around the world."

"Well, if he does," everyone thought, "he'll sell something everywhere he goes. He'll sell stuff on the trains and on the boats and in the foreign cities. He won't waste a minute looking around. He'll open a catalogue and sell them foreigners everything you can think of."

But things happen in a funny way, and you can never tell about people, even about people like Harry. Anybody is liable to get sick. Death and sickness play no favorites; they come to all

Traditional Success Stories 15

men. Presidents and kings and movie stars, they all die, they all get sick.

Even Harry got sick. Not mildly, not merely something casual like the flu that you can get over in a week, and be as good as new again. Harry got T.B. and he got it in a bad way, poor kid.

Well, the sickness got Harry, and all that money of his in the Valley Bank didn't help him a lot. Of course he did try to rest for a while, but that was out of the question. Lying in bed, Harry would try to sell life insurance to his best friends. Harry's cousin, Simon Gregory, told me about this. He said it wasn't that Harry really wanted more money; it was simply that he couldn't open his mouth unless it was to make a sales talk. He couldn't carry on an ordinary conversation because he didn't know the first thing about anything that didn't have something to do with insurance, or automobiles, or real estate. If somebody tried to talk politics or maybe religion, Harry would look irritated, and he would start to make a sales talk. He even asked Simon Gregory how old he was, and when Simon said that he was twenty-two, Harry got all excited.

"Listen, Simon," he said, "you are my cousin, and I want to do you a favor. You haven't a day to lose if you intend to be financially independent when you are sixty-five. I have just the policy you need. Surely you can afford to pay six dollars and twenty-seven cents a month for the next forty-three years. You won't be able to go to many shows; but what is more important, to see a few foolish moving pictures, or to be independent when you are sixty-five?"

It almost made Simon bawl to hear Harry talking that way, sick as he was.

The doctor told Harry's folks that Harry ought to go down to Arizona for a year or two, that it was his only hope, but when they talked the matter over with Harry, he got sore and said the doctor was trying to get him to spend his money. He said he was all right, just a cold in the chest, and he told his folks to ask the doctor to stay away. "Get some other doctor," he said. "Why should I go down to Arizona?"

Every now and then we would see Harry in town, talking rapidly to someone, trying to sell something, but it would be for only a day or two, and then he would have to go back to bed. He kept this up for about two years, and you ought to see the change that came over that poor boy. It was really enough to make you feel rotten. To look at him you would think he was the loneliest person on earth, but the thing that hurt most was the realization that if you tried to talk to him, or tried to be friendly toward him, he would turn around and try to sell you life insurance. That's what burned a man up. There he was dying on his feet, and still wanting to sell healthy people life insurance. It was too sad not to be funny.

Well, one day (this was years ago) I saw Simon Gregory in town, and he looked sick. I asked him what the trouble was, and he said Harry had died and that he had been at the bedside at the time, and now he was feeling rotten. The things Harry talked about, dying. It was terrible. Insurance, straight to the end, financial independence at sixty-five.

Harry's photograph was in *The Evening Herald,* and there was a big story about his life, how smart Harry had been, how ambitious, and all that sort of thing. That's what it came to, but somehow there was something about that crazy jackass that none of us can forget.

He was different, there is no getting away from it. Nowadays he is almost a legend with us, and there are a lot of children in this town who were born after Harry died, and yet they know as much about him as we do, and maybe a little more. You would think he had been some great historical personage, somebody to talk to children about in order to make them ambitious or something. Of course most of the stories about him are comical, but just the same they make him out to be a really great person. Hardly anyone remembers the name of our last mayor, and there haven't been any great men from our town, but all the kids around here know about Harry. It's pretty remarkable when you bear in mind that he died before he was twenty-three.

Whenever somebody fails to accomplish some unusual undertaking in our town, people say to one another, "Harry would have done it." And everybody laughs, remembering him, the way he rushed about town, waking people up, making deals. A couple of months ago, for example, there was a tight-wire walker on the stage of the Hippodrome Theatre, and he tried to turn a somersault in the air and land on the tightwire, but he couldn't do it. He would touch the wire with his feet, lose his balance, and leap to the stage. Then he would try it over again, from the beginning, music and all, the drum rolling to make you feel how dangerous it was. This acrobat tried to do the trick three times and failed, and while he was losing his balance the fourth time, some young fellow away back in the gallery hollered out as loud as he could, "Get Harry. Harry is the man for the emergency." Then everybody in the theatre busted out laughing. The poor acrobat was stunned by the laughter, and he began to swear at the audience

Traditional Success Stories   17

in Spanish. He didn't know about our town's private joke.

All this will give you an idea what sort of a name Harry
made for himself, but the funniest stories about him are the ones
that have to do with Harry in heaven, or in hell, selling earthquake insurance, and automobiles, and buying clothes cheap.
He was a worldbeater. He was different. Everybody likes to laugh
about him, but all the same this whole town misses him, and
there isn't a man who knew him who doesn't wish that he was
still among us, tearing around town, talking big business, making things pop, a real American go-getter.

[SEE EXERCISE ON PAGE 219]

"Although simple men think in terms of happiness and are likely
to identify it with material success, they too know at heart that
wealth is no guarantee of happiness; and almost all pay at least
lip service to 'the finer things of life.'"*

HERBERT J. MULLER

* From *The Uses of the Past* by Herbert J. Muller. Copyright 1952 by Oxford University
Press, Inc. Reprinted by permission.

Success: A Search for Values

Traditional Success Stories

4

5

6

7

8

9

Traditional Success Stories

10

11

Jean-Jacques Sempé

Success: A Search for Values

The poem entitled "The Ruler of the Queen's Navee" is actually a song from H.M.S. Pinafore, *a light opera by William S. Gilbert and Arthur Sullivan first performed on May 25, 1878. This song is sung by Sir Joseph Porter, First Lord of the Admiralty (a job roughly equivalent to the U.S. Secretary of the Navy) when he comes on stage in Act I and introduces himself. In telling of his rise to this high position, the poet is really making a sharp comment on how a man can reach the top* without *working his way up.*

The Queen whose navy (navee) Sir Joseph rules is Victoria of Great Britain.

The Ruler
of the Queen's Navee

William S. Gilbert

When I was a lad I served a term
As office boy to an attorney's firm.
I cleaned the windows and I swept the floor,
And I polished up the handle of the big front door.
   I polished up that handle so carefullee
   That now I am the Ruler of the Queen's Navee!

As office boy I made such a mark
That they gave me the post of a junior clerk.
I served the writs with a smile so bland,
And I copied all the letters in a big round hand—
   I copied all the letters in a hand so free,
   That now I am the Ruler of the Queen's Navee!

In serving writs I made such a name
That an articled clerk I soon became;
I wore clean collars and a brand-new suit
For the pass-examination at the Institute.
   And that pass-examination did so well for me,
   That now I am the Ruler of the Queen's Navee!

Traditional Success Stories 23

Of legal knowledge I acquired such a grip
That they took me into the partnership.
And that junior partnership, I ween,
Was the only ship that I ever had seen.
   But that kind of ship so suited me,
   That now I am the Ruler of the Queen's Navee!

I grew so rich that I was sent
By a pocket borough into Parliament.
I always voted at my party's call,
And I never thought of thinking for myself at all.
   I thought so little, they rewarded me
   By making me the Ruler of the Queen's Navee!

Now, landsmen all, whoever you may be,
If you want to rise to the top of the tree,
If your soul isn't fettered to an office stool,
Be careful to be guided by this golden rule—
   Stick close to your desk and never go to sea,
   And you *all* may be Rulers of the Queen's Navee!

[SEE EXERCISE ON PAGE 227]

"I came; I saw; I conquered."

JULIUS CAESAR

24   *Success: A Search for Values*

The Great American Dream for many years has been that
anybody can become a millionaire. (It may still be the Great
Dream.) If one did not become a millionaire, then at least
one could be, in the dream, financially "comfortable."
The Dream has always been appealing to native-born
Americans, and it has been strong enough to bring immi-
grants to this country ever since the days of the early
settlers.

   Anthony Marotta, the "hero" of the following selection
who became a business success by selling hero sandwiches,
could almost be the perfect example of the man who starts
a little business, works long hours for many years, and
finally makes enough not only to live comfortably but also
to make a sentimental trip back to the "old country."

*You Got to Be a Hero**

Robert Crichton

No question about it: To move from a rinky-dink neighborhood
grocery into the upper tax brackets in only 10 years, you must be
something special. That's Tony Marotta, supporting himself quite
comfortably as a sandwich king.

   Last spring Mr. and Mrs. Anthony Marotta of Lattingtown,
N. Y., drove to the hamlet of Piazzola in the south of Italy in their
rented Alfa Romeo. Lattingtown is a fashionable section of Long
Island, tucked away between Oyster Bay and Locust Valley.
Piazzola is in the poor part of the region of Potenza, and Potenza
is *poor.* Everyone in Lattingtown has money. No one in Piazzola
has money. It is that simple.
   "You recognize anything?" Mrs. Marotta said.
   He recognized it all. There was little in Piazzola to forget,
and nothing had changed since he had left. It is a small place, a
drab of stone houses clinging for life to the edge of a nearly dry
stream bed and an infrequently used road. Mr. Marotta didn't
answer the question because he found himself upset. He had ex-

---

*   Reprinted by permission of the author. Reprinted with permission of *The Saturday Even-*
ing Post © 1967 The Curtis Publishing Company.

Traditional Success Stories 25

pected to be pleasantly amused by his native village, but he found himself feeling sad and even a little frightened.

They passed beneath some olive trees his father had planted and went down a steep path into the house his father had built. It was dark inside, but when their eyes grew accustomed to the light they could see the animals in the room.

"Goats," his wife said. "Goats in the living room."

"There were *always* goats in the living room," Mr. Marotta said. "Let's get out of here."

The people of Piazzola miss nothing; they read outsiders. They knew the Marottas were American by the cut of their clothes, and that they were rich by the leather of their shoes. That someone had sprung from Piazzola, and now was rich, didn't surprise them. Going away and getting rich is part of the Italian folk legend, and something they were prepared to understand.

What they would find hard to understand, however, is that although last year Anthony Marotta paid an income tax of $26,000, he is not, by American standards, rich. What they could never understand is that although he lives in a $75,000 house surrounded by corporation lawyers, prominent physicians and company presidents, he makes his money roughly in the same manner they do—standing on his feet all day, working with his hands.

Anthony Marotta makes and sells hero sandwiches. No matter how many ways you slice it, which is what Marotta does, he is a semiskilled manual laborer. The fact that he owns his own sandwich shop, Marotta's House of 1,000 and 1 Italian Delights, adds immeasurably to his income. But that he makes as much as he does, that he clears between $25,000 and $30,000 a year, is a distinct tribute to Tony Marotta himself. It is also a tribute to the fantastic fecundity of the American economy. Marotta is under no illusions about that. He is aware of the fact that if he, the Great Hero Maker, were to open an identical shop in Glasgow, Scotland, he would be hard pressed to earn $3,000 a year. The British economy simply isn't geared to provide enough people willing or able to pay the equivalent of 80 cents for a sandwich. In the United States there is never a day when Marotta can find the time to make as many sandwiches as he could sell. . . .

If you want to live like Tony Marotta, and nine tenths of the world hungers and thirsts for just that, there are certain rules to be followed. Most of them are so old-fashioned that they seem curiously revolutionary.

The House of 1000 and 1 Italian Delights, in midtown Manhattan on East 47th Street, is not a prepossessing place. Flanked on one side by bars and on the other by the Ace and Flow delicatessens (which pick up a solid amount of trade from Marotta's overflow, a thought that rankles him no end), it looks exactly like what it is—a place to get a good hero sandwich cheap. I got there at eight o'clock in the morning, and Marotta was already there, working with that total absorption of men who like to work.

"Oh, yes. You," he said. He motioned to a case of imported tunafish. "You better start opening some of those." He is one of those men who can't really talk unless he is working, nor talk to someone who isn't. Although Marotta is 61, he had gotten up at five o'clock that morning because he always gets up then. He has a belief that all Italians who come from the little farms, the *contadini,* have inherited some kind of life force, some time fuse, that forces them to rise with the sun. When he could no longer find an excuse to stall around his house, he had climbed into his fire-truck-red Mustang convertible and driven into the city. He had already been at work an hour when I arrived. Evidently the Puerto Ricans are also gifted with this life-time fuse, because Marotta's two assistants, Ralph Garcia and Julio Rodríguez, were also in the store, working as swiftly as the boss.

They work fast because they never allow themselves to forget what lies ahead, what they have come to think of as the attack, the frontal assault, the tide and then the flood tide of humanity that will push its way through the doors at noon, *demanding* to be fed. If for some reason Marotta decided one day not to sell his heroes, his customers would tear the place apart. Most of the people who eat in his place each day don't know who Marotta is. His isn't a private restaurant; it's an institution.

The work in the early morning is all preparation and anticipation of the demand to come. While not everything in the store is hero sandwiches—there are hot plates such as veal and peppers, eggplant *parmigiano,* spaghetti with pepperoni sausage and the like—the backbone of the business is still the hero, what is known in various parts of the country as a grinder, submarine, torpedo, poor boy, belly buster, hoagie, you name it. To make one right, which few people do, and to make one fast, takes a preparation in advance that is taxing.

Take, for example, Marotta's Special. This is the star of the house, billed on the menu as FIT FOR A KING! LARGE 80c. GIANT $1.15. The special consists of three slices of capocollo (spiced smoked pork), two or three slices of imported provolone cheese, four to five slices of imported hard Genoa salami. Depending on the time of year, the capocollo can be replaced by mortadella

Traditional Success Stories 27

(Italian fancy bologna) or pepperoni, a hot sausage. All of this is stretched out in shingle fashion on the bottom half of a freshly sliced loaf of Italian bread and then trimmed — smothered is more accurate — with anchovies, marinated eggplant, Italian peppers, shredded lettuce and fresh tomatoes. If the customer wants it, he can have mayonnaise, pickle, coleslaw, chopped onion, lashings of olive oil and wine vinegar, and whatever Italian antipasto Marotta may have hanging around that day, added to the hero at no extra charge. It is truly, as Marotta boasts, a meal in a sandwich. There is also a formidable challenge in making it well, so that it is somehow clean and crisp, under the pressure of time. I tried for two days, and mine always came out soggy and unacceptable. . . .

In 1951 Tony's brother Ralph, also in the food business, invited Tony to witness an interesting sight. A food truck was pulled up in front of a hole-in-the-wall and was unloading enough crates of hams, wheels of cheese, and loaves of bread to feed a large restaurant for a week. Inside the place, hulking men were eating hulking sandwiches they called belly busters.

"What the hell is *this*?" Marotta said. A second epiphany, a new world about to open.

"*This*," Ralph said, "is the way to sell salami."

The man was selling 25 cents' worth of food for 50 cents and couldn't supply all he could sell. And Marotta knew at once that he could make an even better sandwich cheaper.

It was time to leave the grocery business behind him. For one thing he was tired of getting up at three o'clock to be at the fresh-produce market at four, the meat market at five, to open the store at seven and to close it at eight at night. Soon after he had opened the store, his first wife died in childbirth, and although his daughter Norma lived, Tony welcomed those long hours at first as a place to hide his loneliness.

For another thing, he met, arguing over the price of sardines, Silvia Ambrogi, an Italian girl from Gubbio, an extraordinarily energetic, loquacious woman. . . . In 1955, after 23 years on Bleecker St., Tony sold his grocery store and with the money opened Marotta's Hero Shop on Front Street in the financial district, on a site where several restaurants had gone broke before him. Within one hour, when word flashed up and down among the clerks on Wall Street that there was a place where they could get stuffed for 50 cents, the place was a triumph.

One point here: this word "hero." The Marottas claim to have invented it. When Ralph opened his shop he put a sign in the window: YOU GOT TO BE A HERO TO EAT ONE, and then called

28   *Success: A Search for Values*

it a "hero" shop. So did Tony. If they did, it's a great word. It isn't every day that one coins a word that enters the language.

The place was also too small. From the first week Tony and Silvia, who had gone to work with him then (one of the reasons she had married him was to get *out* of work; little did she know what lay ahead), knew that no matter how fast and hard they worked there was a limit to the money they could make. Then began a pattern that is almost devilish in conception.

Confident now that if you sell a truly good hero the world will find a way to your door, Marotta began leasing space in an unpromising location in an unpromising building (cheap), taking an option to buy the building (cheap). The instant success of his newest shop would make the location suddenly desirable. At this point Marotta would sell the business to eager buyers, and with their money make a down payment on the building, and then by leasing the space back to the new owners at five or six times what he paid, pay off the rest of the building and go on to bigger and better stores.

The system works fairly well. Tony bought the Front Street building, for example, for $65,000. Last year he sold it for $350,000, which is not a bad parlay for a sixth-grade dropout from the village of Piazzola. All built on hero sandwiches.

In 10 years Marotta opened and sold 13 shops and finally tired of it. Three years ago he opened 1,000 and 1 Italian Delights and this, he swears, is the last. He paid $125,000 for the building, and spent $165,000 renovating it. Considering the money he would have to spend for rent of his space, and the money he gets from rent for the apartments he built upstairs, he has possession of the building without putting out any money and runs his restaurant almost rent-free.

At 2:30 P.M. not long ago, when Marotta could finally come up for air, I asked him about this matter of pennies still being the basic unit of all small business. From what I had seen, no one ever asked the price of a hero or seemed to be sure what it was. If Marotta had charged 60 or 65 cents for, say, a mortadella hero, no one would have known or minded the difference, just so long as the final price, with a beer or soda thrown in, came to about a dollar. . . .

Marotta knows that because of his attention to pennies, two cents on this order, one cent per can on that order, everything adding up, he can compete with quality which in turn results in a gross business that approaches several hundred thousand dollars a year.

The money he makes embarrasses him in a way. I wanted

Traditional Success Stories 29

to know the exact cost of a Marotta Special, and he was afraid to tell me because he was afraid his customers might get angry. When I told him that I was unable to duplicate the Marotta Special in my house, with my labor, for the price he charged in his restaurant, he relented.

The bread costs five cents. Three slices of capocollo, nine cents. Two slices of provolone, eight cents. Four slices Genoa salami, 10 cents. Imported peppers, marinated eggplant, anchovies, chopped lettuce, oil and vinegar, fresh tomatoes, 13 cents — 45 cents for a hero that sells at 80 cents. This does not include labor, taxes and overhead, but still, with these, Marotta averages a profit of 20 to 25 percent on every hero he sells. Since a day's take, conservatively, is 800 customers who average one dollar each, it isn't hard to figure that Marotta is capable of making real money — sometimes, I am forced to conclude, a good deal more than Marotta has chosen to tell me. It embarrasses him.

It was six o'clock. It was time to go, but he stopped to put one last basket of fresh green peppers to marinate in a vat of white wine, and then took off his apron and turned out the light. Just before he did, however, he turned at the door and took one last, long look around at the empty shop.

"Well, another day, another dollar," he said.

"You make me laugh," I said, and he laughed.

"Yeah." He knew what I meant. "It's pretty funny, isn't it?" . . .

We got into his Mustang and drove out the Long Island Expressway. He was tired, but not tensely tired. His business was done for the day, he didn't carry it home in his head. . . .

In the house Silvia was waiting for us. She had spent the earlier part of the afternoon having lunch and playing bridge at the Locust Valley Women's Club and had just come from St. Christopher's, an orphanage in the area, where she hoped she had been able to dispense a little of the love and attention she was denied as a child.

It is an amazing country in this way. There is nowhere else that I know of that is really like it. Silvia Marotta knows this and, what is best, can admit it. . . .

"This will sound funny. You know what I miss?" We waited. "Goats. I still miss the goats."

"Oh, no," Silvia said. She seemed to be serious. "No goats. That's what we got away from."

She brought us a cocktail, and now Marotta seemed very tired. He had been up at five. He had been working on his feet for 12 hours, using his back and his hands and his legs. He is 61 years old. He owns a number of buildings now, he has a shop that Ralph Garcia has run with no reduction in profit, he has money in the bank. Why should a man of 61, a hero sandwich maker, be sitting in this lavish room, almost a little too tired to sip his drink? So I asked him the question that it was inevitable to ask, and he looked at me with shock, as if I had said something truly indecent and even a little mad.

"Quit work?" he said to me. "Whattaya mean, quit work?" He held his hands out and looked at them as if I had suggested they be amputated. "Work? That's *me*. That's what I do. That's Tony Marotta. I work."

[SEE EXERCISE ON PAGE 233]

Reproduced by permission of Warren Miller and *The New Yorker.* © **1967 The New Yorker Magazine, Inc.**

Traditional Success Stories   31

Few people become self-made millionaires at 29 years of age. Almost none are women, though they can reach higher positions than were ever before possible.

Pat Palmer reached the "top" by working in a service industry rather than by manufacturing a product. As population—and affluence—have increased, the service industries have grown and prospered. Pat Palmer took advantage of situations she found. In her exercise of ingenuity and single-minded devotion to a job she was also like many other people, including those with far less money.

Success Rushed Up
to Pat Palmer

Self-made Millionaire at 29

By MARTIN ABRAMSON

It is a popular notion that there is discrimination against women in business, that the discrimination is greater if they are young and greatest if they appear to be wide-eyed innocents.

Yet these very qualities were of immeasurable value in helping Pat Palmer hit the jackpot in real estate.

Pat is one of the new breed of women who have shown that in an expanding economy they can attain millionaire status through their own achievements in business rather than by inheriting from a rich father or squeezing alimony from a wealthy ex-husband.

In her small niche, Pat has another distinction: She is only 29 and thus the youngest of this new breed.

Probably the oddest aspect of Miss Palmer's success story is that she never intended to become either a businesswoman or a real-estate broker. Her chosen career was that of concert and opera singer, and she found her financial harvest through a combination of improbable circumstances.

A pleasant, dark-haired woman whose air of unruffled calm masks a boiling ferment of energy, Pat is a native of Boston who lost her father in early childhood. Her mother had the problem of bringing up three children on a modest inheritance, so she taught them the art of money management and responsibility at an early age—which in Pat's case turned out to be a blessing.

Pat was a stand-out in school concerts at Boston Latin High and was advised by her music teachers that she could make the grade professionally if she went to New York and got an experienced vocal coach to tutor her. Her mother was told that living there would be more expensive than in Boston but decided to move anyway to give Pat her chance.

THE FAMILY settled into a midtown

sub-let apartment but after a few months got word that the original tenant was coming back. The 15-year-old Pat took on the assignment of finding another apartment and, during her search, dropped into a real-estate office that had an opening for a part-time secretary.

"Luckily, I knew how to type, so I applied for the job and was accepted," she recalls. She worked after school, four hours a day at a salary of $25 a week. The money went to her voice coach.

When one of the salespeople took ill, Pat filled in. She showed such a natural acumen for selling and for negotiating leases that she was given a temporary saleswoman's license. Later, she passed the examination for a broker, but even as her income increased, she regarded it only as a backstop for her real career in music.

Like all other major American cities, New York was then suffering from an acute apartment shortage in its choice residential areas.

"I noticed that most real-estate people were taking advantage of their seller's market," Pat told me. "They were rude to people and pushed many of them into apartments and houses they didn't want just because they could collect larger commissions. They didn't bother going out to check on apartments or homes that were being vacated because they could wait for them to be called in and fill them from their long waiting lists."

'Innocent
Look' Helped

PAT PALMER decided to get the jump on them by starting an "apartment locating service." She was emboldened to strike out on her own be-

cause her mother had suffered a heart attack and the heavy burden of medical costs made it imperative that she increase her income.

Her technique was to trudge up and down the streets of Manhattan, ringing the doorbells of building superintendents and owners of townhouses, advise them that she had started a new, one-woman agency and urge them to inform her of any upcoming vacancies.

Pat filled her first listings with fellow music students and neophyte singers and dancers hungry for apartments. Later, she advertised her listings but was careful to apply the personal touch in matching person to apartment.

It took a great deal of extra effort, but, as she points out, "I was never what you call a social individual and I had no real friends in New York to spend time with anyway." To build up her business, she worked seven days a week the year round, usually from 8 a.m. to midnight. For a few years, she never went to a party, never had a date and never took even a single day off.

Star-Studded
Client List

THE PERSONAL TOUCH paid off. Secretaries and bit players whom Pat had placed in modest apartments recommended her indefatigable service to bosses and stars who wanted luxury apartments or were willing to buy $200,000 co-ops and sumptuous vacation homes.

Her customer list subsequently included celebrities like Sophia Loren, Richard Nixon, Robert Merrill, Marlene Dietrich, Patrice Munsel, Joan

Traditional Success Stories   33

Crawford, Frank Sinatra, and members of the Rockefeller family. She
began to compile detailed lists of stars'
preferences in home living so she would
know exactly what to recommend if
she got a sudden call that they wanted
to rent temporarily in New York.

"An apartment for Sophia Loren,
for instance, must be truly elegant,"
she observes. "The finest paintings
must be available, also the most lux-
urious carpets and antiques. Sophia
must have one whole room for her
clothes, another for her secretary, another for her husband to work in, and
three or four servants' rooms. Cost is
no object."

Pat Palmer's emergence as the female phenomenon of real estate disturbed some of her colleagues, intrigued others. One of those intrigued
was the owner of a tea company who
also owned a choice, six-story town-
house on East 67th Street and wanted

to retire from both tea and real estate.
He offered Pat an option to buy his
building for an incredibly small down
payment.

She set up her office on the first
floor, moved the tenants to other
buildings and converted the town-
house into a commercial structure.
This brought her a windfall in higher
rents, and she used it to buy into other
buildings.

Usual Luxuries
Don't Faze Her

The girl from Boston now has sole
title to the East 67th Street building
(which is valued at over $400,000),
owns three other buildings of com-
parable value, and manages six more.
Meanwhile, her regular real-estate
operation has expanded so that she
rents and sells in several cities across
the country as well as in resort areas
abroad.

[SEE EXERCISE ON PAGE 241]

RICHEST OF THE AMERICAN RICH

In its May issue, FORTUNE calculates that 153 identifiable Americans are worth at least $100 million, and 66 can lay claim to $150 million or more. The top centimillionaires:

$1 BILLION TO $1.5 BILLION

J. Paul Getty, 75; Getty Oil Co.

Howard Hughes, 62; Hughes Aircraft, Hughes Tool

$500 MILLION TO $1 BILLION

H. L. Hunt, 79; oil
Dr. Edwin H. Land, 58; Polaroid
Daniel K. Ludwig, 70; shipping

Alisa Mellon Bruce, 66
Paul Mellon, 60
Richard King Mellon, 68

$300 MILLION TO $500 MILLION

N. Bunker Hunt, 42; oil
John D. MacArthur, 71; Bankers Life & Casualty

William L. McKnight, 80; Minnesota Mining & Manufacturing
Charles S. Mott, 92; General Motors
R. E. ("Bob") Smith, 73; oil, real estate

$200 MILLION TO $300 MILLION

Howard F. Ahmanson, 61; Home Savings & Loan Assn.
Charles Allen Jr., 65; investment banking
Mrs. W. Van Alan Clark Sr., 80; Avon Products
John T. Dorrance Jr., 49; Campbell Soup
Mrs. Alfred I. du Pont, 84
Charles W. Engelhard Jr., 51; mining and metal fabricating
Sherman M. Fairchild, 72; Fairchild Camera, IBM
Leon Hess, 54; Hess Oil & Chemical
William R. Hewlett, 54; Hewlett-Packard
David Packard, 55; Hewlett-Packard
Amory Houghton, 68; Corning Glass
Joseph P. Kennedy, 79

Eli Lilly, 83; Eli Lilly & Co.
Forrest E. Mars, 64; Mars candy
Samuel I. Newhouse, 73; newspapers
Marjorie Merriweather Post, 81; General Foods
Mrs. Jean Mauze (Abby Rockefeller), 64
David Rockefeller, 52
John D. Rockefeller III, 62
Laurance Rockefeller, 57
Nelson Rockefeller, 59
Winthrop Rockefeller, 56
Cordelia Scaife May, 39
Richard Mellon Scaife, 35
DeWitt Wallace, 78; Reader's Digest
Mrs. Charles Payson (Joan Whitney), 65
John Hay Whitney, 63

$150 MILLION TO $200 MILLION

James S. Abercrombie, 76; oil, Cameron Iron Works
William Benton, 68; Encyclopaedia Britannica
Jacob Blaustein, 75; Standard Oil of Indiana
Chester Carlson, 62; xerography
Edward J. Daly, 45; World Airways
Clarence Dillon, 85; investment banking
Doris Duke, 55
Lammot du Pont Copeland, 62
Henry B. du Pont, 69
Benson Ford,* 48; Ford Motor
Mrs. W. Buhl Ford II (Josephine Ford), 44; Ford Motor
William C. Ford, 43; Ford Motor
Helen Clay Frick, 79

William T. Grant, 91; W. T. Grant stores
Bob Hope, 64
Arthur A. Houghton Jr., 61; Corning glass
J. Seward Johnson, 72; Johnson & Johnson
Peter Kiewit, 67; construction
Allan P. Kirby, 75; Alleghany Corp.
J. S. McDonnell Jr., 69; McDonnell Douglas, aircraft
Mrs. Lester J. Morris, 65
E. Claiborne, 57; A. H. Robins, drugs
W. Clement Stone, 65; insurance
Mrs. Arthur Hays Sulzberger, 75; New York Times
S. Mark Taper, 66; First Charter Financial Corp.
Robert W. Woodruff, 78; Coca-Cola

* Notably absent from FORTUNE's compilation: Henry Ford II, who presumably has given up a considerable portion of his fortune to his ex-wife and two grown daughters.

Reprinted from the May 1968 issue of *Fortune Magazine* by special permission; © 1968 Time Inc.

Traditional Success Stories

STRENGTH IN 77 SECONDS

That's all it takes to help build powerful muscles, trim body

No strenuous exercises...no elaborate gym equipment...no lengthy, tedious work-outs. You don't need time, space, or energy to multiply your strength...to broaden your shoulders . . . to increase your lung capacity . . . to trim your waistline . . . to develop vigor. Now the same method of Isometric-Isotonic Contraction that trained the German Olympic Team and other world-famous athletes can help YOU build a powerful physique. Yes, even if you are 30, 50 years old or more. Unlike ordinary isometric contraction devices, the TENSOLATOR® combines both Isometric *and* Isotonic benefits in a series of quick 7-second exercises that you do once a day in your own room — less than 2 minutes in all! Muscles grow stronger, shoulders broaden, chest expands, waist tapers down — and you feel like a new man. Fast? We guarantee impressive results in 10 days or your money back without question. Send for the big brochure that shows step-by-step illustrations of the Tensolator Method. Enclose this ad with your name, address, zip code (required for mailing!) and 25¢ to cover postage and handling to: THOYLO CORPORATION, Dept. SU-32, 509 Fifth Avenue, New York, N.Y. 10017.

Reproduced by permission of the Thylo Corporation.

The personal Rolls-Royce—$19,600

Personal? Well, unlike some older Rolls-Royces, the new Silver Shadow is not designed for a chauffeur. It is built specifically for the owner-driver. The man who gets a patrician pleasure from being master of a fine machine.

There is nothing subdued about the Silver Shadow. Beneath its outward grace is the spirit of *gran turismo*. Yet it is uncannily quiet even at turnpike speeds. The British magazine *Autocar* reports—"you can talk normally or listen to the radio at 100 mph."

Above all, you feel safe. The Silver Shadow is the only car you can buy that has three separate hydraulic braking circuits. Its disc brakes are steel hands in a velvet glove. A sensing system balances braking front and rear. You slow down as smoothly as you accelerate.

There is also an automatic levelling device. This allows soft springing without ever giving you that nightmare feeling of driving a double bed.

Easy to drive

The drive selector is electric. You use your fingertips, never the palm of your hand. And the front seats enhance your feeling of perfect control.

You reach down. A little knob adjusts your seat *electrically* eight ways. You can even go up and down to give yourself the clearest possible view of the fenders. And the *backs* of the front seats are individually adjustable. The driver can sit erect while his companion reclines.

Other switches, other things

One switch operates a network of tiny wires that demists the rear window. Another raises the radio aerial. Yet another balances front and rear speakers. You can even open the gas tank by pressing a button on the dash.

And there are friendly warning lamps for practically everything. One actually tells you if a stoplight burns out. Another flashes on when your fuel supply falls below three gallons.

Even more sensible, the whole car is only seventeen feet long. It turns full circle in little more than twice its length, and with its power-assisted steering, almost parks itself.

Yet, despite its sensible size, the new Silver Shadow still makes your passengers feel surprisingly expansive. The body and chassis are in one. This new monocoque construction has let us build a lower car yet expand interior space in all directions. A minor miracle.

The sybaritic comforts

The doors close as good doors should. With reassuring conviction. You ensconce yourself in English leather. The panelling is French walnut. The carpets are trimmed with hide. Air-conditioning is standard equipment and there's an unusual split-level ventilation system. You can warm your feet and cool your face at the same time.

And everything has, of course, been done for the comfort of your lady passengers. Leather seams in the upholstery are turned inwards so they can't be felt through a thin dress. And there are illuminated vanity mirrors on each side of the rear compartment.

How to know more than you need to know

If you want to know just about everything there is to know about this jewel of a car, write for your copy of the Rolls-Royce Owner's Manual.

This 142-page hard-cover book has fifty-three diagrams and illustrations and costs $12.50. You get your twelve-fifty back when you order a Silver Shadow, plus six per cent, which is only cricket.

The man to write to is Mr. Norman Miller, Executive Vice President, Rolls-Royce Inc., Room 465, 45 Rockefeller Plaza, New York, N.Y. 10020.

But don't be misled. No owner's manual can take the place of a test drive. The Silver Shadow's performance is a silky mystery that is greater than the sum of its parts. Your Rolls-Royce dealer cannot describe it any better than we can. But he can deliver it.

See dealer listing on a closely following page. Suggested prices P.O.E., exclusive of local taxes, if any. Slightly higher in Alaska and Hawaii. ©1968 Rolls-Royce Inc.

Making the society column of a newspaper is undoubtedly the mark of success for some people. Reading about those in such a column must also be important to some, or newspapers would not continue to run such articles. Surely the greatest height of success must be to have the moon cooperate by shining properly at one's party.

Person to Person*

Moon Cooperated for Greenes' Party

By HELEN WELLS

Herald Special Writer

It must be that **Nancy** and **Bob Greene** "live right." On Sunday when they had 150 friends at their beautiful home on Pine Tree Drive for cocktails and buffet on their patio, the night was perfect with Miami's famous moon peeping through the redwood arbor overhead.

This was an informal dinner party with Nancy in a Christmas red cocktail dress. A holiday green runway covered the swimming pool patio

where the lavish buffet table sat laden with ham, beef and everything good. Round tables covered with white cloths printed with red poinsettias were centered with enormous red candles 18 inches tall and two inches in diameter.

All her Miami Beach friends were greeting pretty **Anette Richard,** here for the first time since she and her late husband, **Walter,** moved to Bel Air, Calif., 17 years ago. Anette was squired by **Charles Martin,** also here from California, to do a Gentle Ben TV show and a movie.

---

* **Reprinted by permission of the** *Miami* **(Florida)** *Herald.*

Traditional Success Stories 39

The last-minute success described in the following selection makes this story almost unbelievable. If it were not in a newspaper, one might think easily that someone made it up, and that he had an active imagination. It is the story of the chasing after a dream, which certainly is admirable, and of an almost phenomenal perseverance.

We cheer because the Escapules struck it rich. We would never have heard of them if they had not.

EIGHT DAYS TO FORECLOSURE AND FAMILY STRIKES SILVER*

'WE NEVER LOST FAITH. WE KNEW THAT RICHES WERE DOWN THAT HOLE.'

Miami Herald-Los Angeles
Times Wire

TOMBSTONE, Ariz.—Eight days from foreclosure, a father and son with faith in their silver claim hit paydirt to the tune of $4.5 million.

Ernest B. Escapule, 71, and his son, Ernie, 45, had debts totaling $34,000. The son's electricity and phone service were disconnected for lack of payment. Their families were living on beans and tortillas.

"But we never lost faith," said Ernie. "We knew riches were down that hole."

They were right. They hit an eight-foot-wide vein of high-quality silver, and their fortunes changed as swiftly as did those of the gunmen, gamblers, and get-rich-quick prospectors of this town's wildest days of old.

The Escapules now have a lease option on their Santa Ana claim—purchased by a Houston oil firm—for $4.5 million.

* **Reprinted by permission of the** *Miami* (Florida) *Herald.*

"We won a photo finish," said Ernie Escapule Thursday as he stood beneath the steel-gallus frame over his diggings on the claim.

How far down the eight-foot vein goes no one knows. Tests show it could easily plunge 3,000 feet and deeper, Escapule said.

And value of the silver in the hole is averaging $2,000 to $3,000 a ton.

The Escapules' forefathers came to Tombstone when the first silver strike here electrified the world in 1877.

"The family has been sitting on these claims ever since silver went sour here at the turn of the century," the old man said.

"Others quit but we stayed, even when the price of silver dropped to 27 cents an ounce. We knew some day it had to come along again." Two years ago the father and son began digging at the Santa Ana.

"Dad is uncanny," Ernie said. "He

can smell silver in the ground. We have claims all over the countryside. We've had the Santa Ana for nearly 40 years but never worked it. When we started digging on the Santa Ana we struck silver at 26 feet."

Since Feb. 2, when the Austral Oil Co. of Houston signed its lease option agreement with the Escapules, prospectors have poured into Tombstone from all over the nation and Canada.

More than 1,500 claims have been staked in the last month.

The reason for the stampede is that the government recently abandoned a fixed price of $1.29 an ounce for silver and the price of the ore nearly doubled overnight. The Escapules expect it to reach $3 to $5 an ounce by the end of the year.

To keep his family going in recent years, Ernie Escapule has driven trucks, worked as a mechanic, even cut lawns, and his wife has been working for $52 a week in a Tombstone cleaners.

"Now," said Ernie, "it looks like we'll be able to buy a yacht, a big house and enjoy some of the real luxuries of life."

[SEE EXERCISE ON PAGE 247]

Reproduced from *Saturday Review,* January 30, 1965, by permission of the artist, Mort Gerberg. Copyright 1965 Saturday Review, Inc.

Traditional Success Stories　41

> *Books and magazine articles abound to tell people how to get ahead in business, how to manage to live within a budget, how to run a party, how to look attractive. Many of them are predictable; after reading some of them you can tell almost in advance what others will say on the subject.*

If at First
You Don't Succeed . . . Skip It*

The story you are about to read is not true. It was made up by Mike Royko, who is a columnist for The Chicago Daily News.

By MIKE ROYKO
Miami Herald-Chicago Daily News Wire

CHICAGO—I recently ran into a successful business executive in a bar. His hand shook so violently that his drink spilled on his impeccable suit. He explained that something terrible had happened.

"As you know," he said, "I am a successful business executive, top-drawer.

"I have worked hard to become one. I have followed all of the advice of the experts.

"There has been nothing written in a financial page or a business section on the subject of how to be a successful executive that I have not read. And we receive more advice from experts than anyone else, even golfers, drunks, teenagers and other unfortunates.

"Look at my appearance. I am youthful—yet mature. Nobody can tell how old I am. Some people think I'm an elderly 30. Others say I'm a youthful 60. Perfect.

"Physical deterioration is a threat to the successful executive. I've read that 50 times.

* **Reprinted by permission of the author.**

"So I have fought it. I am now in better condition than I was when I was 25 years old. I have grown a foot since my 30th birthday. I walk like a panther.

"I am also perfectly groomed. This is important. Look at my haircut. I get it done at a stylist shop. Four times a week.

"Look at this suit. One of the experts said an executive must spend a certain amount of money every year on clothes. I have suits I have never worn, but I keep buying more.

"Another thing is my battery. As an executive, I must get it recharged when it wears down. I take regular vacations. Then I take sabbaticals. My battery is always charged.

"A long time ago, I read that I should be a good public speaker. I have worked at it. I now sound exactly like Hugh Downs.

"I read that it is important for me to appreciate good food, art, books, and sports—but not to become a cultural phony. I've that, too.

"Someone else said business executives should avoid irrelevant read-

42   *Success: A Search for Values*

ing. I've been so careful I haven't read a thing I've enjoyed for five years.

"I've kept a close watch on my career timetable. I've made the proper number of job changes for my age and industry. I even quit a job I loved because a chart in Newsweek Magazine said it was time.

"I have battled anxiety, tension, worry, stress, just as the experts said I should. Some nights I haven't slept a wink figuring out ways to avoid worry.

"I read that executives must 'get involved.'" So I got involved. I have a wide range of community interests — politics, civic affairs, urban renewal, PTA, my church, government, charity, civil rights, schools. I take part in everything.

"I also have avoided letting my home become a jealous rival of my office. A successful executive must not be torn between the two. Yet I have not sacrificed family contacts for my career.

"That's where my wife comes in. She has grown with me, which is important, everyone says.

"She realizes that she, too, is a member of the management team.

"She is not too sexy but she is not drab or dowdy. She does not drink to excess but she is not a teetotaler. She isn't shy but she isn't aggressive. She

not only is a good talker, but also is a good listener.

"She is always prepared to entertain or to spend a quiet evening alone. She has social ease and a wide variety of interests in sports, civic affairs, cultural and current events.

"She has become so perfect that I can't stand to be around her.

"As you can see, I've done it all. Recently I even read an ad in one of the papers from a dance studio. It said: 'Every executive should know how to dance. Dancing is a social must and important to a business career.' I now can do everything from the tango to the American Indian.

"I think it was the dancing that did it. That plus the grooming, physical conditioning, civic interests, public speaking, vacations, sabbaticals, checkups, visits to the tailor, relevant reading, and watching my wife grow with me."

What happened?
"Some time ago, I forgot what my job is. I've been going to the office for weeks, not knowing what I should do. I'm afraid to ask. Indecision is bad for an executive."
That's terrible.
"That's not the worst of it. You see, today they called me in."
Fired?
"No. Promoted."

[SEE EXERCISE ON PAGE 251]

Traditional Success Stories   43

> *One of the qualities special to American society has been the widespread lack of social-class distinction—in fiction, if not always in fact.*
>
> *There have been traditionally two ways for the poor (if not always honest), young person to attain wealth and position: a boy could marry his boss's daughter, and a girl could marry her boss. Both are variations of the Cinderella story in which the handsome, wealthy prince falls in love at first sight with the poor, but always pretty, girl.*
>
> *Sometimes the story actually has come true. This particular wedding was big news because the bridegroom had great wealth (Rockefeller) and position (son of the governor of New York state). His bride was a Norwegian girl who had once worked as a maid in the home of her new husband.*

Anne Marie and Steven*

The world was tense and it was August. The news was of wars and the threats of wars; the tempers of man ran taut. . . . Last week, thanks be to Eros, the god of love, there was another kind of story, in Norway, and the world leaned back and enjoyed it. . . .

It was cool in Norway, and the story was simple. The boy— but whoever began a love story by describing a boy? The girl was Anne Marie Rasmussen. The world knew about her, but she was well worth another look—blond, tall, lissome, and 21. The boy, to get around to him, was named Steven Rockefeller, taller than she and 23, and the son of the governor of New York, Nelson Rockefeller. Steven one day will be a multimillionaire, and Anne Marie is the daughter of the village grocer and fish packer in Sogne, in southern Norway.

Anne Marie was born in Sogne and it was there, last Saturday, that she was married to Steven.

The world knew how these two had met—how Anne Marie had gone to America three years ago almost to the day, to perfect her English, and how she had taken a job as a maid in the Rockefeller home on Manhattan's Fifth Avenue, and there met Steven, when he came home on vacation from Princeton. They hadn't paid much attention to each other at first (the boy and the girl

---

* Reprinted from "Anne Marie and Steven," *Newsweek* (August 31, 1959), p. 36.

never do, in stories like this), but then, on vacation in Maine, they met again, and this time it really happened.

In very proper fashion, Steven had gone to Norway this summer to meet Anne Marie's parents. He had bought a motorcycle, and, the young couple, wearing slacks and sweaters, had ridden off over the dusty, winding roads.

When their romance hit the front pages, some 200 reporters and photographers from almost everywhere crowded into Anne Marie's home village. The wedding was as perfect as it could be. Fittingly as far as the Norwegians were concerned—it had rained for the occasion. The Norwegians have sayings like everyone else, and one of them is that rain on the wedding day means riches for the bride. . . .

Cheers from the Crowds: As the wedding procession passed out of the church doors, photographers fired flash bulbs from a platform set up among the tombstones in the church graveyard. Murmurs of delight rose from the 180 guests, and there were cheers among the 5,000 others waiting outside. Steven's father, Governor Rockefeller, smiled and warmly shook the hand of the bride's father, Kristian Rasmussen (who had footed the $1,500 wedding bill).

There were more cheers, and happy waves from the wedding group as it took off for a reception nearby at Kristiansand's businessmen's club, known locally as "The White House."

Anne Marie and Steven spent their wedding night in a secluded country hotel. Then, in three chartered Scandinavian Airlines planes, the Rockefeller party flew to New York.

After a honeymoon, the newlyweds would set up housekeeping in New York. Steven and Anne Marie planned to live in a modest apartment. Without a maid. And they planned to live happily, ever after.

Traditional Success Stories   45

This tale from India is another kind of love story. It comes from the Mahabharata, *one of the great epics of ancient India, and is of the type that is as well known to Hindus as Bible stories are to Christians and Jews. The names are unfamiliar—Savitri is the princess and Satyavan the man she chooses to marry—but the story has familiar ingredients: a sad prophecy fulfilled, a faithful and clever wife, a happy ending.*

Savitri's success depends on her quick thinking as she talks to the god of death, Yama. It is almost impossible not to feel a sense of satisfaction that goodness is rewarded when the quick-witted Savitri triumphs.

How Savitri Retrieved
Her Husband from Death*

Translated by Oroon Ghosh

There was once a king by the name of Asvapati, who had an only child, the spirited girl Savitri. She was beautiful but because she was so spirited had no suitor who was eager to marry her. So Asvapati told her, "My dear girl, you will have to seek out a husband for yourself. Take a chariot and an escort and roam wherever you like till someone catches your fancy." Savitri did as she was told. And her favor fell on Satyavan. Satyavan was the son of an exiled king, Dumyatsen. Dumyatsen had become blind. Satyavan was then very young. And taking advantage of these circumstances Dumyatsen's enemies had driven him out. He began to live, with his wife, Satyavan, and a few retainers in a forest near Asvapati's capital. And it was here that Savitri found them.

Savitri went back and told Asvapati, "Father, I have fallen in love with Satyavan. I will marry him and no one else."

The heavenly sage Narada, who could read the future, happened to be in court at that time. He said to Savitri, "My child,

---

* From *The Dance of Shiva and Other Tales from India,* translated by Oroon Ghosh. Copyright © 1965 by Oroon Ghosh. Reprinted by permission of The New American Library, Inc., New York.

46   *Success: A Search for Values*

choose another bridegroom. For Satyavan will surely die within one year."

But Savitri said, "I will marry no one but Satyavan. For a girl never really gives her heart but once, and I have given my heart to Satyavan."

So Savitri and Satyavan were married. They lived very happily for a year. Satyavan used to go out every day and cut wood. Savitri used to cook and care for her blind father-in-law and mother-in-law and all the retainers. And they all loved her very much.

Now, Savitri had been counting the days. On the day that Satyavan was to die she said to him, "My lord, I will accompany you to the forest."

Satyavan knew nothing of his impending death. Savitri had never accompanied him into the deep forest before. So he was surprised. He said, "Savitri, you have never accompanied me into the deep forest before. Why do you want to go today?"

Savitri replied, "I have never asked anything of you before. Don't deny me this small thing."

So Satyavan, who loved his wife dearly, said, "It shall be as you say so far as I am concerned. But ask the king, my father, and the queen, my mother, whether they would require you or not. For I will be out the whole day and will return, as usual, only in the evening."

But Dumyatsen and his queen said, "Let Savitri go with you, son. She has never asked for anything of us. If a fancy has taken her, let her have her way."

So Savitri accompanied Satyavan into the deep forest. Toward noon Satyavan said, "Savitri, I can hardly stand. This is strange, for I have never felt like this before. I have a terrible headache."

And Savitri sat on the ground and replied, "My lord, lie down, putting your head on my lap. Rest awhile, and everything will be all right."

Satyavan did so and fell into a coma. And Savitri saw at once before her a tall, dark figure with bloodshot eyes. He was dressed in red; his hair was tied in a knot on the top of his head; in his right hand was a noose.

The tall, dark figure said, "I am Yama, the god of death. The time has come for Satyavan to die. I am taking him with me."

And he made a pass with the noose. Satyavan's soul left him. Yama took it along with him, walking southward. Savitri followed him. At first Yama took no notice. But after some time he said, "Girl, why are you following me?"

Traditional Success Stories 47

Savitri said, "Oh, Yama! I want to go where my husband goes. For what greater love has a woman than the love of her husband? You are a just and righteous god and you know that very well."

Yama replied, "Savitri, your courage and constancy have won my admiration. I will give you a boon. Ask anything but the life of Satyavan."

Savitri said, "Then restore King Dumyatsen's eyesight."

Yama replied, "Good! Dumyatsen will get back his eyesight. Now go back, girl. The path is long and arduous."

But Savitri did not listen to him. She continued to follow Yama. After some time Yama said, "Girl, are you not getting tired?"

Savitri replied sweetly, "Why should I get tired, for I am following my husband. Besides, I am with a good and righteous god. Can his company be tiresome?"

Yama laughed loudly and said, "Savitri, you know how to flatter well. But it was well said. For I am indeed a righteous god. Ask another boon of me but not the life of Satyavan."

Savitri replied, "Then restore Dumyatsen's kingdom to him."

"It shall be done," cried Yama. "Now go back, Savitri. Stop pursuing your futile aim, for you will never get Satyavan back. His time to go to the other world has come."

But Savitri paid no heed to Yama. Toward evening Yama said, "Girl, you have been walking for hours. You have neither eaten nor drunk anything. Don't you feel tired? Now be good and go back."

Savitri replied, "Oh, Yama! You are not only just and righteous, but kindly and good. Have mercy on me."

Yama said, "Savitri, I cannot give you Satyavan back, but ask anything else. I will give you another boon. Then you must go."

Savitri replied, "Oh, Yama! Then give my father a son so that his line continues."

Yama said, "So be it. But Savitri, you have not asked anything for yourself. You are a sweet and courageous girl. I would like to give you something for yourself. So ask anything but the life of Satyavan and I shall give it to you."

Savitri cast her eyes down and said, "Oh, Lord Yama! Then give me a strong, handsome son."

Yama smiled and replied, "You will bear a strong and handsome son, Savitri. Now go back."

But Savitri shot back at once, "Oh, Yama! You are not only

good, but righteous. How can a girl have a son when her husband is dead?"

Yama laughed loudly and long and said, "Savitri, you have outwitted Yama. You are not only courageous and constant, but also good and clever and quick-witted. For all these qualities I will give Satyavan back to you."

So saying, he vanished. Savitri went back where Satyavan lay. Needless to say, after some time he awoke, as if from a deep sleep. Needless to say that all of Savitri's wishes were fulfilled. And in the fullness of time, Savitri sat on the throne by her husband, a wise, powerful, and righteous counselor in all his affairs. And so great was her reputation that women in India are blessed to this day with the words, "Be like Savitri!"

[SEE EXERCISE ON PAGE 255]

Ain't It So?

Now haven't you found it the truth,
And doesn't it grievously irk?
Pure luck helps your neighbor succeed,
But you must depend on hard work.

PAUL TULIEN

Mixed Meanings

Ambition: What makes us work so hard to get ahead.
Greed: The other fellow's ambition.

FRANK ROSE

Traditional Success Stories   49

Through the media of television, radio, newspaper, and movies we are "introduced" to thousands of people. We may even think we "know" some of the people by reading accounts of their lives and loves, by seeing them in daily activities, or by watching them participate in special events. Yet among those people we actually meet and talk with, we can know only a small part of each man and woman. Sometimes it is a shock to realize how very little we "know" about even our best friends.

Richard Cory*

Edwin Arlington Robinson

Whenever Richard Cory went down town,
We people on the pavement looked at him:
He was a gentleman from sole to crown,
Clean favored, and imperially slim.

And he was always quietly arrayed,
And he was always human when he talked;
But still he fluttered pulses when he said,
"Good-morning," and he glittered when he walked.

And he was rich—yes, richer than a king—
And admirably schooled in every grace:
In fine, we thought that he was everything
To make us wish that we were in his place.

So on we worked, and waited for the light,
And went without the meat, and cursed the bread;
And Richard Cory, one calm summer night,
Went home and put a bullet through his head.

[SEE EXERCISE ON PAGE 261]

---

* The following poem by Edwin Arlington Robinson is reprinted by permission of Charles Scribner's Sons: "Richard Cory" from *The Children of the Night*.

Ozymandias is a Greek translation of Ramses II (1301–1234 B.C.), one of the most famous pharaohs of Egypt. A master tactician and warrior, he extended his empire all the way to ancient Syria. Later, he was able to maintain peace during his long reign and devoted himself to enormous building projects.

The most spectacular of these projects was at Abu Simbel where a temple was carved inside a mountain at the side of the Nile. Outside, four statues of Ramses, each one 67 feet high, faced the river, and the legs of each statue sheltered smaller statues of his family.

Today, the entire group has been raised 200 feet to the top of a cliff in order to prevent the statues and temple from being covered by the river when the Aswan High Dam is completed. Many countries have contributed money and technicians in order to perform this amazing engineering feat that is saving the temple and carvings made over 3000 years ago.

Ozymandias

Percy Bysshe Shelley

I met a traveller from an antique land
Who said: Two vast and trunkless legs of stone
Stand in the desert . . . Near them, on the sand,
Half sunk, a shattered visage lies, whose frown,
And wrinkled lip, and sneer of cold command,
Tell that its sculptor well those passions read
Which yet survive, stamped on these lifeless things,
The hand that mocked them, and the heart that fed:
And on the pedestal these words appear:
"My name is Ozymandias, king of kings:
Look on my works, ye Mighty, and despair!"
Nothing beside remains. Round the decay
Of that colossal wreck, boundless and bare
The lone and level sands stretch far away.

Traditional Success Stories 51

Ozymandias Revisited*

Morris Bishop

I met a traveller from an antique land
Who said: Two vast and trunkless legs of stone
Stand in the desert. Near them on the sand,
Half sunk, a shatter'd visage lies, whose frown
And wrinkled lip and sneer of cold command
Tell that its sculptor well those passions read
Which yet survive, stamp'd on these lifeless things,
The hand that mocked them and the heart that fed;
And on the pedestal these words appear:
"My name is Ozymandias, king of kings!
Look on my works, ye Mighty, and despair!"
Also the names of Emory P. Gray,
Mr. and Mrs. Dukes, and Oscar Baer,
Of 17 West 4th Street, Oyster Bay.

[SEE EXERCISE ON PAGE 265]

---

* Reprinted by permission of G. P. Putnam's Sons from *Spilt Milk* by Morris Bishop. Copyright 1929, 1942 by Morris Bishop.

PART 2
Group Success

Introduction

The hermit who comes down from his mountain retreat once a year for supplies or the recluse whose body is discovered amid a litter of 10-year-old newspapers are people so unusual that they become the subject of news stories and surprised conversation.

For every person who protests that he wants to be left alone to "do his own thing," there are still hundreds, or thousands, who subscribe to John Donne's famous words, "No man is an island." There is a sense of interdependence that makes people stay together and work together as a single family unit or as a whole nation. Every culture in every era has had this same sense of togetherness, either for simple survival or for complex and nonutilitarian reasons.

Sometimes startling things happen when people act together. A park may be built overnight, or shops and homes along a whole block may be burned down; men may descend in a submarine to explore the ocean's depths, or an entire city of people may be taken to the forest and shot. For peace or for violence, for good or for evil, people continue to band together.

The coach in the dressing room at half time often expresses the same ideas as the minister in his pulpit. The story has dozens of variations, though it is essentially the same. "March together and you shall have gold," the conquistadores were told. "Reason together and you shall have peace," the diplomats are likely to say.

It is harder to feel affection, sympathy, or hate for a group than it is to direct an emotion toward an individual. Every youngster has his favorite ball player, every middle-aged lady has her favorite movie star. Never mind that the player is part of a team and that the movie star would never appear on screen were it not for a small army of technicians. The team wins the game, but it is the quarterback who gets a big play in the newspapers.

Team efforts, despite their necessity, do not have the glamour of individual efforts, and group successes, even with their many accomplishments, lack the magnetic attraction of personal successes.

Because it is difficult to be as interested in many people as in a single person, group efforts often are told best by focusing on a single member. Thus, this section about group successes includes some selections that at first glance appear to be about individuals; but these individuals are either representative of many or become the focal point of a group activity.

Humorous or serious, the result of imagination or of reality, these group successes are not offered as representative of what you should, or should not, believe in. Rather, the choices you make about which successes are good and which are not good only indicate your developing personal values.

"Most successful suit sale we ever had, I should say."

Reproduced by permission of the artist and *The New Yorker*. Copyright © 1938, 1966 The New Yorker Magazine, Inc.

58   *Success: A Search for Values*

Bureaucracy, red tape, the triumph of governmental rules
over the individual: the story is familiar in many countries.
What chance has an individual over "the system"?
   Zoshchenko writes of his native Russia and shows how
rules supposedly made for the benefit of the people some-
times work in the opposite way. His story may have taken
place in another time and another country, and the over-
shoe may perhaps be another object, or perhaps not a
"thing," but an idea.

The Overshoe*

Mikhail Zoshchenko
Translated by Sidney Monas

Of course, losing an overshoe in a trolley car is not difficult.
Especially if there's pushing from the side, and at the same time
some bruiser steps on your heel from behind—there you are,
without an overshoe.

Losing an overshoe is the simplest thing in the world.

My overshoe got lost in a hurry. You might say I didn't even
get a chance to catch my breath.

I boarded the trolley—both overshoes, as I now recall, were
where they should be.

But when I left the trolley—I look: one overshoe's there, not
the other. My shoes, there. And my socks, I see, are there. And
my underwear's where it should be. But no overshoe. One overshoe is missing.

And, of course, you can't run after a trolley car.

I took off the overshoe that remained, wrapped it in a newspaper, and went along. After work, I think, I'll do a little investi-
gating. To keep from losing my property. Somewhere I'll dig it up.

After work I went to look. But first I took counsel with a
friend of mine who was a motorman.

He straightaway gave me some hope.

"You say you lost it in the trolley. That was lucky," he says.

---
* Reprinted from *Scenes from the Bathhouse* by Mikhail Zoshchenko, translated by Sidney
Monas, by permission of The University of Michigan Press. *Scenes from the Bathhouse* and
other stories of Communist Russia by Mikhail Zoshchenko translated, with an Introduction,
by Sidney Monas. Stories selected by Marc Slonim.

Group Success   59

"In another public place, I couldn't guarantee anything. But to lose something in a trolley—that's a sacred matter. Now there is a little office we have called Lost and Found. Go there and get it. It's a sacred matter!"

"Well," says I, "thanks." A load had been lifted from my shoulders. You see, that overshoe was practically new. This was only the third season I'd been wearing it.

The following day, I go to the room.

"Is it possible, brothers," I say, "to get my overshoe back. I lost it in the trolley."

"Possible," they say. "What kind of an overshoe?"

"Oh," I say, "the ordinary kind. Size number twelve."

"We have," they say, "twelve thousand number twelves. Describe its features."

"The features," I say, "are just the usual ones. The back, of course, is a bit torn. There's no lining on the inside. The lining wore out."

"We have," they say, "a little over a thousand overshoes like that. Aren't there any special marks?"

"Special marks," I say, "yes, there are. The toe looks as though it were cut clean off, but it's still hanging on. And the heel," I say, "is almost gone. The heel's worn out. But the sides," I say, "there's still nothing wrong with the sides."

"Be seated," they say, "right here. Now we'll go look."

And right away they bring out my overshoe.

Naturally, I was beside myself with joy. Really touched.

Here, I think, there's an outfit marvelously at work. And, I think, how many intelligent, responsible people have gone to so much bother about just one overshoe.

I say to them: "Thanks," I say, "you're friends for life. Give it right here. Now it's found. I thank you."

"No," they say, "respected comrade, we cannot give it to you. We," they say, "don't know: maybe it wasn't you who lost it."

"Of course it was me," I say. "I can give you my word of honor."

They say: "We believe you and fully sympathize, and it's quite probable it really was you who lost this overshoe. But we cannot give it up. Bring us some certification that you really did lose this overshoe. Let your house manager verify that fact, and then without any superfluous red tape we shall give back to you that which you legitimately lost."

"Brothers," I say, "sacred comrades, they just don't know about this fact at home. Maybe they wouldn't give me such a paper."

60 *Success: A Search for Values*

"They'll give," they say, "it's their business to give. What else are they for at your place?"

I cast one more glance at the overshoe and left.

The following day I approached the president of our house.

"Give me," I say, "a paper. My overshoe's going to pot."

"Did you really lose it?" he says. "Or are you just twisting things? Maybe you just want to lay hold of some extra consumers' goods?"

"God almighty!" I say. "I lost it."

He says: "Of course, I can't just go on your word. Now if you'd bring me some verification from the trolley park that you lost an overshoe—then I'd give you a paper. Otherwise I can't."

I say: "But they'll just send me to you."

He says: "Well, then, write me a declaration."

I say: "What should I write?"

He says: "Write the following: 'On this day an overshoe was lost . . .' And so on. You see, I'll add a note that you've lived here all along, until the matter's cleared up."

I wrote the declaration. The following day I received a formal verification.

With this verification I went to the Lost and Found. And there, just imagine, without any trouble and without any red tape they gave me back my overshoe.

It was only when I put on my overshoe that I began to feel thoroughly moved. "Here," I think, "real people are at work! Why, would they ever have spent so much time on my overshoe anywhere else? Why, they would have just tossed it out of the trolley. But here a whole week hasn't made any difference— they gave it back."

The only trouble is that during this week while all the fuss was going on, I lost my first overshoe. All that time I was carrying it around in a package under my arm, and I don't remember where I left it. The main point is that it wasn't in a trolley. That's the awful part, that it wasn't in a trolley. Well, where to look for it?

For all that, I still have the other overshoe. I've put it on my bureau. If things ever get gloomy again, why, I'll just look at the overshoe and they'll seem brighter. *There*, I'll think, an office is marvelously at work.

I will keep this overshoe for remembrance. Let posterity admire it.

[SEE EXERCISE ON PAGE 269]

Robot at M.I.T. Builds Towers Out of Toy Blocks*

A COMPUTERIZED TV CAMERA

WITH CLAWS IDENTIFIES SIZES

AND SHAPES OF OBJECTS

By Robert Reinhold

An engineering team at Massachusetts Institute of Technology has unveiled a computerized arm-and-eye assembly that constructs towers and arches out of pieces it selects from a random pile of toy building blocks.

Using metal claws for an arm, a television camera for an eye and a computer for its "brain," the automaton performs its building chores by identifying blocks of various shapes and sizes and arranging them on the basis of what it "sees."

An ordinary automatic machine might be able to build towers and arches out of blocks, too, but it would be necessary for a human operator to be on hand to manipulate the machine step by step.

The M.I.T. automaton begins by having the arm trace out an imaginary object in space. This allows the television "eye" to determine the relative position of the arm in front of it.

Then, as the arm begins to stack blocks, the programmed computer makes decisions on how to maneuver them to carry out a given task — such

as building the highest possible tower. If a mistake is made, as in the case of a misplaced block, the camera "sees" it and "informs" the computer, which then issues new instructions to the arm.

The system was developed by M.I.T.'s Artificial Intelligence Group, directed by Prof. Marvin Minsky and Prof. Seymour Papert. The work is supported by the Advanced Research Projects Agency of the Department of Defense.

The same agency is supporting similar projects at two other institutions — Stanford University and Stanford Research Institute, a subsidiary of the university. If automations are made sufficiently sophisticated, they are expected to have important applications in space and underwater explorations — both hostile environments for humans.

Like the others, the M.I.T. system is still highly experimental. But Dr. Minsky envisages building far more sophisticated devices capable of perceiving textures, color and depth. This would be essential to the accomplishment of complicated real-world tasks.

The programing of the computer is the most complex aspect of the proj-

---

* © **1968/1969 by the New York Times Company. Reprinted by permission.**

62 Success: A Search for Values

Prof. Marvin Minsky, a leader in project, with the robot. Reproduced by permission of Massachusetts Institute of Technology.

ect. To analyze the visual scene, the computer must "know" a good deal about the shapes of objects, surface textures, shadows, perspective, lighting and other features of the surroundings.

In previous work, the M.I.T. team has programed a computer to play somewhat better than average chores and to perform well on tests in school-type subjects, such as high-school algebra and word problems.

[SEE EXERCISE ON PAGE 273]

Group Success

How Plays Shape Up on Great White Way

NEW YORK — (UPI) —
Current attractions, leading players, theaters and ticket situations:

APA REPERTORY COMPANY Lyceum; repertoire of De Ghelderode's "Pantagleize," satire on revolutions; "The Show-Off," revival of George Kelly's comedy about a man who wants to seem important; "Exit the King," Ionesco tragedy about monarch preparing for death; "The Cherry Orchard," Chekhov's classic of Russian social decay; available.

"CABARET" Jill Haworth, Jack Gilford; Imperial; prize musical set in 1930 Berlin, based on play "I Am a Camera;" available.

"CACTUS FLOWER" Betsy Palmer, Lloyd Bridges; Royale; Don Juan dentist meets match in his plain Jane assistant; available.

"CYRANO DE BERGERAC" Repertory Theater of Lincoln Center; Beaumont Rostand's romantic classic about long-nosed poet-warrior; subscription but available; through June 1.

"FIDDLER ON THE ROOF" Harry Goz; Majestic; musical of Jewish father in czarist Russia with problem of marrying off several daughters; some available.

"GEORGE M!" Joel Grey; Palace; semi-biographical musical about showman George M. Cohan with score consisting of famous Cohan songs; new hit, plan ahead.

"GOLDEN RAINBOW" Steve Lawrence, Eydie Gorme; Shubert; musical in which widowed Las Vegas sharpie fights sister-in-law's effort to control his young son; available.

"HAIR" Gerome Ragni, James Rado; Biltmore; off-Broadway hippie show moved to Broadway, described as "tribal love-rock musical," designed to shock; available.

"HAPPINESS IS JUST A LITTLE THING CALLED A ROLLS ROYCE" Pat Harrington, John McGiver; Barrymore; comedy about ambitious young lawyer's career and romantic involvements; available.

"HELLO, DOLLY!" Pearl Bailey, Cab Calloway; St. James; musical about female matchmaker who reserves wealthy client for herself; capacity.

"HOW NOW, DOW JONES" Anthony Roberts, Marlyn Mason; Lunt-Fontanne; boy-meets-wins-girl musical in Wall Street locale; available.

"I DO! I DO!" Carol Lawrence, Gordon MacRae; 46th Street; two-character musical based on "The Fourposter;" vicissitudes of a long marriage; available.

"I NEVER SANG FOR MY FATHER" Hal Holbrook, Alan Webb, Lillian Gish, Longacre; drama of conflicts within family based on what to do with the old folks and generation gap themes; available.

"JOE EGG" Donal Donelly; Atkinson; British comedy about problems of couple with 10-year-old spastic daughter; available.

Tactical Missiles: A report from General Dynamics

Evening the odds against surprise attack:

Even for those who weren't there, newsreels of World War II and the Korean War have made this scene familiar:

Troops are moving along a road or field. Suddenly, an enemy plane swoops out of the sky with machine guns and cannons blazing. Troops scatter for cover. A few fire at the disappearing plane—but in vain.

Today, the foot soldier does not have to head for cover. He has an equalizer. Now the scene would go like this:

An enemy plane is seen in the distance. An infantryman shoulders a weapon that resembles a bazooka. Through an eyepiece he sights the plane, squeezes a trigger and a missile whooshes out of the tube. Seconds later, the plane explodes.

Such a weapon is now moving into the hands of field troops. It is made by General Dynamics and called Redeye. It is a tactical guided missile designed to be used by one man.

The bullet that gets a second chance:

A bullet or shell is affected by gravity and wind, but, by and large, once fired it continues in the direction it was originally pointed.

A sharp eye, a steady arm and an accurate gun are all you need to hit a stationary target.

A moving object has to be "led"—the gunner judges where the moving object will be in a few fractions of a second and points his bullet there.

But to "lead" an airplane traveling at the speed of sound, miles high and able to change its direction in a hurry, you need a guided missile.

An effective surface-to-air weapon must be capable of fast reaction. Its warhead must be powerful enough to destroy an attacking plane. Its speed and range must be enough to reach the attacking aircraft before the plane's offensive weapons can be launched against ground troops.

But the real key is in the word *guided*. The guided missile, like its evasive target, can be steered and sometimes steer itself. In fact, you might call a tactical guided missile a "bullet that gets a second chance."

Let's take a look at three produced by General Dynamics—Terrier, Tartar as well as Redeye—to see how some tactical missiles work. All are essentially defensive weapons.

Terrier and Tartar are supersonic, solid-fueled missiles used by the United States Navy. Both have what is known as "semi-active homing" guidance. This involves a complex of shipboard radar and computers, combined with sensing, computing and controlling devices within the missile itself.

When search radar aboard a ship finds an oncoming target, a radar illumination beam, controlled through a central computer, seeks out the attacking plane. The radar waves reflected from the airplane are picked up by a sensor in the nose of the missile, which will chase its target to intercept even if the plane changes course several times.

Terrier:

Terrier is the bigger of the two. On its launcher aboard a Navy cruiser, it is about 27 feet long. The first 15 feet are the missile proper. The second 12 contain a booster rocket for propulsion.

Terrier is always ready to go. Almost within the instant that the illumination beam fastens on the approaching aircraft, Terrier is triggered.

The booster blasts the missile off the launching rack. The finder is already receiving the reflected beam from the target. Two small charges within the missile have already ignited. Their burn-

Terrier (27 feet)

ing gases turn two small turbines. One provides power for the guidance and control systems. The other operates a hydraulic pump whose fluids move the small guidance fins on the missile's tail.

As the booster burns out and then drops away, a sustainer rocket within the missile proper commences firing to continue necessary velocity to intercept.

Tartar:

Tartar is similar to Terrier, but more compact (15 feet long and about 1,200 pounds compared to 27 feet and about 3,000 pounds for Terrier).

Its booster and sustainer are combined into a single-rocket engine. When

Above: Cruiser fires a Terrier. **Right:** Diagram shows radar waves sent from a ship and reflected from a plane being received by sensor in nose of the missile. Even if the plane takes evasive action, the missile will change course to intercept.

Group Success

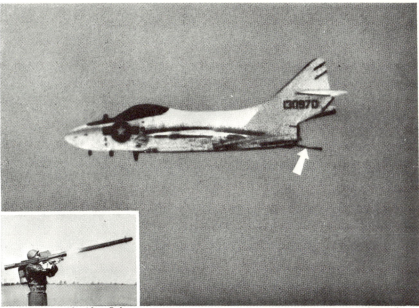

1. An infantryman (above) fires a Redeye missile at a target drone airplane.

2. This is an actual photo of a Redeye missile (arrow) entering the jet exhaust of a drone airplane. Immediately after this photograph was taken, the plane exploded.

Tartar gets its signal, the engine generates high initial thrust to shoot aloft, then reduces its force to provide the long sustained velocity to reach and chase a distant target.

Both Terrier and Tartar, in spite of their size, can be fired repetitively almost as fast as a bolt-operated rifle.

Stored in automated magazines, they can be lifted onto a launcher, hooked into the central computer radar control and fired within seconds.

Ships equipped with Terrier or Tartar can defend themselves against an armada of attacking aircraft today far more effectively than would have been possible against a single aircraft ten years ago.

Tartar (15 feet)

Redeye:

Redeye is designed to destroy low-flying aircraft rather than high-altitude supersonic attackers. Four feet long and three inches in diameter, it weighs only 28 pounds complete with its launcher.

Redeye's heat-seeking guidance is wholly self-contained. Reaction time is little more than it takes the soldier to lift the launcher to his shoulder, find the attacking aircraft in the sighting scope and squeeze the trigger. By that time, Redeye's infrared sensor has locked onto the source of heat it must follow.

A small charge projects the missile from its launching tube. At a distance far enough to protect the soldier from rocket blast, a fuse lights the major rocket charge. Miniature computer circuitry within the missile directs a set of

Redeye launcher

Redeye missile (4 feet)

steering fins which enable Redeye to change direction as necessary and chase the target at supersonic speed until it intercepts it.

During the long history of combat, the advantage of surprise has almost invariably lain with the attacker. The modern tactical missile now more than evens the odds for the defender. At General Dynamics we are already developing newer ones with still more punch.

———

General Dynamics is a company of scientists, engineers and skilled workers whose interests cover every major field of technology, and who produce: aircraft; marine, space and missile systems; tactical support equipment; nuclear, electronic and communication systems; machinery; building supplies; coal, gases.

GENERAL DYNAMICS

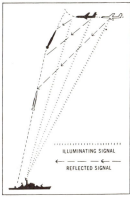

Diagram shows how missile changes course as the target changes course.

[SEE EXERCISE ON PAGE 277]

The occasional, dramatic space feats of any nation cause wonder, thrill, and excitement. There is much that is daring about space exploration and much that appeals to the imagination.

Although the first man to walk in space was a Russian, that amazing act did not have the same impact as the actual broadcast of the first American climbing out of his capsule and calmly talking to his fellow astronauts as he "walked" from the Pacific to the Atlantic Ocean. Although Major White was alone in open space for those 20 minutes, his success was shared by the thousands who planned, built, and worked on the intricate equipment that made success possible.

As U.S. Speeds Up the Space Race—*

It was more than a dramatic spectacle when U.S. spacemen "walked" and "flew" in orbit. Real significance, as top authorities see it—By forging ahead in key areas, U.S. showed it has a chance to win the moon race. More important, some believe, U.S. made major strides toward military mastery of space.

In just 20 dramatic minutes on June 3, the U.S. showed the world that it now has what it takes to start closing the "space gap" with Russia.

In those moments, a man left a spaceship at 17,500 miles an hour and for the first time made his own way through the skies with a hand-held "jet gun." That man was American Air Force Maj. Edward H. White II, age 34.

Another American, piloting their Gemini IV spaceship, flew a series of unprecedented maneuvers and at one time "chased" a second vehicle through space for more than an hour. He was Air Force Maj. James A. McDivitt, age 35.

* **Reprinted from** *U.S. News & World Report,* **June 14, 1965. Copyright 1965, U.S. News & World Report, Inc.**

It was more than simple "stunting" in space.

The U.S. broke Russia's near-monopoly of significant achievement by man in space, made a breakthrough toward military mastery of space and unveiled a speeded-up program that indicated U.S. willingness to take new risks in order to catch up with Russia.

Experts the world over agreed:

The U.S., at the very start of a planned four-day voyage, showed new versatility and scored its most important accomplishment to date in manned space technology.

The two U.S. astronauts—both "rookies"—rocketed up from Cape Kennedy at 10:16 a.m. Eastern standard time in full view of a "live" television audience in 13 countries around the world.

At 2:45 p.m., less than five hours later, astronaut White started a "space walk" that carried him across the Eastern Pacific and the continental United States, from Pacific Coast to Atlantic Coast, in 20 minutes. Details of that feat are described on the following pages. . . .

[SEE EXERCISE ON PAGE 283]

Group Success 67

I'M THANKFUL TO BE FIRST
Historic Voices from Space

What follows is from the transcript of the "live" conversation on June 3 between Edward H. White II, "walking" in space; James A. McDivitt, inside the capsule, and Virgil I. ("Gus") Grissom in Houston:

WHITE: My maneuvering unit is good. The only problem I have is that I haven't got enough fuel. I've exhausted the fuel. I was able to maneuver myself down to the bottom of the spacecraft. I'm looking down now and it looks as if we're coming up on the coast of California. I'm going in slow rotation to the right. There is absolutely no disorientation.

McDIVITT: One thing about it, when Ed gets out there and starts wiggling around, it sure makes the spacecraft tough to control.

GRISSOM: Is he taking any pictures?

McDIVITT: Of the ocean. That's about my guess.

GRISSOM: Take some pictures.

WHITE: I'm going to work on getting some pictures now.

McDIVITT: O.K. Get out in front where I can see you again. I've only got about three with my Hasselblad [McDivitt's camera]. Where are you?

WHITE: Right out in front now. I don't have the control I had any more, with my fuel gone.

GRISSOM: And you've got about 5 minutes to go.

WHITE: I want to get out and shoot some more pictures. There's no difficulty in recontacting the spacecraft. I'm thankful in having the experience to be first. Right now I'm on top of your window, Jim.

McDIVITT: Move slowly and I'll take your picture.

WHITE: Right now I could maneuver much better if I just had the gun, but I'll manage.

McDIVITT: Ed, just free-float around. Right now we're pointing just about straight down at the ground.

WHITE: O.K. I'm looking back now. I'm coming back down on the spacecraft. I can sit out here and see the whole California coast.

FLIGHT SURGEON: The medical data looks great here.

GRISSOM: He's just ripping through at a great rate. Here on the ground we are watching a scope of the heart action and respiration.

McDIVITT: Hey, Ed, smile.

WHITE: I'm looking right down your gun barrel, eh?

McDIVITT: Let me take a close-up picture of you. [Pause]. You smeared up my windshield, you dirty dog. You see how it's all smeared up there?

WHITE: I did? Well, hand me out a piece of Kleenex, and I'll clean it.

McDIVITT: I don't know exactly where we are, but it looks like we're over Texas. As a matter of fact that looks like Houston down below. Gus, I don't know if you can read us, but we're right over Houston.

WHITE: I'm looking right down on Houston.

McDIVITT: Run outside and look up at us, Gus. Yes, that's Galveston Bay, right there. Hey, Ed, can you see it on your side of the spacecraft?

WHITE: I'll get a picture. Can't you see me? I'm right behind the spacecraft now. I shot about three or four.

McDIVITT: Is that right? Well, I've taken a lot of you, but they're not very good. You're in too close for

most of them. I finally put the focus down to about 8 feet or so. Let's see what the flight director has to say.
VOICE: The flight director says get back in.
McDIVITT: Gus, this is Jim. Got any message for us?
GRISSOM: Yes, get White back in.
McDIVITT: Ed, we're coming over the West area, and they want you to come back in now.
GRISSOM: Roger, we've been trying to talk to you for a while.
WHITE: This is fun.
McDIVITT: Well, back in, c'mon.
WHITE: I'm coming.
McDIVITT: We've still got $3\frac{1}{2}$ days to go, buddy.
WHITE: I'm coming.
GRISSOM: You've got about 4 minutes to Bermuda.
McDIVITT: O.K., Ed. Don't wear yourself out now. Just come on in.
WHITE: The spacecraft really looks like it's [garbled] because whenever a little piece of dirt or something goes by it always heads right for that door and goes on out.
McDIVITT: O.K. Oops! Take it easy now. The pull on the spacecraft is fantastic.
WHITE: O.K. I'm on top of the capsule right now.
McDIVITT: O.K. You're right on top. Come on in, then.
WHITE: Aren't you going to hold my hand?
McDIVITT: No, come on in. Ed, come on in here!
WHITE: All right. I'm trying to get a better picture of the spacecraft. But I'll open the door and come through there. Just let me fold the camera and put the gun up.
McDIVITT: O.K. Let's not lose this camera of yours now. I don't quite have it. A little bit more. Easy, easy. O.K., I've got it. C'mon, let's get back in here before it gets dark.
WHITE: I'm hesitating.
McDIVITT: Come on now.
WHITE: It's the saddest moment of my life.
McDIVITT: You're going to find this out when you have to come down from this whole thing.

How a U.S. Astronaut "Walked" from Hawaii to Florida in 20 Minutes

Maj. Edward H. White II left his Gemini capsule during its third orbit, more than 100 miles over the Pacific not far from Hawaii. His speed was 17,500 miles an hour.

The spaceman was wearing a pressure suit of 22 separate layers, including one of felted nylon to protect him from meteoroids zipping through space at 10 miles a second. Thermal gloves protected his hands and a triple-thickness visor guarded against the sun.

The 171-pound astronaut was tethered to his capsule by a 25-foot "um-

Group Success

bilical cord" wrapped in gold-plated tape. This life line actually consisted of an oxygen hose, a communication cable and a nylon rope designed to withstand a 1,000-pound pull.

Once out of the capsule, astronaut White inched slowly along its side, then let go. He moved around with the help of a "Buck Rogers" type spacegun. To go forward, Major White pointed the gun at his intended direction and squeezed a trigger. Thrust was provided by jets of compressed oxygen that fired from nozzles aimed behind him. Mounted atop the spacegun was a color camera.

The astronaut was "weightless"—in delicate balance against the earth's gravitational pull. He had no sensation of speed and felt no air rushing by in the vacuum of space. The sun heated up one side of his suit to 250 degrees Fahrenheit, while the other side, in the shadow, chilled to 150 degrees below zero. But he was well protected.

Astronaut White maneuvered at the end of his tether during the few minutes it took to pass over the U.S., taking photographs as he raced along.

Command pilot James A. McDivitt, meanwhile, was keeping the Gemini on even keel, trying to photograph White.

Pilot McDivitt asked the "space walker" to move in closer. White did, and bumped against the capsule. Cried McDivitt in mock anger: "You're smearing up my windshield, you dirty dog."

Astronaut and capsule continued hurtling through space, over Mexico, Arizona, New Mexico, Texas, the Gulf of Mexico and Florida. Over Texas Major White saw the city of his birth, San Antonio. His journey over the continental U.S. itself took less than 8 minutes.

First word for the spaceman to return to his capsule came long before he reached Miami. But Major White wanted to keep walking and had to be coaxed back in. McDivitt pleaded: "Don't wear yourself out. Just come back in." White then could be heard laughing. What was to have been a 12-minute venture continued for 8 additional minutes—and an additional 2,400 miles.

The "space walker" had sped, in those 20 minutes, a distance over the earth of perhaps 6,000 miles. Safely back inside the Gemini capsule, astronaut White jettisoned some of his special equipment and the two men then settled down to eating, sleeping, experimenting and reporting to earth.

70   *Success: A Search for Values*

*It is one thing to read about an event in history written by
historians years after it occurred. It is quite another thing
to read the account of someone who participated in that
event.*

*The passage that follows was written by a man present at
the first meeting between the powerful Aztec ruler Montezuma and Hernando Cortés, called Malinche by the man he
had crossed the sea to meet. That meeting resulted in the
achievement of one goal: it gave Cortés the key to conquest.
It was also the way to success of other goals: taking the gold
of the Indians in the name of Spain and introducing Christianity to the people of what is now Mexico.*

From *The Bernal Díaz Chronicles**

Translated by Albert Idell

CHAPTER 1

THE EXPEDITION UNDER

FRANCISCO HERNÁNDEZ DE CÓRDOBA

1 . . . I am Bernal Díaz del Castillo, a resident and magistrate of the most loyal city of Santiago of Guatemala, one of the
discoverers and conquerors of New Spain and its provinces, native of the noble and distinguished town of Medina del Campo,
son of Francisco Díaz del Castillo, who was magistrate there and
known as The Gallant, and of María Díaz Rejón, his legitimized
woman, may they have glorious sainthood.

I write for myself and for all my companions, the real conquerors, who served His Majesty in discovering, conquering,

---

* **From *The Bernal Diaz Chronicles* translated by Albert Idell. Copyright © 1956 by Albert
Idell. Reprinted by permission of Doubleday & Company, Inc.**

Group Success   71

pacifying, and colonizing New Spain, which is one of the best
sections discovered in the New World, and this we did by our
own efforts, without His Majesty knowing of it.

With the help of God, I write the truth as I remember it, without flattering certain captains or putting down others.

CHAPTER 16

FIRST MEETINGS

WITH MONTEZUMA

1 . . . As the great Montezuma had eaten and knew that our
captain and all the rest of us had done the same a good while
before, he came to our quarters in great state with a large number of chiefs and relatives. When Cortés heard that he was approaching, he went out to the middle of the salon to receive him.
Montezuma took him by the hand, and seats richly decorated
with gold were brought. Montezuma told our captain to be seated,
and both sat down. Then Montezuma began a good speech, saying that he was happy to have in his house and kingdom gentlemen who were as brave as Cortés and ourselves. He said that two
years ago he had heard of another captain who had come to
Champotón, and the year before he had heard of still another
captain who came with four ships, and each time he had wanted
to see them. Now that he had us with him, he was ready to serve
us and give us all that he had, for truly we must be those of whom
his ancestors had spoken long ago when they said that men would
come from where the sun rises to be lords over these lands, for
we had fought so valiantly at Potonchán and Tabasco and
against the Tlaxcalans; pictures of all the battles, true to life,
had been brought to him.

Cortés answered through the interpreters, who were always
with him, especially Doña Marina, that we did not know how to
repay him for the great favors we had received from him daily.
Truly we had come from where the sun rises, and we were servants of a great lord, the emperor Don Carlos, to whom many
great princes were subject, and who had sent us to these parts
because he had heard of Montezuma and wanted to beg him to
become a Christian, so that his soul and the souls of all his
vassals might be saved. Later on Cortés would explain how this

72   *Success: A Search for Values*

should be done, and other good things that he would hear, such
as had already been explained to his ambassadors Tendile,
Pitalpitoque, and Quintalbor when we were on the sand dunes.[1]

At the end of this talk Montezuma had ready rich gold jew-
elry, in many patterns, which he gave to our captain. He also
gave to each captain trinkets of gold and three *cargas*[2] of cloth
richly decorated with feathers. To each soldier he gave two *cargas* of cloth – all with a grace that gave him the appearance of
being in every way a great lord.

After other polite speeches between Montezuma and Cortés,
since it was his first visit and difficult for him, they cut their
conversation short. Montezuma had ordered his major-domos to
provide us with maize and grinding stones, as well as Indian
women to make tortillas, and chicken, fruit, and grass for the
horses.

Then Montezuma took leave with great courtesy toward our
captain and ourselves. We accompanied him as far as the street,
but Cortés ordered us not to go far from our quarters until we
knew better what to expect.

2 . . . The next day Cortés decided to go to Montezuma's
palace, first sending to find out what he should do and how we
should go. He took with him Pedro de Alvarado, Juan Velázquez
de León, Diego de Ordáz, Gonzalo de Sandoval, and five of us
soldiers.

Montezuma advanced to the middle of the hall to welcome
us, accompanied by many of his nephews; no other chiefs could
enter or communicate with him unless it was on important mat-
ters. He and Cortés showed each other great courtesy, taking one
another by the hand, and Montezuma sat him at the right of
his throne and asked us to be seated on chairs that he ordered
brought in.

Then Cortés explained that now that he had come to see and
speak with such a great prince as he, he was satisfied, as we all
were, for he had carried out the journey and mission that our
great king and lord had ordered. What he had chiefly come to say
had already been said to Montezuma's ambassadors when they
had brought us the moon of silver and sun of gold on the sand
dunes, which was that we were Christians and adored one true
God, called Jesus Christ, Who died to save us. He told how He

---

[1] The emissaries of Montezuma had met earlier with the army of Cortés and arranged for
the meeting being described here. [Ed. note]
[2] A measurement. [Ed. note]

Group Success

was resurrected on the third day and was in heaven, the same that had made the sky and the earth, the sea and the sands. What they took for gods were not gods at all, but devils, which were very bad things. Wherever we had raised crosses they dared not appear, as he would notice as time went on.

Cortés also told about the creation of the world and how all of us were brothers, children of Adam and Eve, and he said that it was wrong to adore idols and to sacrifice men and women, because we *were* brothers. As time went on our lord and king would send men who led holy lives, better than ourselves, who would explain everything, for we had come only to notify them. Then, as he saw that Montezuma wished to answer, Cortés broke off and said to us, "With this we have done all we could for a first attempt."

Montezuma answered, "Señor Malinche, I have understood what you have said to my servants about three gods and the cross, and the other things you have spoken about in the towns through which you passed. We have not answered any of it, for here we have always worshiped our own gods and hold them to be good; so must yours be. For the present do not talk to us about them any more. This about the creation of the world we have believed for ages past. For this reason we are sure that you are those whom our ancestors predicted would come from where the sun rises. I feel that I owe a debt to your great king and will give him of what I have, for, as I have said before, I have heard for two years of captains coming in ships from the direction from which you came, and they said they were servants of that great king of yours. I would like to know if you are all of the same group."

Cortés said yes, that we were all brothers, and that the others had come to discover the way, the seas, and the ports, so that he would know them well when we came.

Montezuma referred to the voyages of Francisco de Córdoba and Grijalva, and said that since that time he had thought about taking some of those men that came, to honor them in his cities. Now his gods had fulfilled his desires, for we were in his house, which we could call our own. If before he had sent to tell us not to enter his city, it was because his vassals were afraid and said that we made thunderbolts and lightnings, that we killed many Indians with our horses and were angry *teules*, and other such childish things; but now that he could see us, he knew that we were of bone and flesh, and that we had sound understanding and were brave men. For these reasons he thought much more highly of us now, and would share with us what he had.

Cortés and all of us replied that we thanked him for his

74   *Success: A Search for Values*

good will, and Montezuma laughed—for he was very festive in his princely manner—"Malinche, I know that the Tlaxcalans, with whom you have made friends, have told you that I am like a god or *teul,* and that everything in my houses is all gold, silver, or precious stones. I know that you understand, and took it as a joke. Look at me now. My body is of bone and flesh, like yours. My houses are made of wood, stone, and lime. It is true that I have inherited the riches of my ancestors and am a great king, but I am sure that you took as a joke all the crazy stories and lies that have been told about me, just as I did your thunders and lightnings."

Cortés also laughed as he answered that enemies always say things without truth about those they dislike, and that he was certain that in these parts there was no other lord so magnificent, and that it was not without cause that he had been so described to our emperor.

While this conversation continued, Montezuma secretly ordered a great chief, one of his nephews, to have his stewards bring some pieces of gold that must have been put aside to give to Cortés, and ten *cargas* of fine clothing, which he divided among Cortés and the four captains, and to each of us soldiers he gave two necklaces of gold, each worth about ten pesos, and two *cargas* of cloth. The value of all the gold he gave them was more than a thousand pesos, and he gave it cheerfully, with the air of a great and powerful lord.

As it was now past noon and we did not want to appear to be asking for more, Cortés said, "Lord Montezuma, you always have the custom of doing us one favor after another. Now it is time for Your Highness to eat."

Montezuma replied that we had first done a favor to him by having come to visit him; and so we left and went to our quarters.

We remarked about his good manners and his thoughtfulness, and we felt that we should show him the greatest respect and raise our quilted caps to him when we passed, and we always did.

[SEE EXERCISE ON PAGE 289]

Group Success 75

Many of the riches of New Spain, often acquired by plunder, were sent back to Europe. While most of the loaded ships made the trip safely, storm and reefs took their toll. For hundreds of years these riches have lain beneath the ocean; only the relatively recent development of diving equipment has made them accessible. Few skin divers do not dream of finding such a wreck, and the following account concerns those men who did have such a success.

In the 1940s, Kip Wagner, then a Florida construction man, picked up the first clues to the location of ten richly laden vessels that had been wrecked on the Florida reefs more than 250 years before. He gathered a small group of other men and formed the Real Eight Corporation, named for the Spanish coin ocho reales, or pieces of eight.

Their long, sometimes disappointing, usually grueling underwater search was sensationally rewarded with the find described in this passage. In addition, they recovered a gold necklace appraised by a museum at $50,000, and three million dollars worth of treasure!

From "Underwater Bonanza"
in *Pieces of Eight**

By Kip Wagner,
as told to L. B. Taylor, Jr.

Del was out with us one weekend—we all joined the full-time crew on Saturdays and Sundays, or whenever we could—and toward the end of the day he pointed off to the south.

"I've got a feeling, fellows," he began, and we all gathered around to glean whatever prophetic pearls he was about to spill, "that we're going to hit it big again soon—right over there." We estimated the spot he aimed at to be about 800 to 900 feet south of the area we had been working.

"Yep," he drawled with a note of assurance, "if we go over there we'll find a heap of gold."

* From the book *Pieces of Eight* by Kip Wagner as told to L. B. Taylor, Jr. Copyright, ©, 1966 by Real Eight Company, Inc. and L. B. Taylor, Jr. Reprinted by permission of E. P. Dutton & Co., Inc.

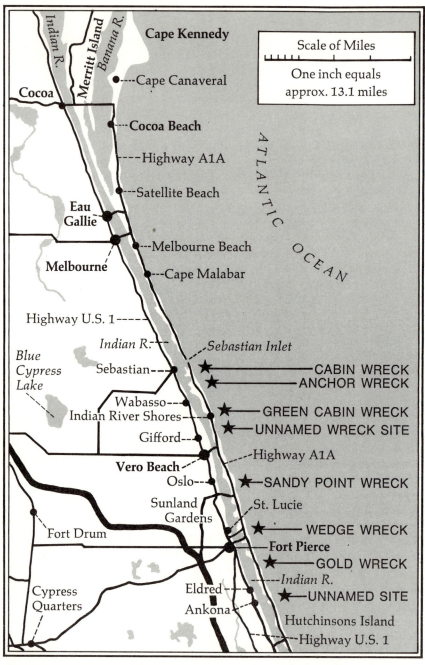

East Coast of Florida from Merritt Island to Fort Pierce, showing locations of the eight wrecks licensed to the Real Eight Corporation. Adapted by permission of E. P. Dutton & Co., Inc.

Group Success 77

Sure enough, and may I be struck on the spot if it's not the gospel, Bob and the boys motored over to the location in the next couple of days, and on May 30, found 130 gold coins four fathoms down—not 50 feet from the site Del had pinpointed! It was phenomenal. How can you explain it?

As everyone was off work the next day, Bob called and told us of the strike. Everyone but Harry was aboard the next morning when we sailed at 8:48 A.M., and anchored a little over an hour later, about 1,000 feet off-shore. Within 20 minutes Conkey came up with a gold doubloon. His find opened the floodgates to the most fantastic single day we have ever recorded. I hadn't been diving lately because of a bad back, but I couldn't resist the temptation, and down I went. It was a beautiful day, and the waters were as clear as any I could remember. Visibility was 40 or 50 feet in all directions. Conditions were perfect. The sands were so white it looked as if the surf had scrubbed the grains with detergent.

And then I saw it—a sight every man should see just once in his life. The blaster had cut a hole about 30 feet in diameter, and there, in this vast pocket of the ocean floor, lay a carpet of gold; believe me, a carpet of gold! It was the most glorious picture one can imagine. Not even Hollywood could have upstaged this natural underwater scene. Off to one side, against a rock-coral formation, the coins, so help me, were even lying in neat stacks of three and four. The water magnification made it seem as though the entire bottom was lined with gold.

We were spellbound. Here was a bunch of seasoned, hardened treasure hunters who had been making finds for more than five years, and we couldn't move. It was like a great painting by one of the old masters. It just held us in awe. When we finally did snap back to reality, we surfaced and made sure everybody on board got a chance to view this wonder before we began picking up the coins.

So abundant were the doubloons that we literally scooped them by the double handful and loaded buckets to the brim with them. Not only were the coins plentiful, but they were in mint condition—and they were big ones—mostly eight-escudo pieces, about the size of an American silver dollar. Most of the gold we had found the year before was smaller—one- and two-escudo pieces.

Before we had vacuumed the area clean, we hollered to Mel, Rupe and the others on the *Dee-Gee* to come over and join in the fun. Moe went down and came up with gold glistening in each of his palms and a smile splitting his ears. All day long we poured

78   *Success: A Search for Values*

the coins onto the decks of the *Derelict* in a steady cascade of
gold. We were one tired bunch of divers when we finally knocked
off at 5:20 that afternoon, but we had the comforting knowledge
that we had recovered more treasure in one day than anyone in
history—in recorded history at least.

We entrusted the day's take to Lou and Dan for sorting and
counting that night, and when they arrived at Dan's house, he
told his wife Jane, "We hit it pretty good today, honey. Get out the
card table." By now she had gotten used to seeing silver coins
by the bushel and other treasure, but gold was still a relatively
scarce commodity in our group. Jane later described the scene
to me, and I think it's worth recounting from her point of view:

"When Dan told me they had made another strike, I was
happy, of course, but then Lou went home for supper so I figured
it wasn't that important, and I scurried off to our kitchen. A little
while later Lou came back and I could hear a lot of clinking on
the table, so I went out to see what they had found. It took my
breath away. The tabletop was completely covered with coins.
I thought at first they must be counterfeit. There couldn't be that
much gold in the world!

"The thing that struck me more than anything was the non-
chalant manner in which my husband and Lou were counting
and stacking the coins—as if they were so many buttons or pennies from the piggy bank. Everything was so matter-of-fact to
them. Here was, by conservative guess, several hundred thousand dollars worth of gold on my card table, and they could still
maintain poker faces! Eagerly, I helped them sort and catalog
each coin, and if you can imagine the sensation, my fingers actually got tired from counting doubloons."

Few people, I'd venture, have experienced fatigue from such
a chore, nor would they have minded it. Neither did Jane. It was
one in the morning when everything had been properly assessed
and stacked. The total count from our record day was 1,128 gold
coins.

The breakdown went like this: 351 eight-escudo pieces, 378
four-escudo pieces and 215 two-escudo pieces from the Mexico
City mint; 167 eights, 3 fours, and 13 twos from the mint at Lima,
Peru. There was also one four-escudo imperial. This is a coin that
workers took extra care to strike from new dies, so as to form as
near perfect impressions as were possible. Imperials were then
presented to royalty. This one was dated 1711. Its value is estimated at from $2,000 to $5,000.

Not only had it been a banner day for quantity, but also
nearly half of the coins were eight-escudo pieces—which are

Group Success   79

worth more on the market. In good condition, and these all met
that qualification and more so, this denomination sells for $1,000
to $3,000—and we had 518 of them! How much was our total
take worth for the one day? You figure it out.

With most treasure hunters, like fishermen, they see the big
take and are ready to haul it in when the elements, or luck, en-
gulf them, leaving only the tall stories to tell again and again.
I've heard countless tales of divers getting within close range of
a recovery only to be thwarted by bad weather or some similar
misfortune. With us, the story had a new twist. We had found
treasure, and *then* the conditions worsened, leaving us with
tongues hanging out and fingernails bitten to the quick. Such was
the case on our first coin clump finds in 1961, and on so many
other instances—and such was the case the day after this fabu-
lous gold recovery. The waters kicked up, clouding visibility, and
told us in no uncertain terms that we had found enough for a
while, now sit back and cool it. We had no choice. The whitecaps
would have slapped us all over the ocean had we tried to go out.
We could only wait. What a great equalizer nature is. . . .

[SEE EXERCISE ON PAGE 295]

80   *Success: A Search for Values*

Atomic bombs, invasions, senatorial investigations, millions in foreign aid are all hardly the subjects of comedy. Yet, the deft twist of a novelist can make them laughable, even if it is only long enough for the reader to sense the irony in reality.

The following chapter from the middle of the novel The Mouse That Roared *has enough unreality cloaked in plausibility to be considered literary satire.*

Tully Bascomb leads an expeditionary force of 20 longbowmen from his country, the mythical duchy of Grand Fenwick, ruled by the Duchess Gloriana XII, to make war upon the United States. His ultimate aim is to obtain the economic aid from the U.S. that always seems to be given to countries the U.S. defeats in war.

Contrary to Tully's expectations, the landing in New York City is unopposed, though he has no way of knowing that was because an air raid practice drill was in progress and, therefore, no one was on the streets. A further unexpected success is the capture of Dr. Kokintz and his Quadium bomb.

From *The Mouse That Roared**

Leonard Wibberley

CHAPTER 10

Few in the history of human warfare have been so difficult to convince that they had been taken prisoner by an enemy as was Dr. Kokintz when captured by Tully Bascomb in the name of Grand Fenwick. He had, it is true, good reason for his disbelief. For one thing, he had been expecting sandwiches and he had got, instead, broadswords. For another, he had anticipated that a twentieth-century air-raid warden would be up to see him with coffee and comfort. Instead he was confronted by two fourteenth-century men at arms, clad in chain mail, and covered from shoulders to calves with surcoats on which were emblazed a

---

*   From *The Mouse That Roared* by Leonard Wibberly, by permission of Little, Brown and Co. Copyright, 1955, by Leonard Wibberly.

Group Success   81

double-headed eagle, rampant. Finally, in common with the
whole United States, he had no idea that the nation had been invaded, and invaded by the duchy of Grand Fenwick.

Even for a man who kept in touch with current events, the
situation would have been astonishing. For Dr. Kokintz, who as
a scientist was more familiar with the future and the past than
the present, it was beyond immediate comprehension.

"No sandwiches," he said for the third time, blinking at
Tully as if he had risen through the floor boards and was likely
to disappear by the same route at any minute. Tully told him for
the third time, with creditable patience, that there were no
sandwiches and that he was a prisoner of war.

"I do not understand it," the doctor said, shaking his head
from side to side quite slowly. "I do not understand it. I believe
I must have been working too hard and am suffering from hal-
lucinations. You two"—pointing to them—"are a hallucination.
You are the result of my working too hard. The mind, when over-
pressed with realities, takes refuge in fantasy at times, and that
is undoubtedly what has happened to me. You may also be the
result of vitamin shortage. That sometimes has a good deal to
do with it. However, if I close my eyes and breathe deeply, you
will undoubtedly disappear."

He closed his eyes, took two or three deep breaths and
opened them again furtively. But the two men at arms were still
there, still clad in surcoats and mail, and still staring at him out
of hostile blue eyes.

"So," said Dr. Kokintz. "It is not a hallucination and I am a
prisoner of war. But perhaps the matter will resolve itself if sub-
jected to reason. Please tell me: who is the United States at war
with?"

"The duchy of Grand Fenwick," replied Tully.

"The duchy of Grand Fenwick," repeated the doctor. He
said the words quite slowly as if weighing them, to see whether
they had any substance. "Certainly this is a hallucination," he
concluded. "I was born in the duchy of Grand Fenwick. How can
I be a prisoner of war of the place where I was born?"

"Look," said Tully grimly, conscious of the passing of the
minutes. "This is not a hallucination. This is deadly earnest. The
duchy of Grand Fenwick declared war on the United States over
two months ago. We have invaded New York. You are our prisoner, and we are going to take you back to Grand Fenwick with us."

"But why did the duchy of Grand Fenwick declare war on
the United States?" Dr. Kokintz asked.

"Over wine," replied Will. "You Americans are imitating

82   *Success: A Search for Values*

our wine, putting out some kind of a rotgut brew and calling it
Pinot Grand Enwick. That's why."

"Over wine," said Kokintz. "For what other reason would
one expect a nation to go to war with the United States?" He
shrugged his shoulders as if the matter was now entirely clear.

"Enough of this," rapped Tully. "You're coming with us as
a prisoner of war. You and that bomb you made. Where is the
bomb?"

"Bomb?" said the doctor, the word pulling him sharply to
his senses out of the dream into which he felt he had slipped.
"Bomb? What bomb are you talking about? I don't know of any
bomb."

"This bomb here," said Tully, thrusting the copy of the
New York Times in front of him. "The one that will blow up
everything if it is exploded."

The physicist glanced for one second from them to the lead
box on the bench. Suddenly he made a grab at it, but Tully was
there before him and snatched the oblong container up in his
big hand.

"Is this it?" he asked triumphantly. He thrust it out at arm's
length, and the weight was such that he nearly dropped it. Indeed, it was slipping from his hand when he caught it with the
other, letting his sword clatter to the floor to do so. Dr. Kokintz
rose to his toes like a ballet dancer, and then subsided, his eyes
closed tight behind his thick glasses.

"Please," he said, wiping a hand across his forehead. "Please
be very careful. That box you have in your hand is dangerous."

"Is this the bomb?" Tully repeated, shaking it a little in
emphasis.

"Please," pleaded Kokintz. "Careful. Handle it as if it were
a baby mouse. Yes. That is the bomb. If you shake it like that,
or rattle it, or drop it, or jar it, or disturb it in any way, it is likely
to explode. And if it explodes it will blow up all of New York and
Philadelphia and Boston. It will kill every living soul for several
hundred miles around. And over and above that, it will release a
dreadful gas which will keep on killing everything it comes in
touch with for years and years to come. So I beg of you, put it
down gently and spare the lives of millions of innocent people."

Will had been watching the scene with growing suspicion.
He did not know what all this talk of a bomb was about. But if
Tully said there was a bomb, then there must be a bomb. On the
other hand it was hard to believe that the box his leader held
in his hand could wipe out the whole of Grand Fenwick and
more, which was what this Dr. Kokintz was trying to say.

Group Success   83

He raised his sword now and reached for the bomb. "Give it to me," he said, "and I'll cut it open and see what's inside. I think this man is lying, and that thing, which even if it was filled with gunpowder wouldn't wreck much more than this room, has got nothing in it but earth or sand."

"No! No!" screamed Dr. Kokintz. "No. Please. I beg of you. Don't hit it." He flung himself on Will and seized his sword arm in both hands.

"I don't think he is lying," said Tully quietly. "I think this is it. We ought to be going, but there's just one thing I want to ask. Why did you make this?" And he held the box contemptuously out towards the scientist.

"It is a peace weapon of the United States of America," Dr. Kokintz replied. "The only peace weapon of its kind; far more effective than the atom bomb or any other peace weapon devised so far."

"A peace weapon?" said Tully in some surprise, turning the box over in his hand. He looked over at Will who was leaning on his broadsword. "Well," he continued, "the sword Will there is leaning on is a peace weapon, only of course it's not as good as this one because you can't kill so many people with it. You know we in Grand Fenwick, being a small country, need a really good peace weapon, which is another reason for taking this contraption along with us. So let's go. Down the stairs. March."

Dr. Kokintz shrugged and walked to the door. But when he got there he turned around.

"What about my canary?" he said. "There will be no one to look after it."

"There won't be much need for anyone to look after it," replied Tully. "This city is going to be atom bombed pretty soon. Someone else using a peace weapon, and the sooner we get out of here, the better."

"Atom bombed!" exclaimed Will and Kokintz together.

"That's right. Read this." Tully showed them the *New York Times* again, pointing out the sentence on the front page which stated that the alert of the whole east coast of the United States, in preparation for atomic attack, was likely to be held in the next twenty-four hours. "The alert's on," he said, "so the attack should take place any minute."

"But this is only a practice alert," expostulated Kokintz. "The air-raid warden told me so. There is not going to be any real attack."

Tully looked at him hard for a second and then read the story again. It didn't say definitely that there was going to be a real

84   Success: A Search for Values

atomic attack. In fact the deeper he read into it, the more evident it became that he alert was for practice only.

"Maybe you're right," he agreed at length, "and if so I'm much relieved about it. But while this practice alert is on we have still to get down to the *Endeavor* and get you out of here with this bomb. So, march."

"But my canary," said the doctor.

"Take your canary with you. But hurry," Tully ordered.

Kokintz snatched up the cage and walked swiftly out of the room. At the head of the stairs he turned to Tully. "Do not stumble and fall," he said. "Otherwise all New York will fall with you."

[SEE EXERCISE ON PAGE 299]

"Now if we can just invent a way to put it out."

From *Through History with J. Wesley Smith*. Reprinted from *Saturday Review*, November 11, 1961. Copyright 1961 Saturday Review, Inc.

Group Success 85

This photograph and article appeared on the editorial page of a large, urban newspaper.

MAKING PARK PROMISE GOOD*

No one likes public pressure from a group of people pleading a special cause. Yet no group of people, denied what it was promised, can be expected to maintain its patience.

This justifies the result obtained by Liberty City residents who conducted a well-mannered demonstration before the Metro Commission. The community had been promised a park and a swimming pool seven months ago, and nothing had happened.

Liberty City, an unhappy example of urban desolation in Greater Miami, will get its park and pool. Angered Metro commissioners have renewed the promise. The story is the familiar one of bureaucratic procrastination. Sometimes a little clamor helps.

* Reprinted by permission of the *Miami* (Florida) *Herald.*

[SEE EXERCISE ON PAGE 305]

Success: A Search for Values

Both Dr. Martin Luther King's public position and his often-stated ideas made him a controversial figure among whites and blacks. Yet he was never ignored in life, and he has acquired additional status in death. This passage is in keeping with the way Dr. King lived: it urges people to positive and peaceful action in order to achieve their goals.

From "Where We Are Going" in *Where Do We Go from Here: Chaos or Community?**

Martin Luther King, Jr.

Negroes nurture a persisting myth that the Jews of America attained social mobility and status solely because they had money. It is unwise to ignore the error for many reasons. In a negative sense it encourages anti-Semitism and overestimates money as a value. In a positive sense the full truth reveals a useful lesson.

Jews progressed because they possessed a tradition of education combined with social and political action. The Jewish family enthroned education and sacrificed to get it. The result was far more than abstract learning. Uniting social action with educational competence, Jews became enormously effective in political life. Those Jews who became lawyers, businessmen, writers, entertainers, union leaders and medical men did not vanish into the pursuits of their trade exclusively. They lived an active life in political circles, learning the techniques and arts of politics.

Nor was it only the rich who were involved in social and

---

* From pp. 154-157 in *Where Do We Go from Here: Chaos or Community?* by Martin Luther King, Jr. Copyright © 1967 by Martin Luther King, Jr. Reprinted by permission of Harper & Row, Publishers.

Group Success

political action. Millions of Jews for half a century remained relatively poor, but they were far from passive in social and political areas. They lived in homes in which politics was a household word. They were deeply involved in radical parties, liberal parties and conservative parties—they formed many of them. Very few Jews sank into despair and escapism even when discrimination assailed the spirit and corroded initiative. Their life raft in the sea of discouragement was social action.

Without overlooking the towering differences between the Negro and Jewish experiences, the lesson of Jewish mass involvement in social and political action and education is worthy of emulation. Negroes have already started on this road in creating the protest movement, but this is only a beginning. We must involve everyone we can reach, even those with inadequate education, and together acquire political sophistication by discussion, practice and reading. Jews without education learned a great deal from political meetings, mass meetings and trade union activities. Informal discussions and reading at home or in the streets are educational; they challenge the mind and inform our actions.

Education without social action is a one-sided value because it has no true power potential. Social action without education is a weak expression of pure energy. Deeds uninformed by educated thought can take false directions. When we go into action and confront our adversaries, we must be as armed with knowledge as they. Our policies should have the strength of deep analysis beneath them to be able to challenge the clever sophistries of our opponents.

The many thousands of Negroes who have already found intellectual growth and spiritual fulfillment on this path know its creative possibilities. They are not among the legions of the lost, they are not crushed by the weight of centuries. Most heartening, among the young the spirit of challenge and determination for change is becoming an unquenchable force.

But the scope of struggle is still too narrow and too restricted. We must turn more of our energies and focus our creativity on the useful things that translate into power. This is not a program for a distant tomorrow, when our children will somehow have acquired enough education to do it for themselves. We in this generation must do the work and in doing it stimulate our children to learn and acquire higher levels of skill and technique.

It must become a crusade so vital that civil rights organizers do not repeatedly have to make personal calls to summon support. There must be a climate of social pressure in the Negro com-

88   *Success: A Search for Values*

munity that scorns the Negro who will not pick up his citizenship rights and add his strength enthusiastically and voluntarily
to the accumulation of power for himself and his people. The
past years have blown fresh winds through ghetto stagnation,
but we are on the threshold of a significant change that demands
a hundredfold acceleration. By 1970 ten of our larger cities will
have Negro majorities if present trends continue. We can shrug
off this opportunity or use it for a new vitality to deepen and en-
rich our family and community life.

How shall we turn the ghettos into a vast school? How shall
we make every street corner a forum, not a lounging place for
trivial gossip and petty gambling, where life is wasted and human experience withers to trivial sensations? How shall we make
every houseworker and every laborer a demonstrator, a voter,
a canvasser and a student? The dignity their jobs may deny them
is waiting for them in political and social action.

We must utilize the community action groups and training
centers now proliferating in some slum areas to create not merely
an electorate, but a conscious, alert and informed people who
know their direction and whose collective wisdom and vitality
commands respect. The slave heritage can be cast into the dim
past by our consciousness of our strengths and a resolute determination to use them in our daily experiences. Power is not the
white man's birthright; it will not be legislated for us and delivered in neat government packages. It is a social force any
group can utilize by accumulating its elements in a planned,
deliberate campaign to organize it under its own control. . . .

[SEE EXERCISE ON PAGE 307]

PART 3

Personal Success

Introduction

The symbols of success change with the times. Maybe the old symbols do not even apply any more. Instead of money or social status, perhaps the new symbols are leading a sit-in, experimenting with drugs, or "coping out."

One thing seems certain: there is growing dissatisfaction with a culture that stresses only materialism. The disenchantment is not new, of course, nor is it exclusively the property of this country. However, more and more to be different is becoming acceptable, and increasingly the emphasis is on a different way of thinking, on reassessing the old values.

Those people who study such things have been writing recently that for growing numbers of people success on the job is no longer a matter of making more money. Instead, "success" means feeling personally involved in what is going on and experiencing a sense of worth in what one is doing.

Success may mean striving for a goal, as well as achieving it. The story of the man who looks forward to retirement only to find himself bored and looking for a new challenge has become familiar. Indeed, retirement, for many people, now means the chance to start a new job or a new project.

If these new beliefs have wide appeal, then it is necessary to examine the idea of success from new angles, to take a long and careful look at just what kind of person or deed *is* admirable and worthy of imitation.

If we are ready to disgard the cowboy-as-hero, who should take his place? If notches on a gun or enemy flags painted on the side of an airplane are not the measure of achievement, what is? In the search for new meanings of "success," and new symbols for it, ideas crowd upon ideas.

> — ARMY SURRENDERS! WAR IS OVER!

> — "Jimmy took his first steps alone today."

Which is really a success: the big event involving millions of people or the small one of interest only to a few? To an historian, perhaps the first one is more important, but Jimmy's first walk is no less a wonder though it is a repetition of what millions have already accomplished. As the event momentarily becomes the

91

Success: A Search for Values

focus for those within Jimmy's family, it takes on importance for them.

Perhaps success is, after all, a changing thing, a goal that continues to move along the scale of personal values. It is not always big, or unusual, or spectacular, or even terribly important. It wears so many faces and appears in so many guises, and it can come in such an unlimited number of ways, that a single picture of success is not possible.

If there is one main point, or one mark of unity among the selections in this third part of the book, it is that of variety. In the story and the poem, in the cartoon and the ad, in the real and the imaginary, this section celebrates the individual: his right to be himself, his determination to choose a goal he believes in, his success in many different ways, his obligation to himself.

Gandhi said, "Turn the searchlight inward." Socrates said it another way: "The unexamined life is not worth living." Both men were asking that the individual look within himself and try to understand what he thinks, feels, and believes. It is by knowing who he is that each person determines his own values, and by determining his values, he knows who he is.

© 1957 United Feature Syndicate.

Personal Success   93

> *Poetry can make its point in a way that prose cannot; the humorous can do what the serious cannot. The following is a poem that sometimes reads like prose, and the humor in it is faintly serious. One characteristic of Ogden Nash's poetry is that the writer sometimes coins words — most close enough to the actual word to be easily understood, but different enough to fit the rhyme or rhythm of the poem.*

Kindly Unhitch
*That Star, Buddy**

Ogden Nash

I hardly suppose I know anybody who wouldn't rather be
    a success than a failure,
Just as I suppose every piece of crabgrass in the garden
    would much rather be an azalea,
And in celestial circles all the run-of-the-mill angels would
    rather be archangels or at least cherubim and seraphim,
And in the legal world all the little process servers hope
    to grow up into great big bailiffim and sheriffim.
Indeed, everybody wants to be a wow,
But not everybody knows exactly how.
Some people think they will eventually wear diamonds
    instead of rhinestones
Only by everlastingly keeping their noses to their ghrinestones,
And other people think they will be able to put in more
    time at Palm Beach and the Ritz
By not paying too much attention to attendance at the
    office but rather by being brilliant by starts and fits.
Some people after a full day's work sit up all night getting
    a college education by correspondence,
While others seem to think they'll get just as far by
    devoting their evenings to the study of the difference
    in temperament between brunettance and blondance.
Some stake their all on luck,

---

* From *Verses from 1929 On* by Ogden Nash, by permission of Little, Brown and Co. Copyright, 1935, by Ogden Nash.

And others put their faith in their ability to pass the buck.
In short, the world is filled with people trying to achieve
    success,
And half of them think they'll get it by saying No and
    half of them by saying Yes,
And if all the ones who say No said Yes, and vice versa,
    such is the fate of humanity that ninety-nine per cent
    of them still wouldn't be any better off than they
    were before,
Which perhaps is just as well because if everybody was
    a success nobody could be contemptuous of anybody
    else and everybody would start in all over again trying
    to be a bigger success than everybody else so they
    would have somebody to be contemptuous of and so on
    forevermore,
Because when people start hitching their wagons to a star,
That's the way they are.

[SEE EXERCISE ON PAGE 311]

GRANDMOTHER, 62, RUNS 100 MILES FOR A T-SHIRT*

CHICAGO (AP) — Mrs. Frida Sigle, 62 years old, and a grandmother of six, proudly wears her Y.M.C.A. T-shirt. She is the first woman at the Irving Park Y to be awarded one for completing 100 miles on the track.

Mrs. Sigle goes to the "Y" twice a week, exercises for 20 minutes, runs two miles, swims for about an hour, then takes a sauna bath.

After that, she goes home, finishes her housework and prepares dinner for her husband, Fred.

* **Reprinted from Associated Press Newsfeatures.**

Personal Success

POLICEMAN IN BROOKLYN LASSOES ZEBRA IN BAY*

A policeman lassoed a zebra in Gowanus Bay, Brooklyn, yesterday while the badly frightened animal treaded water. The animal, one of 23 zebras, seven giraffes and three gazelles that arrived from South Africa Friday aboard the chartered vessel Dumbaia, was destined for a 30-day quarantine before being sold to dealers for resale to zoos.

The police surmised that when a curious longshoreman opened the sliding door of the zebra's crate to peek in, the animal lunged forward and jumped into the water off Pier 31.

Patrolman Edward Donahue arrived as a group of longshoremen and some of the vessel's crew were prodding the animal with sticks toward the dock. He tied a loop in a length of rope, swung it over the zebra's neck and held it while crewmen lowered a boat and fastened a sling under the zebra's stomach.

* © **1968 by The New York Times Company. Reprinted by permission.**

96   *Success: A Search for Values*

Many people today see a kind of poetic justice in the occasional stories of lucrative oil or mineral deposits discovered on Indian tribal lands, for in their rush to drive the Indian from his land and force him to accept the white man's ways, those who "conquered" this country, and especially the West, crushed cultures from which they could have learned much.

This tale of the wild horse roundup is an unusual "inside" view of a lost art. Perhaps it is the story of the triumph of a horse over humans, or perhaps it is a story symbolic of a defiant spirit that lives within many people who refuse to be conquered and forced to behave as they do not wish.

The Ghost Horse*

Chief Buffalo Child Long Lance

With the first touch of spring, we broke up our Indian camp and headed southwest across the big bend of the upper Columbia, toward the plateau between the Rockies and the Cascades. It was on this high plateau that the world's largest herd of wild horses had roamed for more than a hundred and fifty years. Several hundred head of them were still there. It was these horses that we were after, to replace the herd which the storm had driven from our camp.

We struck the herd in the season of the year when it was weakest: early spring, after the horses had got their first good feed of green grass. Since these wild creatures can run to death any horse raised in captivity, it is doubly a hard job to try to ensnare them on foot. But, like wolves, wild horses are very curious animals. They will follow a person for miles out of mere curiosity. And, when chased, they will invariably turn back on their trails to see what it is all about; what their pursuers look like, what they are up to.

The method our warriors used to capture wild horses was first to locate a herd and then follow it for hours, or perhaps days, before making any attempt to round it up. This was to get the horses used to us and to show them that we would not harm them.

---

* From *Long Lance* by Chief Buffalo Child Long Lance. Copyright 1928, © 1956 by Holt, Rinehart and Winston, Inc. Reprinted by permission of Holt, Rinehart and Winston, Inc.

Personal Success 97

We had been trailing fresh tracks for five days before we finally located our first herd away up on the Couteau Plateau of central British Columbia. There, grazing away on the side of a craggy little mountain on top of the plateau, was a herd of about five hundred animals. Their quick, alert movements showed that they would dash off into space like a flock of wild birds at the slightest cause for excitement. A big steel-dust stallion ruled the herd. Our warriors directed all of their attention to him, knowing that the movements of the entire herd depended on what he did.

When we had approached to within about five hundred yards, our braves began to make little noises, so that the horses could see us in the distance. Then they would not be taken by surprise and frightened into a stampede at seeing us suddenly at closer range.

"Hoh! Hoh!" our braves grunted softly. The steel-dust stallion uttered a low whinny, and all the herd raised their heads high into the air. Standing perfectly still, they looked at us with their big, nervous nostrils wide open. They stood looking at us for moments, without moving a muscle. Then as we came too near, the burly stallion dashed straight at us with a deep, rasping roar.

Others followed him, and on they came like a yelling war party, their heads swinging wildly, their racing legs wide apart, and their long tails lashing the ground. But before they reached us the speeding animals stiffened their legs and came to a sudden halt in a cloud of dust. While they were close they took one more good look at us. Then they turned and scampered away.

But the big steel-dust stallion stood his ground alone for a moment and openly defied us. He dug his front feet into the dirt far out in front of him, and wagged his head furiously. Then he stopped long enough to see what effect his antics were having upon us. He blazed fire at us through the whites of his turbulent, flint-colored eyes. Having displayed his courage and defiance, he turned and pranced off, with heels flying so high and so lightly that one could almost imagine he was treading air.

Our braves laughed and said, "Ah, ponokamita, vain elkdog, you are a brave warrior. But trot along and have patience. We shall yet ride you against the Crows."

For five days we chased this big herd of horses, traveling along leisurely behind them. We knew that they would not wander far, and that they would watch us like wolves as long as we were near.

By the fifth day they had become so used to us that they merely moved along slowly when we approached them, nibbling

98   *Success: A Search for Values*

the grass as they walked. All during this time our braves had been taming them by their subtle method. At first they just grunted, but now they were dancing and shouting at them. This was to let the horses know that, although men could make a lot of noise and act fiercely, they would not harm them.

On the tenth night of our chase our warriors made their final preparations to capture the herd. They had maneuvered the horses into the vicinity of a huge half-natural corral which they had built of logs against the two sides of a rock-bound gulch. From the entrance of this corral they had built two long fences, forming a runway, which gradually widened as it left the gate of the corral. This funnel-shaped entrance fanned out into the plateau for more than half a mile, and was cleverly hidden with evergreens.

The mouth at the outer end of the runway was about one hundred yards wide. From this point on, the runway was further extended and opened up by placing big tree tops, stones, and logs along the ground for several hundred yards. This was to direct the herd slowly into the mouth of the fenced part of the runway. Once wedged inside, the horses would be trapped; and the only thing left for them to do would be to keep on going toward the corral gate.

There was subdued excitement in our hidden camp on this tenth night of our chase, for it was the big night, when we would "blow-in" the great, stubborn herd of wild horses. No one went to bed. Shortly before nightfall more than half of our braves quietly slipped out of our camp and disappeared. According to prearranged directions, they fanned out to the right and left in a northerly route. They crept noiselessly toward the place where the herd had disappeared that afternoon. All during the early night we heard wolves, arctic owls, night hawks, or panthers crying out in the mystic darkness of the rugged plateau. These were the signals of our men, informing one another of their movements.

Then, about midnight, everything became deathly quiet. We knew that our braves had located the herd and surrounded it. They were now lying on the ground, awaiting the first streaks of dawn and the signal to start the drive.

One of our subchiefs, Chief Mountain Elk, went through our camp, quietly giving instructions for all hands to line themselves along the great runway to "beat in" the herd. Every woman, old person, and child in the camp was called to take part in this part of the drive. We children and the women crept to the runway and

Personal Success 99

sprawled along the outside of the fence. The men went beyond the fenced part of the runway and concealed themselves behind the brush and logs, where it was more dangerous.

We crouched on the ground and shivered quietly for an hour or more before we heard a distant "Ho-h! . . . Ho-h!" It was the muffled driving cry of our warriors, the cry which they had been uttering to the horses for ten days. Thus, the horses did not stampede, as they would have done had they not recognized this noise in the darkness of the night.

We youngsters lay breathless in expectancy. We had all picked out our favorite mounts in this beautiful herd of wild animals. We felt like the white boy lying in bed waiting for Santa Claus. Our fathers had all promised us that we should have the ponies that we had picked, and we could hardly wait. My favorite was a calico pony, a beautiful roan with three colors splashed on his shoulders and flanks like a crazy-quilt of exquisite design. He had a red star on his forehead between his eyes. I had already named him Naytukskie-Kukatos, which in Blackfoot means One Star.

Presently we heard the distant rumble of horses' hoofs—a dull booming which shook the ground on which we lay. Then, "Yip-yip-yip, he-heeh-h-h," came the night call of the wolf from many different directions. It was our braves signaling to one another to keep the herd on the right path. From out of this medley of odd sounds we could hear the mares going, "Wheeeee-hagh-hagh," calling their colts.

Our hearts began to beat fast when we heard the first loud "Yah! Yah! Yah!" We knew that the herd had now entered the brush portion of the runway and that our warriors were jumping up from their hiding-place. They made fierce noises in order to stampede the horses and send them racing headlong into our trap.

Immediately there was a loud thunder of hoofs. Horses were crying and yelling. Above the din we heard one loud, full, deep-chested roar which we all recognized. It sounded something like the roar of a lion. It was the steel-dust stallion, furious king of the herd. In our imagination we could see his long silver tail thrown over his back, his legs lashing apart, and the whites of those terrible eyes glistening. We wondered what he would do if he should crash through that fence into our midst.

But now he came, leading his raging herd, and we had no more time to think about danger. Our job was to lie still and wait until the lead stallion had passed us. Then we were to jump to the top of the fence and yell and wave fiercely. This was to keep the maddened herd from crashing the fence and to hasten them into our trap.

"Therump, therump, therump." On came the storming herd. As we youngsters peeped through the brush-covered fence, we could see their sleek backs bobbing up and down in the starlit darkness like great billows of raging water. The turbulent stallion was leading them with front feet wide apart and his forehead sweeping the ground like a pendulum. His death-dealing heels were swinging to the right and left with each savage leap of his mighty frame.

Once he stopped and tried to breast the oncoming herd, but it struck and knocked him forward with terrific force. He rose from his knees, and uttered a fearful bellow of defiance. The herd that had watched his very ears for their commands was now running wildly over him.

I believe that, if at that moment there had been a solid iron wall in front of that stallion, he would have dashed his brains out against it. I remember looking back into the darkness for a convenient place to hop, if he should suddenly choose to rush headlong into the noise that was driving him wild with helpless rage. I heard a whistling sound, and as I looked back to the runway I saw the steel-dust king stretching himself past us like a huge greyhound. With each incredible leap, his breath shrieked like a whistle.

No one will ever know why he so suddenly broke away from his herd. But on he went, leaving the other horses behind like a deer leaving a bunch of coyotes. A few seconds later the rest of the herd came booming past. I had never seen so many horses before. We stuck to our posts until it was nearly daylight, and still they came straggling along.

When we climbed down from the fence and went to the corral at daylight, we saw four of our best warriors lying bleeding and unconscious. When our mothers asked what was the matter, someone pointed to the corral, and said, "Ponokomita—akai—mahkahpay!" ("That very bad horse!")

We saw a dozen men trying to put leather on that wild steel-dust stallion. With his heavy moon-colored mane bristling over his bluish head and shoulders, he looked more like a lion than a horse. His teeth were bared like a wolf's. Four men had tried to get down into the corral and throw rawhide around his neck. While the other wild horses had scurried away to the corners of the corral, this ferocious beast of a horse had plunged headlong

Personal Success 101

into them and all but killed them before they could be dragged away.

He had proved to be a rare kind of horse – a killer. A man might live a hundred years among horses without ever seeing one of those hideous freaks of the horse world. He had already killed two of his own herd there in our corral.

Our braves were taking no more chances with him. They were high up on top of the seven-foot corral fence, throwing their rawhide lariats in vain attempt to neck the beast. He would stand and watch the rawhide come twirling through the air. Then, just as it was about to swirl over his head, he would duck his shaggy neck and remain standing defiantly on the spot.

It was finally decided to corner him with firebrands and throw a partition between him and the rest of the herd. Then our braves could get busy cutting out the best of the other animals, before turning the rest loose. This was done, and by nightfall we had captured and hobbled two hundred of the best horses in the Northwest.

The next day our braves began breaking the wild horses to halter. They used the Indian method, which is very simple. While four men held a stout rawhide rope which was noosed around the animal's neck, another man would approach the horse's head gradually, "talking horse."

"Horse talk" is a low grunt which seems to charm a horse and make him stand perfectly still for a moment or so at a time. It sounds like "Hoh-Hoh," uttered deep down in one's chest. The horse will stop his rough antics and strain motionless on the rope for a few seconds. While he is doing this and looking straight at the approaching figure, the man will wave a blanket at him and hiss, "Shuh! Shuh!" It takes about fifteen minutes of this to show the horse that no motion or sound which the man makes will harm him.

When the man has reached the head of the horse, his hardest job is to give him the first touch of man's hand. Of this the horse seems to have a deathly fear. The man maneuvers for several minutes before he gets a finger on the struggling nose. Then he rubs it and allows the horse to get his smell or scent. When this has been done, the brave loops a long, narrow string of rawhide around the horse's nose. He carries it up behind the ears, brings it down on the other side, and slips it under the other side of the nose loop. This makes something like a loose-knotted halter which will tighten up on the slightest pull from the horse.

This string is no stronger than a shoe-lace. Yet, once the

warrior has put it on the horse's head, he tells the other men to let go the strong rawhide thong. From then on he alone handles the horse with the small piece of string held lightly in one hand. Whenever the horse makes a sudden pull on the string, it grips certain nerves around the nose and back of the ears. This either stuns him or hurts him so badly that he doesn't try to pull again.

With the horse held this way, the warrior now stands in front of him and strokes the front of his face and hisses at him at close range. It is the same noise that a person makes to drive away chickens—"shuh, shuh"—and perhaps the last sound an untrained person would venture to use in taming a wild, ferocious horse. Yet it is the quickest way of gaining a horse's confidence.

When the warrior has run his fingers over every inch of the horse's head and neck, he starts to approach his shoulders and flanks with his fingers. The horse will start to jump about again, but a couple of sharp jerks on the string stop him. As he stands trembling with fear, the warrior slowly runs his hand over his left side. When this is finished he stands back and takes a blanket and strikes all of the portions of his body that he has touched. With each stroke of the blanket, he shouts, "Shuh!"

When he has repeated this on the other side of the horse, he starts to do his legs. Each leg, beginning with his left front leg, must be gone over by the warrior's hand, with not an inch of its surface escaping his touch. This is the most ticklish part of the work; for the horse's feet are his deadly weapons. But two more jerks on the string quiet the horse's resentment. Within another fifteen minutes every inch of the horse's body has been touched and rubbed.

Now, there is just one other thing to do, and that is to accustom the horse to a man hopping on his back and riding him. This is done in about five minutes.

The warrior takes the blanket and strikes the horse's back a number of blows. Then he lays the blanket gently on his back. The horse will at first start to buck it off, but another jerk on the string, and he is quieted. The warrior picks the blanket up and lays it across his back again. The horse will jump out from under it, perhaps twice, before he will stand still. When he has been brought to this point, the man throws the blanket down and walks slowly to the side of the horse and places both hands on his back and presses down lightly. He keeps pressing a little harder and harder, until finally he places his elbows across the horse's back and draws his body an inch off the ground. A horse may jump a little, but he will stand still the next time.

After the warrior has hung on his back by his elbows for

Personal Success   103

several periods of about thirty seconds each, he will gradually pull himself up, up, up. Finally he is ready to throw his right foot over to the other side. It is a strange fact that few horses broken in this manner ever try to buck. Usually the horse will stand perfectly still. The man will sit there and stroke him for a moment and then gently urge him to go. Then the horse will awkwardly trot off in a mild, aimless amble, first this way and that. He appears so bewildered and uncertain in his gait that one would think it was the first time he had ever tried to walk on his own feet.

Four months after we had captured the horses we were again back on our beloved plains in upper Montana. Our horses were the envy of every tribe who saw us that summer. They all wanted to know where we got them. Our chief told the story of this wild-horse hunt so many times that it became a legend among the Indians.

But at the end of the story our venerable leader would always look downcast. In sadly measured words, he would tell of the steel-dust stallion with the flowing moon-colored mane and tail, which he had picked out for himself. He would spend many minutes describing this superb horse, yet he would never finish the story, unless someone asked him what became of the animal.

Then he would slowly tell how our band had worked all day trying to rope this beast, and how that night they had left him in the little fenced-off part of the corral. But the next morning when they visited the corral, he had vanished. The horse had climbed over more than seven feet of fence which separated him from the main corral. There, with room for a running start, he attacked the heavy log fence and rammed his body clear through it. Nothing was left to tell the tale but a few patches of blood and hair and a wrecked fence.

That should have ended the story of the steel-dust beast, but it did not. The horse became famous throughout the Northwest as a lone traveler of the night. He went down on the plains of Montana and Alberta, and in the darkest hours of the night he would turn up at the most unexpected points in the wilderness of the prairies. He had lost his mighty bellow. And no person heard a sound from him again. He haunted the plains by night, and was never seen by day.

This silent, lone traveler of the night was often seen silhouetted against the moon on a butte, with his head erect, his tail thrown over his back. The steel-blue color of his body melted completely into the inky blueness of the night. His tail and mane stood out in the moonlight like shimmering threads of lighted

104 *Success: A Search for Values*

silver, giving him a halo which had a ghostly aspect. He became known throughout the Northwest as the Shunkatonka-Wakan —The Ghost Horse.

[SEE EXERCISE ON PAGE 315]

*The Ego Trap**

Robert Trent Jones golf courses are designed for a specifically American clientele. British "links" are much more difficult; the rough is left alone to become a tangled jungle and bad shots are penalized ferociously. In addition, British courses follow natural land contours, which means that on one shot the ball will be well above the golfer's feet, on another well below. This does not make par-breaking easy.

"If we were to build a course like that," Jones says, "the next day the greens committee would decide to level the fairways. The American wants to excel. He is more apt to adapt his playing field to where his ego can be satisfied by excelling than to accept a challenge. The British golfer does not consider a bogey a failure. The American golfer does."

LEONARD SCHECTER

* © **1968 by The New York Times Company. Reprinted by permission.**

Personal Success   105

> *When a short story is so famous that it starts an annual
> contest based on it, that is success. By many measures—
> enjoyment, literary quality, retellings—the short story
> which follows is one of the most successful ever written. A
> single story that has made an author known to more people
> and more places would be difficult to find.*
>
> *This a tale of a smart man outsmarted and of a man-who
> lives by his wits. Although it is part of the tradition of tall
> tales about animals (and men), the dialect adds to the story's
> authenticity. Certainly the people, or the animal, of this
> story are not likely to be forgotten.*

The Notorious Jumping Frog
of Calaveras County*

Mark Twain

In compliance with the request of a friend of mine, who
wrote me from the East, I called on good-natured, garrulous old
Simon Wheeler, and inquired after my friend's friend, Leonidas
W. Smiley, as requested to do, and I hereunto append the result.
I have a lurking suspicion that *Leonidas W.* Smiley is a myth;
that my friend never knew such a personage; and that he only
conjectured that if I asked old Wheeler about him, it would remind him of his infamous *Jim* Smiley, and he would go to work
and bore me to death with some exasperating reminiscence of
him as long and as tedious as it should be useless to me. If that
was the design, it succeeded.

I found Simon Wheeler dozing comfortably by the bar-room
stove of the dilapidated tavern in the decayed mining camp of
Angel's, and I noticed that he was fat and bald-headed, and had
an expression of winning gentleness and simplicity upon his
tranquil countenance. He roused up, and gave me good day. I
told him that a friend of mine had commissioned me to make

---

* "The Notorious Jumping Frog of Calaveras County" from *Sketches New and Old* by
Mark Twain. Reprinted by permission of Harper & Row, Publishers.

106   *Success: A Search for Values*

some inquiries about a cherished companion of his boyhood named *Leonidas W.* Smiley—*Rev. Leonidas W.* Smiley, a young minister of the Gospel, who he had heard was at one time a resident of Angel's Camp. I added that if Mr. Wheeler could tell me anything about this Rev. Leonidas W. Smiley, I would feel under many obligations to him.

Simon Wheeler backed me into a corner and blockaded me there with his chair, and then sat down and reeled off the monotonous narrative which follows this paragraph. He never smiled, he never frowned, he never changed his voice from the gentle-flowing key to which he tuned his initial sentence, he never betrayed the slightest suspicion of enthusiasm; but all through the interminable narrative there ran a vein of impressive earnestness and sincerity, which showed me plainly that, so far from his imagining that there was anything ridiculous or funny about his story, he regarded it as a really important matter, and admired its two heroes as men of transcendent genius in *finesse*. I let him go on in his own way, and never interrupted him once.

"Rev. Leonidas W. H'm, Reverend Le—well, there was a feller here once by the name of *Jim* Smiley, in the winter of '49—or maybe it was the spring of '50—I don't recollect exactly, somehow, though what makes me think it was one or the other is because I remember the big flume warn't finished when he first come to the camp; but anyway, he was the curiousest man about always betting on anything that turned up you ever see, if he could get anybody to bet on the other side; and if he couldn't he'd change sides. Any way that suited the other man would suit *him*—any way just so's he got a bet, *he* was satisfied. But still he was lucky, uncommon lucky; he most always come out winner. He was always ready and laying for a chance; there couldn't be no solit'ry thing mentioned but that feller'd offer to bet on it, and take any side you please, as I was just telling you. If there was a horse-race, you'd find him flush or you'd find him busted at the end of it; if there was a dog-fight, he'd bet on it; if there was a cat-fight, he'd bet on it; if there was a chicken-fight, he'd bet on it; why, if there was two birds setting on a fence, he would bet you which one would fly first; or if there was a camp-meeting, he would be there reg'lar to bet on Parson Walker, which he judged to be the best exhorter about here, and so he was too, and a good man. If he even see a straddle-bug start to go anywheres, he would bet you how long it would take him to get to—to wherever he was going to, and if you took him up, he would foller that straddle-bug to Mexico but what he would find out where he was bound for and how long he was on the road. Lots of the boys here has

Personal Success   107

seen that Smiley, and can tell you about him. Why, it never made
no difference to *him* — he'd bet on *any* thing — the dangdest feller.
Parson Walker's wife laid very sick once, for a good while, and it
seemed as if they warn't going to save her; but one morning he
come in, and Smiley up and asked him how she was, and he said
she was considerable better — thank the Lord for his inf'nite
mercy — and coming on so smart that with the blessing of Prov'-
dence she'd get well yet; and Smiley, before he thought, says,
'Well, I'll resk two-and-a-half she don't anyway.'

"Thish-yer Smiley had a mare — the boys called her the
fifteen-minute nag, but that was only in fun, you know, because
of course she was faster than that — and he used to win money
on that horse, for all she was so slow and always had the asthma,
or the distemper, or the consumption, or something of that kind.
They used to give her two or three hundred yards' start, and then
pass her under way; but always at the fag end of the race she'd
get excited and desperate like, and come cavorting and straddling
up, and scattering her legs around limber, sometimes in the air,
and sometimes out to one side among the fences, and kicking up
m-o-r-e dust and raising m-o-r-e racket with her coughing and
sneezing and blowing her nose — and *always* fetch up at the stand
just about a neck ahead, as near as you could cipher it down.

"And he had a little small bull-pup, that to look at him you'd
think he warn't worth a cent but to set around and look ornery
and lay for a chance to steal something. But as soon as money
was up on him he was a different dog; his under-jaw'd begin to
stick out like the fo'castle of a steamboat, and his teeth would
uncover and shine like the furnaces. And a dog might tackle
him and bully-rag him, and bite him, and throw him over his
shoulder two or three times, and Andrew Jackson — which was
the name of the pup — Andrew Jackson would never let on but
what *he* was satisfied, and hadn't expected nothing else — and the
bets being doubled and doubled on the other side all the time, till
the money was all up; and then all of a sudden he would grab
that other dog jest by the j'int of his hind leg and freeze to it — not
chaw, you understand, but only just grip and hang on till they
throwed up the sponge, if it was a year. Smiley always come out
winner on that pup, till he harnessed a dog once that didn't have
no hind legs, because they'd been sawed off in a circular saw, and
when the thing had gone along far enough, and the money was
all up, and he come to make a snatch for his pet holt, he see in a
minute how he'd been imposed on, and how the other dog had him
in the door, so to speak, and he 'peared surprised, and then he
looked sorter discouraged-like, and didn't try no more to win the

fight, and so he got shucked out bad. He give Smiley a look, as much as to say his heart was broke, and it was *his* fault, for putting up a dog that hadn't no hind legs for him to take holt of, which was his main dependence in a fight, and then he limped off a piece and laid down and died. It was a good pup, was that Andrew Jackson, and would have made a name for hisself if he'd lived, for the stuff was in him and he had genius — I know it, because he hadn't no opportunities to speak of, and it don't stand to reason that a dog could make such a fight as he could under them circumstances if he hadn't no talent. It always makes me feel sorry when I think of that last fight of his'n, and the way it turned out.

"Well, thish-yer Smiley had rat-tarriers, and chicken cocks, and tomcats and all them kind of things, till you couldn't rest, and you couldn't fetch nothing for him to bet on but he'd match you. He ketched a frog one day, and took him home, and said he cal'lated to educate him; and so he never done nothing for three months but set in his back yard and learn that frog to jump. And you bet you he *did* learn him, too. He'd give him a little punch behind, and the next minute you'd see that frog whirling in the air like a doughnut — see him turn one summerset, or maybe a couple, if he got a good start, and come down flat-footed and all right, like a cat. He got him up so in the matter of ketching flies, and kep' him in practice so constant, that he'd nail a fly every time as fur as he could see him. Smiley said all a frog wanted was education, and he could do 'most anything — and I believe him. Why, I've seen him set Dan'l Webster down here on this floor — Dan'l Webster was the name of the frog — and sing out, 'Flies, Dan'l, flies!' and quicker'n you could wink he'd spring straight up and snake a fly off'n the counter there, and flop down on the floor ag'in as solid as a gob of mud, and fall to scratching the side of his head with his hind foot as indifferent as if he hadn't no idea he'd been doin' any more'n any frog might do. You never see a frog so modest and straightfor'ard as he was, for all he was so gifted. And when it come to fair and square jumping on a dead level, he could get over more ground at one straddle than any animal of his breed you ever see. Jumping on a dead level was his strong suit, you understand; and when it come to that, Smiley would ante up money on him as long as he had a red. Smiley was monstrous proud of his frog, and well he might be, for fellers that had traveled and been everywheres all said he laid over any frog that ever *they* see.

"Well, Smiley kep' the beast in a little lattice box, and he

Personal Success

used to fetch him down-town sometimes and lay for a bet. One day a feller—a stranger in the camp, he was—come acrost him with his box, and says:

"'What might it be that you've got in the box?'

"And Smiley says, sorter indifferent-like, 'It might be a parrot, or it might be a canary, maybe, but it ain't—it's only just a frog.'

"And the feller took it, and looked at it careful, and turned it round this way and that, and says, 'H'm—so 'tis. Well, what's *he* good for?'

"'Well,' Smiley says, easy and careless, 'he's good enough for *one* thing, I should judge—he can outjump any frog in Calaveras County.'

"The feller took the box again, and took another long, particular look, and give it back to Smiley, and says, very deliberate, 'Well,' he says, 'I don't see no p'ints about that frog that's any better'n any other frog.'

"'Maybe you don't,' Smiley says. 'Maybe you understand frogs and maybe you don't understand 'em; maybe you've had experience, and maybe you ain't only a amature, as it were. Anyways, I've got *my* opinion, and I'll resk forty dollars that he can outjump any frog in Calaveras County.'

"And the feller studied a minute, and then says, kinder sad-like, 'Well, I'm only a stranger here, and I ain't got no frog; but if I had a frog, I'd bet you.'

"And then Smiley says, 'That's all right—that's all right—if you'll hold my box a minute, I'll go and get you a frog.' And so the feller took the box, and put up his forty dollars along with Smiley's, and set down to wait.

"So he set there a good while thinking and thinking to himself, and then he got the frog out and prized his mouth open and took a teaspoon and filled him full of quail-shot—filled him pretty near up to his chin—and set him on the floor. Smiley he went to the swamp and slopped around in the mud for a long time, and finally he ketched a frog, and fetched him in, and give him to this feller, and says:

"'Now, if you're ready, set him alongside of Dan'l, with his fore paws just even with Dan'l's, and I'll give the word.' Then he says, 'One—two—three—*git!*' and him and the feller touched up the frogs from behind, and the new frog hopped off lively, but Dan'l give a heave, and hysted up his shoulders—so—like a Frenchman, but it warn't no use—he couldn't budge; he was planted as solid as a church, and he couldn't no more stir than if he was anchored out. Smiley was a good deal surprised, and he was disgusted too, but he didn't have no idea what the matter was, of course.

"The feller took the money and started away; and when he was going out at the door, he sorter jerked his thumb over his shoulder—so—at Dan'l, and says again, very deliberate, 'Well,' he says, '*I* don't see no p'ints about that frog that's any better'n any other frog.'

"Smiley he stood scratching his head and looking down at Dan'l a long time, and at last he says, 'I do wonder what in the nation that frog throw'd off for—I wonder if there ain't something the matter with him—he 'pears to look mighty baggy, somehow.' And he ketched Dan'l by the nap of the neck, and hefted him, and says, 'Why blame my cats if he don't weigh five pound!' and turned him upside down and he belched out a double handful of shot. And then he see how it was, and he was the maddest man —he set the frog down and took out after that feller, but he never ketched him. And—"

[Here Simon Wheeler heard his name called from the front yard, and got up to see what was wanted.] And turning to me as he moved away, he said: "Just set where you are, stranger, and rest easy—I ain't going to be gone a second."

But, by your leave, I did not think that a continuation of the history of the enterprising vagabond *Jim* Smiley would be likely to afford me much information concerning the Rev. *Leonidas* W. Smiley, so I started away.

At the door I met the sociable Wheeler returning, and he buttonholed me and recommenced:

"Well, thish-yer Smiley had a yeller one-eyed cow that didn't have no tail, only jest a short stump like a bannanner, and—"

"Oh, hang Smiley and his afflicted cow!" I muttered, good-naturedly, and bidding the old gentleman good-day, I departed.

[SEE EXERCISE ON PAGE 319]

Personal Success   111

18-Foot Leap Wins Frog-Jumping Title*

ANGELS CAMP, Calif.—(AP)—Tickled onward by his owner, a swamp-bred frog named Corrosion hopped 36 times his length and won the Mark Twain-inspired international frog-jumping contest.

Corrosion, a diminutive six-incher, once called a Bakersfield, Calif., swamp home. He outdistanced more than 500 of his peers to win the 40th annual event.

The four-year-old winner leaped 18 feet and one-half inches, outdistancing his nearest rival by one foot, 4¼ inches.

It marked the fifth victory for owner-trainer Leonard Hall of Concord, Calif., who said there is a for-

* **Reprinted from Associated Press News-features.**

mula to his success.

"Get yourself a good wild frog," Hall said. "We hunted this one."

Hall, a real estate man, said he learned while training Corrosion that "if you tickle him, he'll pick up a bit."

Confidently plunking him on the starting spot before thousands of onlookers, Hall cooed, "Gitchee, gitchee, gitchee" and tickled him with his index finger.

Corrosion bounded away, escaping the traditional dinner-pan finish of some also rans and outclassing "celebrity" frogs.

Big Tom, entered by Oregon Gov. Tom McCall, jumped only six feet, 6½ inches, but that outdistanced "celebrity" finalists entered by politicians from Nevada, Nebraska and New Hampshire.

When you are aspiring to the highest place, it is honorable to reach the second or even the third mark.

CICERO

To maintain that our successes are due to Providence and not to our own cleverness is a cunning way of increasing in our own eyes the importance of our successes.

PAVESE

Used by permission of the artist.

Personal Success   113

A Sure Way to Succeed
from the *Midrash*

A youth grew up in a certain king's household and the king
came to feel a deep affection for him. One day he said to him:
"Ask whatever you wish and I'll give it to you."
The youth thought and thought:
What shall I ask him for? Shall I ask for precious gems, for
gold and silver? He'll surely give them to me. Shall I ask for expensive clothes? These too he'll gladly give to me. What among
them should I choose? Why not ask for his daughter? As his
son-in-law I can then have everything.

Fortune does not change men; it unmasks them.

MME. NECKER

None think the great unhappy but the great.

YOUNG

*The language of the two poems that follow sounds archaic,
and perhaps silly. No wonder. They were written in England
about 400 years ago. (Christopher Marlowe lived from 1564
to 1593 and Sir Walter Raleigh from 1552 to 1618.) They
came from an era in which country life was so admired
that young men-about-town thought it romantic to assume
the role of shepherds and to write delicate verses to their
lady-loves.*

*The clothes they wore, the things they said and did are all
strange to us today. But the human desires and emotions
are very familiar. The young man in the Marlowe poem is
making an offer to the young lady, although the inducements he lists are not the same that would be required
today. Raleigh wrote his poem as an answer to the one by
Marlowe, pointing out (even as a woman might today) that
the fellow is offering everything except what she really
wants.*

(Note: *It may help, in reading the poem, to pronounce
"love" as it was pronounced in the time of these two poets:
rhyme "love" with "move" and "prove.")*

The Passionate Shepherd
to His Love

Christopher Marlowe

Come live with me and be my love,
And we will all the pleasures prove
That hills and valleys, dales and fields,
Or woods or steepy mountain yields.

And we will sit upon the rocks,
And see the shepherds feed their flocks
By shallow rivers, to whose falls
Melodious birds sing madrigals.

And I will make thee beds of roses,
And a thousand fragrant posies;

Personal Success   115

A cap of flowers, and a kirtle [*a woman's gown or skirt*]
Embroider'd all with leaves of myrtle.

A gown made of the finest wool,
Which from our pretty lambs we pull;
Fair lined slippers for the cold,
With buckles of the purest gold.

A belt of straw and ivy buds
With coral clasps and amber studs;
And if these pleasures may thee move,
Come live with me, and be my love.

The shepherd swains shall dance and sing
For thy delight each May morning:
If these delights thy mind may move,
Then live with me, and be my love.

The Nymph's Reply
to the Shepherd

Sir Walter Raleigh

If all the world and love were young,
And truth in every shepherd's tongue,
These pretty pleasures might me move
To live with thee and be thy love.

Time drives the flocks from field to fold
When rivers rage and rocks grow cold,
And Philomel [*the nightingale*] becometh dumb;
The rest complains of cares to come.

The flowers do fade, and wanton fields
To wayward winter reckoning yields;

A honey tongue, a heart of gall,
Is fancy's spring, but sorrow's fall.

Thy gowns, thy shoes, thy beds of roses,
Thy cap, thy kirtle, and thy posies
Soon break, soon wither, soon forgotten,—
In folly ripe, in reason rotten.

Thy belt of straw and ivy buds,
Thy coral clasps and amber studs,
All these in me no means can move
To come to thee and be thy love.

But could youth last and love still breed,
Had joys no date nor age no need,
Then these delights my mind might move
To live with thee and be thy love.

[SEE EXERCISE ON PAGE 323]

Cleopatra's Joke
on Marc Anthony: 40 B.C.*

Plutarch

Marc Anthony went out fishing one day with Cleopatra, and being able to catch nothing in the presence of his mistress, he gave secret orders to fishermen to dive under water and put fish that had already been caught on his hook. He drew them in so fast, Cleopatra perceived the reason. Pretending great admiration, she invited everyone to come out next day and see how skillful he was. While they watched from the boats, as soon as he threw in his hook, she had a diver put a salted fish on it. Feeling a tug, Anthony drew it in and great laughter ensued. Cleopatra said, "General, leave the fishing rod to us poor sovereigns of Pharos and Canopus: your game is cities, provinces and kingdoms."

* **Quotation by Plutarch from** *Captain Cousteau's Underwater Treasure*, **ed. Jacques-Yves Cousteau and James Dugan.**

"... and of course you all remember Lionel Tunstall, the chap voted most likely to succeed. Well, Lionel didn't make it, but let's give him a big hand anyway — he's the waiter with the moustache."

Reproduced with permission of the *Saturday Evening Post*. © 1966 The Curtis Publishing Company.

All the world loves a winner. But everybody is not a winner, either because of circumstances or because of personal characteristics. Miniver Cheevy is one of those in the latter group.

Miniver Cheevy*

Edwin Arlington Robinson

Miniver Cheevy, child of scorn,
　　Grew lean while he assailed the seasons;
He wept that he was ever born,
　　And he had reasons.

Miniver loved the days of old
　　When swords were bright and steeds were prancing;
The vision of a warrior bold
　　Would set him dancing.

Miniver sighed for what was not,
　　And he dreamed, and rested from his labors;
He dreamed of Thebes and Camelot,
　　And Priam's neighbors.

Miniver mourned the ripe renown
　　That made so many a name so fragrant;
He mourned Romance, now on the town,
　　And Art, a vagrant.

Miniver loved the Medici,
　　Albeit he had never seen one;
He would have sinned incessantly
　　Could he have been one.

---

* The following poem by Edwin Arlington Robinson is reprinted by permission of Charles Scribner's Sons: "Miniver Cheevy" (Copyright 1907 Charles Scribner's Sons renewal copyright 1935) from *The Town Down the River.*

Personal Success   119

Miniver cursed the commonplace
    And eyed a khaki suit with loathing;
He missed the medieval grace
    Of iron clothing.

Miniver scorned the gold he sought,
    But sore annoyed was he without it;
Miniver thought, and thought, and thought,
    And thought about it.

Miniver Cheevy, born too late,
    Scratched his head and kept on thinking;
Miniver coughed, and called it fate,
    And kept on drinking.

[SEE EXERCISE ON PAGE 327]

When I was a young man I observed that 9 out of 10 things I did were failures. I didn't want to be a failure, so I did 10 times more work.

GEORGE BERNARD SHAW

We succeed in exterprises which demand the positive qualities we possess, but we excel in those which can also make use of our defects.

DE TOCQUEVILLE

Here is another viewpoint of a "loser," one quite different from Miniver Cheevy's opinion of himself. In this poem it is the gambler (or "dicer") who experiences defeat. However, the poet indicates that even from defeat may come some good, if one takes the right attitude.

Davy, the Dicer

Sir Thomas More

Long was I, Lady Luck, your serving-man,
And now have lost again all that I gat;
Wherefore, when I think on you now and than
And in my mind remember this and that,
Ye may not blame me though I beshrew your cat.
But, in faith, I bless you again, a thousand times,
For lending me now some leisure to make rhymes.

Personal Success   121

> *The mousy, long-suffering wife is almost as much a literary*
> *cliché as the henpecked husband. Jokes about her and let-*
> *ters from her are likely to appear in newspaper advice-to-*
> *the-lovelorn columns. In her are revealed the frustrations*
> *felt by everyone who has to follow orders and do things*
> *against his will, while wishing to—but not daring to—rebel.*

The Way Up to Heaven*

Roald Dahl

All her life, Mrs. Foster had had an almost pathological fear
of missing a train, a plane, a boat, or even a theatre curtain. In
other respects, she was not a particularly nervous woman, but
the mere thought of being late on occasions like these would
throw her into such a state of nerves that she would begin to
twitch. It was nothing much—just a tiny vellicating muscle in
the corner of the left eye, like a secret wink—but the annoying
thing was that it refused to disappear until an hour or so after
the train or plane or whatever it was had been safely caught.

It is really extraordinary how in certain people a simple
apprehension about a thing like catching a train can grow into
a serious obsession. At least half an hour before it was time to
leave the house for the station, Mrs. Foster would step out of the
elevator all ready to go, with hat and coat and gloves, and then,
being quite unable to sit down, she would flutter and fidget about
from room to room until her husband, who must have been well
aware of her state, finally emerged from his privacy and suggested in a cool dry voice that perhaps they had better get going
now, had they not?

Mr. Foster may possibly have had a right to be irritated by
this foolishness of his wife's, but he could have had no excuse
for increasing her misery by keeping her waiting unnecessarily.
Mind you, it is by no means certain that this is what he did, yet
whenever they were to go somewhere, his timing was so accu-

---

* **Copyright 1954 by Roald Dahl. Reprinted from *Kiss Kiss* by Roald Dahl by permission
of Alfred A. Knopf, Inc. Originally appeared in *The New Yorker*.**

rate – just a minute or two late, you understand – and his manner so bland that it was hard to believe he wasn't purposely inflicting a nasty private little torture of his own on the unhappy lady. And one thing he must have known – that she would never dare to call out and tell him to hurry. He had disciplined her too well for that. He must also have known that if he was prepared to wait even beyond the last moment of safety, he could drive her nearly into hysterics. On one or two special occasions in the later years of their married life, it seemed almost as though he had *wanted* to miss the train simply in order to intensify the poor woman's suffering.

Assuming (though one cannot be sure) that the husband was guilty, what made his attitude doubly unreasonable was the fact that, with the exception of this one small irrepressible foible, Mrs. Foster was and always had been a good and loving wife. For over thirty years, she had served him loyally and well. There was no doubt about this. Even she, a very modest woman, was aware of it, and although she had for years refused to let herself believe that Mr. Foster would ever consciously torment her, there had been times recently when she had caught herself beginning to wonder.

Mr. Eugene Foster, who was nearly seventy years old, lived with his wife in a large six-story house on East Sixty-second Street, and they had four servants. It was a gloomy place, and few people came to visit them. But on this particular morning in January, the house had come alive and there was a great deal of bustling about. One maid was distributing bundles of dust sheets to every room, while another was draping them over the furniture. The butler was bringing down suitcases and putting them in the hall. The cook kept popping up from the kitchen to have a word with the butler, and Mrs. Foster herself, in an old-fashioned fur coat and with a black hat on the top of her head, was flying from room to room and pretending to supervise these operations. Actually, she was thinking of nothing at all except that she was going to miss her plane if her husband didn't come out of his study soon and get ready.

"What time is it, Walker?" she said to the butler as she passed him.

"It's ten minutes past nine, Madam."

"And has the car come?"

"Yes, Madam, it's waiting. I'm just going to put the luggage in now."

"It takes an hour to get to Idlewild," she said. "My plane leaves at eleven. I have to be there half an hour beforehand for the formalities. I shall be late. I just *know* I'm going to be late."

Personal Success   123

"I think you have plenty of time, Madam," the butler said kindly. "I warned Mr. Foster that you must leave at nine fifteen. There's still another five minutes."

"Yes, Walker, I know, I know. But get the luggage in quickly, will you please?"

She began walking up and down the hall, and whenever the butler came by, she asked him the time. This, she kept telling herself, was the *one* plane she must not miss. It had taken months to persuade her husband to allow her to go. If she missed it, he might easily decide that she should cancel the whole thing. And the trouble was that he insisted on coming to the airport to see her off.

"Dear God," she said aloud, "I'm going to miss it. I know, I know, I *know* I'm going to miss it." The little muscle beside the left eye was twitching madly now. The eyes themselves were very close to tears.

"What time is it, Walker?"

"It's eighteen minutes past, Madam."

"Now I really *will* miss it!" she cried. "Oh, I wish he would come!"

This was an important journey for Mrs. Foster. She was going all alone to Paris to visit her daughter, her only child, who was married to a Frenchman. Mrs. Foster didn't care much for the Frenchman, but she was fond of her daughter, and, more than that, she had developed a great yearning to set eyes on her three grandchildren. She knew them only from the many photographs that she had received and that she kept putting up all over the house. They were beautiful, these children. She doted on them, and each time a new picture arrived, she would carry it away and sit with it for a long time, staring at it lovingly and searching the small faces for signs of that old satisfying blood likeness that meant so much. And now, lately, she had come more and more to feel that she did not really wish to live out her days in a place where she could not be near these children, and have them visit her, and take them for walks, and buy them presents, and watch them grow. She knew, of course, that it was wrong and in a way disloyal to have thoughts like these while her husband was still alive. She knew also that although he was no longer active in his many enterprises, he would never consent to leave New York and live in Paris. It was a miracle that he had ever agreed to let her fly over there alone for six weeks to visit them. But, oh, how she wished she could live there always, and be close to them!

"Walker, what time is it?"

124   *Success: A Search for Values*

"Twenty-two minutes past, Madam."

As he spoke, a door opened and Mr. Foster came into the hall. He stood for a moment, looking intently at his wife, and she looked back at him — at this diminutive but still quite dapper old man with the huge bearded face that bore such an astonishing resemblance to those old photographs of Andrew Carnegie.

"Well," he said, "I suppose perhaps we'd better get going fairly soon if you want to catch that plane."

"*Yes*, dear — *yes!* Everything's ready. The car's waiting."

"That's good," he said. With his head over to one side, he was watching her closely. He had a peculiar way of cocking the head and then moving it in a series of small, rapid jerks. Because of this and because he was clasping his hands up high in front of him, near the chest, he was somehow like a squirrel standing there — a quick clever old squirrel from the Park.

"Here's Walker with your coat, dear. Put it on."

"I'll be with you in a moment," he said. "I'm just going to wash my hands."

She waited for him, and the tall butler stood beside her, holding the coat and the hat.

"Walker, will I miss it?"

"No, Madam," the butler said. "I think you'll make it all right."

Then Mr. Foster appeared again, and the butler helped him on with his coat. Mrs. Foster hurried outside and got into the hired Cadillac. Her husband came after her, but he walked down the steps of the house slowly, pausing halfway to observe the sky and to sniff the cold morning air.

"It looks a bit foggy," he said as he sat down beside her in the car. "And it's always worse out there at the airport. I shouldn't be surprised if the flight's cancelled already."

"Don't say that, dear — *please*."

They didn't speak again until the car had crossed over the river to Long Island.

"I arranged everything with the servants," Mr. Foster said. "They're all going off today. I gave them half pay for six weeks and told Walker I'd send him a telegram when we wanted them back."

"Yes," she said. "He told me."

"I'll move into the club tonight. It'll be a nice change staying at the club."

"Yes, dear. I'll write to you."

"I'll call in at the house occasionally to see that everything's all right and to pick up the mail."

Personal Success 125

"But don't you really think Walker should stay there all the time to look after things?" she asked meekly.

"Nonsense. It's quite unnecessary. And anyway, I'd have to pay him full wages."

"Oh yes," she said. "Of course."

"What's more, you never know what people get up to when they're left alone in a house," Mr. Foster announced, and with that he took out a cigar and, after snipping off the end with a silver cutter, lit it with a gold lighter.

She sat still in the car with her hands clasped together tight under the rug.

"Will you write to me?" she asked.

"I'll see," he said. "But I doubt it. You know I don't hold with letter-writing unless there's something specific to say."

"Yes, dear, I know. So don't you bother."

They drove on, along Queens Boulevard, and as they approached the flat marshland on which Idlewild is built, the fog began to thicken and the car had to slow down.

"Oh dear!" cried Mrs. Foster. "I'm *sure* I'm going to miss it now! What time is it?"

"Stop fussing," the old man said. "It doesn't matter anyway. It's bound to be cancelled now. They never fly in this sort of weather. I don't know why you bothered to come out."

She couldn't be sure, but it seemed to her that there was suddenly a new note in his voice, and she turned to look at him. It was difficult to observe any change in his expression under all that hair. The mouth was what counted. She wished, as she had so often before, that she could see the mouth clearly. The eyes never showed anything except when he was in a rage.

"Of course," he went on, "if by any chance it *does* go, then I agree with you—you'll be certain to miss it now. Why don't you resign yourself to that?"

She turned away and peered through the window at the fog. It seemed to be getting thicker as they went along, and now she could only just make out the edge of the road and the margin of grassland beyond it. She knew that her husband was still looking at her. She glanced back at him again, and this time she noticed with a kind of horror that he was staring intently at the little place in the corner of her left eye where she could feel the muscle twitching.

"Won't you?" he said.

"Won't I what?"

"Be sure to miss it now if it goes. We can't drive fast in this muck."

He didn't speak to her any more after that. The car crawled on and on. The driver had a yellow lamp directed onto the edge of the road, and this helped him to keep going. Other lights, some white and some yellow, kept coming out of the fog toward them, and there was an especially bright one that followed close behind them all the time.

Suddenly, the driver stopped the car.

"There!" Mr. Foster cried. "We're stuck. I knew it."

"No, sir," the driver said, turning round. "We made it. This is the airport."

Without a word, Mrs. Foster jumped out and hurried through the main entrance into the building. There was a mass of people inside, mostly disconsolate passengers standing around the ticket counters. She pushed her way through and spoke to the clerk.

"Yes," he said. "Your flight is temporarily postponed. But please don't go away. We're expecting this weather to clear any moment."

She went back to her husband who was still sitting in the car and told him the news. "But don't you wait, dear," she said. "There's no sense in that."

"I won't," he answered. "So long as the driver can get me back. Can you get me back, driver?"

"I think so," the man said.

"Is the luggage out?"

"Yes, sir."

"Goodbye, dear," Mrs. Foster said, leaning into the car and giving her husband a small kiss on the coarse grey fur of his cheek.

"Goodbye," he answered. "Have a good trip."

The car drove off, and Mrs. Foster was left alone.

The rest of the day was a sort of nightmare for her. She sat for hour after hour on a bench, as close to the airline counter as possible, and every thirty minutes or so she would get up and ask the clerk if the situation had changed. She always received the same reply—that she must continue to wait, because the fog might blow away at any moment. It wasn't until after six in the evening that the loudspeakers finally announced that the flight had been postponed until eleven o'clock the next morning.

Mrs. Foster didn't quite know what to do when she heard this news. She stayed sitting on her bench for at least another half-hour, wondering, in a tired, hazy sort of way, where she might go to spend the night. She hated to leave the airport. She

Personal Success   127

didn't wish to see her husband. She was terrified that in one way
or another he would eventually manage to prevent her from getting to France. She would have liked to remain just where she
was, sitting on the bench the whole night through. That would
be the safest. But she was already exhausted, and it didn't take
her long to realize that this was a ridiculous thing for an elderly
lady to do. So in the end she went to a phone and called the house.

Her husband, who was on the point of leaving for the club,
answered it himself. She told him the news, and asked whether
the servants were still there.

"They've all gone," he said.

"In that case, dear, I'll just get myself a room somewhere
for the night. And don't you bother yourself about it at all."

"That would be foolish," he said. "You've got a large house
here at your disposal. Use it."

"But, dear, it's *empty.*"

"Then I'll stay with you myself."

"There's no food in the house. There's nothing."

"Then eat before you come in. Don't be so stupid, woman.
Everything you do, you seem to want to make a fuss about it."

"Yes," she said. "I'm sorry. I'll get myself a sandwich here,
and then I'll come on in."

Outside, the fog had cleared a little but it was still a long,
slow drive in the taxi, and she didn't arrive back at the house on
Sixty-second Street until fairly late.

Her husband emerged from his study when he heard her
coming in. "Well," he said, standing by the study door, "how was
Paris?"

"We leave at eleven in the morning," she answered. "It's
definite."

"You mean if the fog clears."

"It's clearing now. There's a wind coming up."

"You look tired," he said. "You must have had an anxious
day."

"It wasn't very comfortable. I think I'll go straight to bed."

"I've ordered a car for the morning," he said. "Nine o'clock."

"Oh, thank you, dear. And I certainly hope you're not going
to bother to come all the way out again to see me off."

"No," he said slowly. "I don't think I will. But there's no
reason why you shouldn't drop me at the club on your way."

She looked at him, and at that moment he seemed to be
standing a long way off from her, beyond some borderline. He
was suddenly so small and far away that she couldn't be sure

128   *Success: A Search for Values*

what he was doing, or what he was thinking, or even what he was.

"The club is downtown," she said. "It isn't on the way to the airport."

"But you'll have plenty of time, my dear. Don't you want to drop me at the club?"

"Oh, yes — of course."

"That's good. Then I'll see you in the morning at nine."

She went up to her bedroom on the third floor, and she was so exhausted from her day that she fell asleep soon after she lay down.

Next morning, Mrs. Foster was up early, and by eight thirty she was downstairs and ready to leave.

Shortly after nine, her husband appeared. "Did you make any coffee?" he asked.

"No, dear. I thought you'd get a nice breakfast at the club. The car is here. It's been waiting. I'm all ready to go."

They were standing in the hall — they always seemed to be meeting in the hall nowadays — she with her hat and coat and purse, he in a curiously cut Edwardian jacket with high lapels.

"Your luggage?"

"It's at the airport."

"Ah yes," he said. "Of course. And if you're going to take me to the club first, I suppose we'd better get going fairly soon, hadn't we?"

"Yes!" she cried. "Oh, yes — *please!*"

"I'm just going to get a few cigars. I'll be right with you. You get in the car."

She turned and went out to where the chauffeur was standing, and he opened the car door for her as she approached.

"What time is it?" she asked him.

"About nine fifteen."

Mr. Foster came out five minutes later, and watching him as he walked slowly down the steps, she noticed that his legs were like goat's legs in those narrow stovepipe trousers that he wore. As on the day before, he paused halfway down to sniff the air and to examine the sky. The weather was still not quite clear, but there was a wisp of sun coming through the mist.

"Perhaps you'll be lucky this time," he said as he settled himself beside her in the car.

"Hurry, please," she said to the chauffeur. "Don't bother about the rug. I'll arrange the rug. Please get going. I'm late."

The man went back to his seat behind the wheel and started the engine.

Personal Success   129

"*Just* a moment!" Mr. Foster said suddenly. "Hold it a moment, chauffeur, will you?"

"What is it, dear?" She saw him searching the pockets of his overcoat.

"I had a little present I wanted you to take to Ellen," he said. "Now, where on earth is it? I'm sure I had it in my hand as I came down."

"I never saw you carrying anything. What sort of present?"

"A little box wrapped up in white paper. I forgot to give it to you yesterday. I don't want to forget it today."

"A little box!" Mrs. Foster cried. "I never saw any little box!" She began hunting frantically in the back of the car.

Her husband continued searching through the pockets of his coat. Then he unbuttoned the coat and felt around in his jacket. "Confound it," he said, "I must've left it in my bedroom. I won't be a moment."

"Oh, *please!*" she cried. "We haven't got time! *Please* leave it! You can mail it. It's only one of those silly combs anyway. You're always giving her combs."

"And what's wrong with combs, may I ask?" he said, furious that she should have forgotten herself for once.

"Nothing, dear, I'm sure. But . . ."

"Stay here!" he commanded. "I'm going to get it."

"Be quick, dear! Oh, *please* be quick!"

She sat still, waiting and waiting.

"Chauffeur, what time is it?"

The man had a wristwatch, which he consulted. "I make it nearly nine thirty."

"Can we get to the airport in an hour?"

"Just about."

At this point, Mrs. Foster suddenly spotted a corner of something white wedged down in the crack of the seat on the side where her husband had been sitting. She reached over and pulled out a small paper-wrapped box, and at the same time she couldn't help noticing that it was wedged down firm and deep, as though with the help of a pushing hand.

"Here it is!" she cried. "I've found it! Oh dear, and now he'll be up there forever searching for it! Chauffeur, quickly—run in and call him down, will you please?"

The chauffeur, a man with a small rebellious Irish mouth, didn't care very much for any of this, but he climbed out of the car and went up the steps to the front door of the house. Then he turned and came back. "Door's locked," he announced. "You got a key?"

130   *Success: A Search for Values*

"Yes—wait a minute." She began hunting madly in her purse. The little face was screwed up tight with anxiety, the lips pushed outward like a spout.

"Here it is! No—I'll go myself. It'll be quicker. I know where he'll be."

She hurried out of the car and up the steps to the front door, holding the key in one hand. She slid the key into the key-hole and was about to turn it—and then she stopped. Her head came up, and she stood there absolutely motionless, her whole body arrested right in the middle of all this hurry to turn the key and get into the house, and she waited—five, six, seven, eight, nine, ten seconds, she waited. The way she was standing there, with her head in the air and the body so tense, it seemed as though she were listening for the repetition of some sound that she had heard a moment before from a place far away inside the house.

Yes—quite obviously she was listening. Her whole attitude was a *listening* one. She appeared actually to be moving one of her ears closer and closer to the door. Now it was right up against the door, and for still another few seconds she remained in that position, head up, ear to door, hand on key, about to enter but not entering, trying instead, or so it seemed, to hear and to analyze these sounds that were coming faintly from this place deep within the house.

Then, all at once, she sprang to life again. She withdrew the key from the door and came running back down the steps.

"It's too late!" she cried to the chauffeur. "I can't wait for him, I simply can't. I'll miss the plane. Hurry now, driver, hurry! To the airport!"

The chauffeur, had he been watching her closely, might have noticed that her face had turned absolutely white and that the whole expression had suddenly altered. There was no longer that rather soft and silly look. A peculiar hardness had settled itself upon the features. The little mouth, usually so flabby, was now tight and thin, the eyes were bright, and the voice, when she spoke, carried a new note of authority.

"Hurry, driver, hurry!"

"Isn't your husband travelling with you?" the man asked, astonished.

"Certainly not! I was only going to drop him at the club. It won't matter. He'll understand. He'll get a cab. Don't sit there talking, man. *Get going!* I've got a plane to catch for Paris!"

With Mrs. Foster urging him from the back seat, the man drove fast all the way, and she caught her plane with a few min-utes to spare. Soon she was high up over the Atlantic, reclining

Personal Success 131

comfortably in her airplane chair, listening to the hum of the motors, heading for Paris at last. The new mood was still with her. She felt remarkably strong and, in a queer sort of way, wonderful. She was a trifle breathless with it all, but this was more from pure astonishment at what she had done than anything else, and as the plane flew farther and farther away from New York and East Sixty-second Street, a great sense of calmness began to settle upon her. By the time she reached Paris, she was just as strong and cool and calm as she could wish.

She met her grandchildren, and they were even more beautiful in the flesh than in their photographs. They were like angels, she told herself, so beautiful they were. And every day she took them for walks, and fed them cakes, and bought them presents, and told them charming stories.

Once a week, on Tuesdays, she wrote a letter to her husband — a nice, chatty letter — full of news and gossip, which always ended with the words "Now be sure to take your meals regularly, dear, although this is something I'm afraid you may not be doing when I'm not with you."

When the six weeks were up, everybody was sad that she had to return to America, to her husband. Everybody, that is, except her. Surprisingly, she didn't seem to mind as much as one might have expected, and when she kissed them all goodbye, there was something in her manner and in the things she said that appeared to hint at the possibility of a return in the not too distant future.

However, like the faithful wife she was, she did not overstay her time. Exactly six weeks after she had arrived, she sent a cable to her husband and caught the plane back to New York.

Arriving at Idlewild, Mrs. Foster was interested to observe that there was no car to meet her. It is possible that she might even have been a little amused. But she was extremely calm and did not overtip the porter who helped her into a taxi with her baggage.

New York was colder than Paris, and there were lumps of dirty snow lying in the gutters of the streets. The taxi drew up before the house on Sixty-second Street, and Mrs. Foster persuaded the driver to carry her two large cases to the top of the steps. Then she paid him off and rang the bell. She waited, but there was no answer. Just to make sure, she rang again, and she could hear it tinkling shrilly far away in the pantry, at the back of the house. But still no one came.

So she took out her own key and opened the door herself.

The first thing she saw as she entered was a great pile of mail lying on the floor where it had fallen after being slipped through the letter hole. The place was dark and cold. A dust sheet was still draped over the grandfather clock. In spite of the cold, the atmosphere was peculiarly oppressive, and there was a faint but curious odor in the air that she had never smelled before.

She walked quickly across the hall and disappeared for a moment around the corner to the left, at the back. There was something deliberate and purposeful about this action; she had the air of a woman who is off to investigate a rumor or to confirm a suspicion. And when she returned a few seconds later, there was a little glimmer of satisfaction on her face.

She paused in the center of the hall, as though wondering what to do next. Then, suddenly, she turned and went across into her husband's study. On the desk she found his address book, and after hunting through it for a while she picked up the phone and dialed a number.

"Hello," she said. "Listen—this is Nine East Sixty-second Street. . . . Yes, that's right. Could you send someone round as soon as possible, do you think? Yes, it seems to be stuck between the second and third floors. At least, that's where the indicator's pointing. . . . Right away? Oh, that's very kind of you. You see, my legs aren't any too good for walking up a lot of stairs. Thank you so much. Goodbye."

She replaced the receiver and sat there at her husband's desk, patiently waiting for the man who would be coming soon to repair the elevator.

[SEE EXERCISE ON PAGE 331]

The common idea that success spoils people by making them vain, egotistic, and self-complacent is erroneous; on the contrary, it makes them, for the most part, humble, tolerant, and mild. Failure makes people cruel and bitter.

MAUGHAM

Personal Success   133

> *Anyone who outsmarts "the establishment" makes a good subject for writers. In this story, Albert Edward Foreman does outsmart the establishment and more: he beats "them" at their own game. The fact that the main character is a Londoner, and that his work experience is alien to us, does not matter. It is still a story about another human being, and his delights and pains are enough like our own so that we can share them.*
>
> *A "verger" is a man who takes care of the inside of a church, assists the clergyman, and acts in general as a caretaker for the building.*

The Verger*

W. Somerset Maugham

There had been a christening that afternoon at St. Peter's, Neville Square, and Albert Edward Foreman still wore his verger's gown. He kept his new one, its folds as full and stiff as though it were made not of alpaca but of perennial bronze, for funerals and weddings (St. Peter's, Neville Square, was a church much favoured by the fashionable for these ceremonies) and now he wore only his second-best. He wore it with complacence, for it was the dignified symbol of his office, and without it (when he took it off to go home) he had the disconcerting sensation of being somewhat insufficiently clad. He took pains with it; he pressed it and ironed it himself. During the sixteen years he had been verger of this church he had had a succession of such gowns, but he had never been able to throw them away when they were worn out and the complete series, neatly wrapped up in

---

* U.S. rights for "The Verger," copyright 1929 by W. Somerset Maugham, from *Cosmopolitan* and *The Complete Short Stories* by W. Somerset Maugham. Reprinted by permission of Doubleday & Company, Inc. Canadian and Philippine rights by permission of the Literary Executor of W. Somerset Maugham and William Heinemann Ltd.

brown paper, lay in the bottom drawers of the wardrobe in his bedroom.

The verger busied himself quietly, replacing the painted wooden cover on the marble font, taking away a chair that had been brought for an infirm old lady, and waited for the vicar to have finished in the vestry so that he could tidy up in there and go home. Presently he saw him walk across the chancel, genuflect in front of the high altar and come down the aisle; but he still wore his cassock.

"What's he 'anging about for?" the verger said to himself. "Don't 'e know I want my tea?"

The vicar had been but recently appointed, a red-faced energetic man in the early forties, and Albert Edward still regretted his predecessor, a clergyman of the old school who preached leisurely sermons in a silvery voice and dined out a great deal with his more aristocratic parishioners. He liked things in church to be just so, but he never fussed; he was not like this new man who wanted to have his finger in every pie. But Albert Edward was tolerant. St. Peter's was in a very good neighbourhood and the parishioners were a very nice class of people. The new vicar had come from the East End and he couldn't be expected to fall in all at once with the discreet ways of his fashionable congregation.

"All this 'ustle," said Albert Edward. "But give 'im time, he'll learn."

When the vicar had walked down the aisle so far that he could address the verger without raising his voice more than was becoming in a place of worship he stopped.

"Foreman, will you come into the vestry for a minute. I have something to say to you."

"Very good, sir."

The vicar waited for him to come up and they walked up the church together.

"A very nice christening, I thought, sir. Funny 'ow the baby stopped cryin' the moment you took him."

"I've noticed they very often do," said the vicar, with a little smile. "After all I've had a good deal of practice with them."

It was a source of subdued pride to him that he could nearly always quiet a whimpering infant by the manner in which he held it and he was not unconscious of the amused admiration with which mothers and nurses watched him settle the baby in the crook of his surpliced arm. The verger knew that it pleased him to be complimented on his talent.

The vicar preceded Albert Edward into the vestry. Albert

Personal Success   135

Edward was a trifle surprised to find the two churchwardens
there. He had not seen them come in. They gave him pleasant
nods.

"Good-afternoon, my lord. Good-afternoon, sir," he said to
one after the other.

They were elderly men, both of them, and they had been
churchwardens almost as long as Albert Edward had been verger. They were sitting now at a handsome refectory table that the
old vicar had brought many years before from Italy and the vicar
sat down in the vacant chair between them. Albert Edward faced
them, the table between him and them, and wondered with slight
uneasiness what was the matter. He remembered still the occasion on which the organist had got into trouble and the bother
they had all had to hush things up. In a church like St. Peter's,
Neville Square, they couldn't afford a scandal. On the vicar's
red face was a look of resolute benignity, but the others bore an
expression that was slightly troubled.

"He's been naggin' them, he 'as," said the verger to himself.
"He's jockeyed them into doin' something, but they don't 'alf like
it. That's what it is, you mark my words."

But his thoughts did not appear on Albert Edward's clean-
cut and distinguished features. He stood in a respectful but not
obsequious attitude. He had been in service before he was appointed to his ecclesiastical office, but only in very good houses,
and his deportment was irreproachable. Starting as a page-boy
in the household of a merchant-prince, he had risen by due degrees from the position of fourth to first footman, for a year he
had been single-handed butler to a widowed peeress and, till the
vacancy occurred at St. Peter's, butler with two men under him
in the house of a retired ambassador. He was tall, spare, grave
and dignified. He looked, if not like a duke, at least like an actor
of the old school who specialised in dukes' parts. He had tact,
firmness and self-assurance. His character was unimpeachable.

The vicar began briskly.

"Foreman, we've got something rather unpleasant to say
to you. You've been here a great many years and I think his lord-
ship and the general agree with me that you've fulfilled the duties
of your office to the satisfaction of everybody concerned."

The two churchwardens nodded.

"But a most extraordinary circumstance came to my knowledge the other day and I felt it my duty to impart it to the churchwardens. I discovered to my astonishment that you could neither
read nor write."

The verger's face betrayed no sign of embarrassment.

136   *Success: A Search for Values*

"The last vicar knew that, sir," he replied. "He said it didn't make no difference. He always said there was a great deal too much education in the world for 'is taste."

"It's the most amazing thing I ever heard," cried the general. "Do you mean to say that you've been verger of this church for sixteen years and never learned to read or write?"

"I went into service when I was twelve, sir. The cook in the first place tried to teach me once, but I didn't seem to 'ave the knack for it, and then what with one thing and another I never seemed to 'ave the time. I've never really found the want of it. I think a lot of these young fellows waste a rare lot of time readin' when they might be doin' something useful."

"But don't you want to know the news?" said the other churchwarden. "Don't you ever want to write a letter?"

"No, me lord, I seem to manage very well without. And of late years now they've all these pictures in the papers I get to know what's goin' on pretty well. Me wife's quite a scholar and if I want to write a letter she writes it for me. It's not as if I was a bettin' man."

The two churchwardens gave the vicar a troubled glance and then looked down at the table.

"Well, Foreman, I've talked the matter over with these gentlemen and they quite agree with me that the situation is impossible. At a church like St. Peter's, Neville Square, we cannot have a verger who can neither read nor write."

Albert Edward's thin, sallow face reddened and he moved uneasily on his feet, but he made no reply.

"Understand me, Foreman, I have no complaint to make against you. You do your work quite satisfactorily; I have the highest opinion both of your character and of your capacity; but we haven't the right to take the risk of some accident that might happen owing to your lamentable ignorance. It's a matter of prudence as well as of principle."

"But couldn't you learn, Foreman?" asked the general.

"No, sir, I'm afraid I couldn't, not now. You see, I'm not as young as I was and if I couldn't seem able to get the letters in me 'ead when I was a nipper I don't think there's much chance of it now."

"We don't want to be harsh with you, Foreman," said the vicar. "But the churchwardens and I have quite made up our minds. We'll give you three months and if at the end of that time you cannot read and write I'm afraid you'll have to go."

Albert Edward had never liked the new vicar. He'd said from the beginning that they'd made a mistake when they gave

Personal Success   137

him St. Peter's. He wasn't the type of man they wanted with a classy congregation like that. And now he straightened himself a little. He knew his value and he wasn't going to allow himself to be put upon.

"I'm very sorry, sir, I'm afraid it's no good. I'm too old a dog to learn new tricks. I've lived a good many years without knowin' 'ow to read and write, and without wishin' to praise myself, self-praise is no recommendation, I don't mind sayin' I've done my duty in that state of life in which it 'as pleased a merciful providence to place me, and if I *could* learn now I don't know as I'd want to."

"In that case, Foreman, I'm afraid you must go."

"Yes, sir, I quite understand. I shall be 'appy to 'and in my resignation as soon as you've found somebody to take my place."

But when Albert Edward with his usual politeness had closed the church door behind the vicar and the two churchwardens he could not sustain the air of unruffled dignity with which he had borne the blow inflicted upon him and his lips quivered. He walked slowly back to the vestry and hung up on its proper peg his verger's gown. He sighed as he thought of all the grand funerals and smart weddings it had seen. He tidied everything up, put on his coat, and hat in hand walked down the aisle. He locked the church door behind him. He strolled across the square, but deep in his sad thoughts he did not take the street that led him home, where a nice strong cup of tea awaited him; he took the wrong turning. He walked slowly along. His heart was heavy. He did not know what he should do with himself. He did not fancy the notion of going back to domestic service; after being his own master for so many years, for the vicar and churchwardens could say what they liked, it was he that had run St. Peter's, Neville Square, he could scarcely demean himself by accepting a situation. He had saved a tidy sum, but not enough to live on without doing something, and life seemed to cost more every year. He had never thought to be troubled with such questions. The vergers of St. Peter's, like the popes of Rome, were there for life. He had often thought of the pleasant reference the vicar would make in his sermon at evensong the first Sunday after his death to the long and faithful service, and the exemplary character of their late verger, Albert Edward Foreman. He sighed deeply. Albert Edward was a non-smoker and a total abstainer, but with a certain latitude; that is to say he liked a glass of beer with his dinner and when he was tired he enjoyed a cigarette. It occurred to him now that one would comfort him and since he did not carry them he looked about him for a shop where he could buy a packet of

Gold Flakes. He did not at once see one and walked on a little. It was a long street, with all sorts of shops in it, but there was not a single one where you could buy cigarettes.

"That's strange," said Albert Edward.

To make sure he walked right up the street again. No, there was no doubt about it. He stopped and looked reflectively up and down.

"I can't be the only man as walks along this street and wants a fag," he said. "I shouldn't wonder but what a fellow might do very well with a little shop here. Tobacco and sweets, you know."

He gave a sudden start.

"That's an idea," he said. "Strange 'ow things come to you when you least expect it."

He turned, walked home, and had his tea.

"You're very silent this afternoon, Albert," his wife remarked.

"I'm thinkin'," he said.

He considered the matter from every point of view and next day he went along the street and by good luck found a little shop to let that looked as though it would exactly suit him. Twenty-four hours later he had taken it and when a month after that he left St. Peter's, Neville Square, for ever, Albert Edward Foreman set up in business as a tobacconist and newsagent. His wife said it was a dreadful come-down after being verger of St. Peter's, but he answered that you had to move with the times, the church wasn't what it was, and 'enceforward he was going to render unto Cæsar what was Cæsar's. Albert Edward did very well. He did so well that in a year or so it struck him that he might take a second shop and put a manager in. He looked for another long street that hadn't got a tobacconist in it and when he found it, and a shop to let, took it and stocked it. This was a success too. Then it occurred to him that if he could run two he could run half a dozen, so he began walking about London, and whenever he found a long street that had no tobacconist and a shop to let he took it. In the course of ten years he had acquired no less than ten shops and he was making money hand over fist. He went round to all of them himself every Monday, collected the week's takings and took them to the bank.

One morning when he was there paying in a bundle of notes and a heavy bag of silver the cashier told him that the manager would like to see him. He was shown into an office and the manager shook hands with him.

"Mr. Foreman, I wanted to have a talk to you about the

Personal Success   139

money you've got on deposit with us. D'you know exactly how
much it is?"

"Not within a pound or two, sir; but I've got a pretty rough
idea."

"Apart from what you paid in this morning it's a little over
thirty thousand pounds. That's a very large sum to have on deposit and I should have thought you'd do better to invest it."

"I wouldn't want to take no risk, sir. I know it's safe in the
bank."

"You needn't have the least anxiety. We'll make you out a
list of absolutely gilt-edged securities. They'll bring you in a better rate of interest than we can possibly afford to give you."

A troubled look settled on Mr. Foreman's distinguished face.
"I've never 'ad anything to do with stocks and shares and I'd
'ave to leave it all in your 'ands," he said.

The manager smiled. "We'll do everything. All you'll have
to do next time you come in is just to sign the transfers."

"I could do that all right," said Albert uncertainly. "But 'ow
should I know what I was signin'?"

"I suppose you can read," said the manager a trifle sharply.

Mr. Foreman gave him a disarming smile.

"Well, sir, that's just it. I can't. I know it sounds funny-like,
but there it is, I can't read or write, only me name, an' I only learnt
to do that when I went into business."

The manager was so surprised that he jumped up from his
chair.

"That's the most extraordinary thing I ever heard."

"You see, it's like this, sir, I never 'ad the opportunity until
it was too late and then some'ow I wouldn't. I got obstinate-like."

The manager stared at him as though he were a prehistoric
monster.

"And do you mean to say that you've built up this important
business and amassed a fortune of thirty thousand pounds without being able to read or write? Good God, man, what would you
be now if you had been able to?"

"I can tell you that, sir," said Mr. Foreman, a little smile
on his still aristocratic features. "I'd be verger of St. Peter's,
Neville Square."

[SEE EXERCISE ON PAGE 337]

140   *Success: A Search for Values*

*Milo Fractionating Center is a company employing 8000
people. Mr. Dalton, author of the book from which these
selections are taken, asked several of the employees this
question: "What are the things that enable men to rise here
in the plant?" The first answer, that of Mr. Bierner, was
made during a formal interview. The others are unofficial
statements.*

From *Men Who Manage**

Melville Dalton

L. Bierner, an inactive divisional superintendent suffering
from heart trouble, aged fifty-seven, and employed by Milo for
thirty-eight years, answered:

Integrity, loyalty, and honesty! Nobody can keep an honest man
down! If you deliver the goods, you'll be pushed. If you help your
superiors they'll help you—they'd be fools not to! I've heard a lot of
stuff in the plant about Catholics and Masons and how you have to
be one or the other. There's nothing to that! It's just in men's heads
and has no basis in fact! If you're loyal, your boss doesn't give a
damn what your religion is—he'll probably be glad you've got some
and that's all. Men come in and raise hell because somebody got
to be a foreman and they didn't. They bring up all this stuff about
being a Mason or a Catholic or something else. There's nothing to
it! The men who say this sort of thing are merely trying to find ex-
cuses for their failing—because they don't have anything on the
ball. All you've got to do is to show people you're a right guy. All
you've got to do is get on the ball and hit it, and nobody will raise
any questions as to what your religion is or what you belong to.
Any unbiassed objective person can see this. The guy who's always
making charges of this kind has nobody to blame but himself—he

---

* **Reprinted by permission of John Wiley & Sons, Inc.**

Personal Success   141

won't take the necessary steps to improve himself. When men complain about not being foremen, I tell them the truth. I tell them so they can improve themselves or go somewhere else, but I never want to ruin or discourage them. I've often turned men down who later improved themselves and were given foremen jobs. There's no substitute for honesty and fair-dealing among men in industry. You talk about people getting up in industry. Do you know that seventy-five per cent of supervisors don't want to advance if it means more work and responsibility? They want money but not what goes with it! . . .

The following . . . partial statements are selected as representing those who in theory would be most eager for promotion —skilled workers, first-line foremen, and staff personnel. Their responses are to the same question . . .

H. Trimble, a sixty-three-year-old first-line foreman with eight years of schooling and thirty-seven years' service with the corporation, answered:

Mostly their own ambition. If they do their work well and anything else that comes along, they'll do all right. A man has to do more than what's expected. First you'll be trusted with a few small jobs to see how you handle them. If you do well—you're on the way up.

I used to be ambitious when I was a young fellow, but I never knowed how to keep my damn big mouth shut. I'd just as soon tell my bosses to go to hell as to look at them. If I'd used my head I could have been someplace. Two different times, after I got to be a foreman, my bosses got big jobs in some of the other plants and wrote to me asking me to come and be a superintendent for them. I had five kids in school and owned my home and just didn't want to tear up and move to a strange place. Besides, back in 1929 when I got the first offer, I was making pretty good money then—about $360 a month. I thought I had the world by the tail with a down-hill haul. When the depression come I lost all my savings and wished I'd taken the job. It pays to have friends but it's my own fault it didn't pay me.

. . .

A night supervisor, aged sixty, J. Cunningham had two years of college and had been with the firm seventeen years. . . .

Well, by God, it's not by ability! I can tell you that! It's who you know that counts, not what you know. Take Dick Pugh. He knows nothing about accounting but he has a man under him who's a trained accountant. Hell, that's not right. Anybody can see it's not. The accountant gets a little over $400 a month while Dick pulls down better than $600. Do you see any justice in that? Look here [showing a list of supervisors], there's one, two, three, four -- nine men who are drawing the pay of foremen and carrying the title. Yet none of 'em have over five men under them. One man could easy boss the whole damn bunch. Why do you think they get away with it? Because they're Masons? Not by a long shot! That's part of it, but there's other reasons. Fisher's uncle is one of the directors. He thinks we don't know that, but that's how he gets by. Jones is a son-in-law of the assistant superintendent. Brown is always flunk-eying out at the Yacht Club. And the soop [Cunningham's super-intendent] gets a hell of a kick out of dancing with Davis' good-looking wife. If she's going to dress well and keep on looking good, Bill's got to make his $515 a month and feel like staying up nights —and a lot of these nights he spends home with the kids. His kids are damn nice. Two little girls. But Bill wants a boy, and Liz [the wife] says there'll be no more kids.

Look at my own job! On nights I'm responsible for the same thing that it takes Blaine, Taylor, Hampton, Vick, and Streeter to do on days. They average about $850 a month while I get only $575. Figure it out—five hundred seventy-five bucks compared with forty-two hundred and fifty. [Total monthly salaries of Blaine, Taylor, Hampton, Vick, and Streeter.] Now you tell me. How do you think men get up in industry? [All salaries mentioned have been increased considerably since the interviews.]

.   .   .

A college graduate, aged thirty-nine, E. Stein was a staff officer who had spent much time in the Central Office. His response was:

The company naturally talks of having a promotion system. But this thing of "ability" is damned hard to pin down. It's easier to get at when you've got something concrete to work on. For example, when you're down on the lower levels in industry—say a machinist or a time-study man—you can always be checked on your worth to the company. Your superiors can see that you're doing some-thing. If you were suddenly asked at the end of a month or a year just what you'd contributed to the company's cause you could point to some statistics. It's not that way when you get up higher. The higher you get, the more your advancement depends on impres-sions that your superiors have of you. And these impressions are based on almost no real evidence. If a high staff officer or a division

Personal Success 143

superintendent were asked what he'd done for the company during the last year he'd have a hell of a time pulling up anything concrete. When you're in a position like that you know all the time that other people want your job and are trying to get it—and you know that impressions are constantly being formed of you. I know it goes on. I see my supervisors here. I find that people up in the front office have impressions of them. They're typed. And the whole damn thing is usually wrong and always unfair. Vaughn or McNair will see my supervisors for maybe twenty minutes once or twice a month and will form impressions of their merit on such evidence as that. Hell, you can't judge a man's capabilities from no more knowledge of him than that! Yet these guys insist on getting first-hand impressions. They know damn well they don't have any fool-proof means of rating men so they're conceited enough to think they can look at a man and size him up—find out how he stacks up alongside others and how much he's worth to the company. And their impressions just boil down to whether they like a man or don't like him. When you walk into a room with them you can see that they're intent on getting every impression of you that they can. You've got to always be on guard about your dress, speech, manners, and general conduct. All that has nothing to do with brains or ability. Look at Edison, or Lincoln, or Henry Ford—they were too busy doing things to be fussy about how they looked. Yet even if I'm an hour late of a morning, I'll shave. Some people will skip their shave if they were up late the night before. But it doesn't pay. I first noticed this when I was in [the Office.] There, the higher you went the more you got involved in politics. Everybody was uneasy and trying to beat everybody else in making a favorable impression. [Stein was recently promoted to the top post in his staff.]

[SEE EXERCISE ON PAGE 342]

JAPANESE CHILD EATS NAILS AFTER VIEWING STUNT ON TV

OKAYAMA, Japan, (UPI) — Municipal authorities here have urged parents to monitor the type of television programs they allow their children to watch.

The warning was brought on by the case of 7-year-old Koichi Higuchi.

Young Koichi ate a handful of nails after having watched a television program showing stuntmen eating nails and glass. The nails were removed from his stomach in an hour-long operation.

144   *Success: A Search for Values*

Academy of Sciences Chooses

50 Members and 10 Associates*
Special to The New York Times

WASHINGTON, April 27 — The National Academy of Sciences has elected 50 new members as well as 10 foreign associates. It also moved towards the formation of a nominating committee to choose its new president.

Dr. Frederick Seitz, its current president, becomes head of Rockefeller University July 1. He will, however, continue as president of the academy until its new president is elected by its 806 members early next year.

The new associates are:

ERWIN BUNNING, University of Tubingen, West Germany.

JACQUES YVES COUSTEAU, Monaco.

EMANUEL FAURE-FREMIET, College de France, Paris.

RAGNAR GRANIT, Stockholm.

GERHARD HERZBERG, National Research Council of Canada.

H. C. LONGUET-HIGGINS, University of Cambridge, England.

A. R. LURIA, Moscow State University.

JACQUES MONOD, Pasteur Institute, Paris.

CARL LUDWIG, University of Gottingen, West Germany.

J. TUZO WILSON, University of Toronto.

The following were elected members of the academy:

KENNETH J. ARROW, Harvard University.

* © **1968 by The New York Times Company. Reprinted by permission.**

MYRON L. BENDER, Northwestern University.

ROBERT W. BERLINER, National Heart Institute.

RICHARD B. BERNSTEIN, University of Wisconsin.

MARLAND P. BILLINGS, Harvard.

GARRETT BIRKHOFF, Harvard.

BART J. BOK, University of Arizona.

NORMAN E. BORLAUG, Rockefeller Foundation.

ALBERTO P. CALDERON, University of Chicago.

MORRIS COHEN, Massachusetts Institute of Technology.

GOTTFRIED S. FRAENKEL, University of Illinois.

THOMAS GOLD, Cornell University.

WILLIAM E. GORDON, Rice University.

VERNE E. GRANT, Texas Agricultural and Mechanical University.

JAMES B. GRIFFIN, University of Michigan.

KARL HABEL, Scripps Clinic and Research Foundation.

LOUIS G. HENYEY, University of California, Berkeley.

WILLIAM C. HERRING, Bell Telephone Laboratories.

ROBERT W. HOLLEY, Cornell University.

RUDOLF KOMPFNER, Bell Telephone Laboratories.

RITA LEVI-MONTALCINI, Washington University and Instituto Superiore di Sanita, Rome.

EDWARD B. LEWIS, California Institute of Technology.

RICHARD C. LEWONTIN, University of Chicago.

Personal Success 145

THOMAS F. MALONE, Travelers Insurance Company.

HENRY W. MENARD Jr., Scripps Institution of Oceanography.

ROBERT K. MERTON, Columbia University.

MATTHEW S. MESELSON, Harvard.

ARTHUR B. PARDEE, Princeton University.

WILLIAM PRAGER, University of California, San Diego.

HENRY PRIMAKOFF, University of Pennsylvania.

HERMANN RAHN, University of Buffalo School of Medicine.

LEO J. RAINWATER, Columbia.

JOHN H. REYNOLDS, University of California, Berkeley.

STUART A. RICE, University of Chicago.

SIDNEY D. RIPLEY 2d, Smithsonian Institution.

HOWARD K. SCHACHMAN, University of California, Berkeley.

GEORGE S. SCHAIRER, Boeing Company.

ISADORE MANUAL SINGER, Massachusetts Institute of Technology.

RICHARD L. SOLOMON, University of Pennsylvania.

GEORGE F. SPRAGUE, Department of Agriculture.

ADRIAN MORRIS SRB, Cornell University.

EDWARD A. STEINHAUS, University of California.

IRVINE ELIOT STELLAR, University of Pennsylvania.

VALENTINE L. TELEGDI, University of Chicago.

DAVID TURNBULL, Harvard.

ORVILLE F. TUTTLE, Stanford University.

EUGENE E. VAN TAMELEN, Stanford.

JEROME RUBIN VINOGRAD, California Institute of Technology.

JOHN WEST WELLS, Cornell.

PAUL CHARLES ZAMECNIK, Hunting Memorial Hospital and Massachusetts General Hospital.

If you win in life, you are a successful man. If you lose, you are an unsuccessful man. But if you go on whether you win or lose, then you have something more than success or failure. You keep your own soul.*

ALAN PATON

* © 1968 by The New York Times Company. Reprinted by permission.

146   *Success: A Search for Values*

Success in science is apt to be one of two kinds: either painstakingly slow and without public acclaim, or painstakingly slow but ending in fame and public acclamation. Countless men and women have experienced the first kind of success. Only a few, such as Jonas Salk, Louis Pasteur, or Marie Curie have known the second kind.

Because we live in a time when the study of science is encouraged from first grade, when promising science students have little difficulty in obtaining college scholarships, when the federal government and philanthropic foundations make millions of dollars available to support scientific study, when industry bids against industry for the services of scientists, and because we live in a time that "reveres" science, it is sometimes hard to believe that a woman as brilliant and as dedicated as Marie Curie had to overcome so many obstacles to pursue her studies. Yet without her discovery of radium, the world would be quite different today.

The First Great Woman
Scientist . . . and Much More*

Susan Raven

People who remember Marie Curie in the last decades of her life thought of her as frail, delicate, almost immaterial— "as if," one of her former laboratory assistants has said, "she could walk through walls." They remember her constantly rubbing her hands, they itched so much. It had been some time before she and her husband realized the harm radiation could do, and in the *époque héroïque*—those five arduous years at the turn of the century when they had painfully investigated the mysterious new element which she had been the first to suspect —they used to walk around with a tiny phial of the stuff loose in

---

* Reprinted from "The First Great Woman Scientist . . . And Much More" by Susan Raven from The Sunday Times Magazine section, December 3, 1967. © 1967 by The New York Times Company. Reprinted by permission.

Personal Success   147

their overall pockets. Her hands were rough and scarred. It was leukemia brought on by radiation which finally killed her; but she lived to the age of 66, working to the end, in spite of the kidney trouble and the operations for cataract. She was gentle and timid, but she had a will of steel, forged in the poverty and setbacks of a long apprenticeship.

She was born Marya Sklodowska, the youngest of the five children of teachers, 100 years ago[1] in Warsaw. Poland was suffering under the oppressive rule of Czarist Russia; Russian was the official language, even for schoolchildren, and the lessons in Polish history had to be hidden from the authorities. Like many forced into deception in childhood, Marya grew up painfully honest.

All her life she remained loyal to the land of her birth. She almost didn't marry Pierre Curie because she believed she should devote her life to science in her native country. She announced the discovery of radium in Warsaw almost as soon as in Paris; she inspired the building of a Radium Institute there, and donated to it a gram of radium; there was always at least one Polish student in her laboratory in Paris, whose fees were paid by her if there was no scholarship available. Her two daughters learned Polish from Polish governesses. To the end of her life, she counted in Polish. In part at least her remarkable career was inspired by the passionate desire common to her generation to work for the greater glory of Poland.

The family was poor, and the Sklodowskis had to share a succession of small apartments with boarding pupils to make ends meet. Marya did her homework and slept in the dining room. She could remember their mother making their leather shoes herself.

Madame Sklodowska, formerly a headmistress, had had to give up her job when Marya was born. She was already suffering from tuberculosis. As a grown woman, Marie Curie could not recall ever being kissed by her. "Restore our mother's health," was a regular family prayer. It was not answered. She died when Marya was 10, and the unresolved grief and guilt her mother's death unavoidably caused was a key factor in the development of her adult personality. No psychologist can explain the springs of genius, or even of talent, but from this childhood loss must stem the extreme emotional reserve that many who knew her later remarked on, and her neglect of her femininity. Inevitably, she identified with her surviving parent.

---

[1]   1868 [Ed. note]

The father did his best to bring up his motherless children alone, taking them on educational expeditions, reading aloud to them from the literatures of several countries, grieving always that he could not give them the education he knew they deserved. The only son, Joseph, won a gold medal at the end of his school-days and entered medical school; but the gifted eldest surviving daughter, Bronya, who also won a gold medal and longed to study medicine, had to become her father's housekeeper. Marya also left the government gymnasium with a gold medal, and top grades in all her 22 subjects—and no possibility of going on to university.

Yet her childhood, though hard, was happy and full. In spite of the hated Russian staff she could not help enjoying school. Her marvelous memory—she could get a poem off by heart after a couple of readings—and her gift for concentration, above all her curiosity and enthusiasm, made her an apt pupil. And she had an exceptionally close relationship with her family, which lasted all their lives.

At 17 she spent a whole year—the only lazy, carefree period of her life—staying with a succession of cousins and uncles in the country. Her letters are full of the pleasures of dancing, of sleighing in winter and bathing in summer, of "such follies that sometimes we deserve to be locked up in an asylum for the insane. . . ." Her vocation was still sleeping inside her.

The young Sklodowskis took private pupils—miserable, ill-paid work, but it enabled them to study at the same time. Joseph enrolled at Warsaw University, which was closed to women. Yet so much was the education of young Poland a mission of their generation that Bronya and Marya were able to join a kind of "floating university" organized by teachers hardly older than themselves; in absolute secrecy they attended lessons in anatomy, natural history, and sociology. She and Bronya began to dream of the Sorbonne, where women were admitted.

"Marya Sklodowska, good references, capable, wants place as governess. Salary 400 rubles a year." It was her idea. It was easier to save away from home. She would be housed and fed, and her salary would finance Bronya's medical studies in Paris. Then, after two or three years, it would be her turn: Bronya would help her. As it happened Marya was a governess for five years. During that time she found her vocation—and, in despair, nearly lost it. She had chosen a hard life, and it is not surprising that her resolution faltered. . . .

Only gradually did she discover that her real interests were

Personal Success   149

mathematics and physics. "When I feel myself quite unable to read with profit, I work problems of algebra or trigonometry, which allow no lapses of attention. . . ." In later life she wrote: "These solitary studies were encompassed with difficulty. The scientific education I had received at school was very incomplete. . . . I tried to complete it in my own way, with the help of books got together by sheer chance. The method was not efficacious, but I acquired the habit of independent work. . . ." There were still great holes in her knowledge when she finally reached the Sorbonne, but the lessons she did learn, the self-discipline, the self-reliance and the infinite capacity for taking pains even in extreme fatigue, were the lessons the discoverer of radium most needed.

There was a distraction. The eldest son of the house, home from Warsaw for the holidays, fell in love with her, and she with him. They approached his parents, who had always been good to her and had, so she thought, looked upon her as a daughter. Shocked and angry, they refused to countenance his marrying a governess. The young man weakly yielded; and Marya received a double blow, to her pride as a human being and her pride as a woman. She recovered; but, at a time when she was beginning to despair of her future, it cut deep. Crushed, she grew timid.

Too proud—or perhaps, still, too hopeful—to resign she stayed on in Szczuki;[2] but her despair grew darker. In a letter urging Joseph to pursue his career in Warsaw, she wrote: "I have lost the hope of ever becoming anybody, all my ambition has been transferred to Bronya and you . . ." and again, "It seems to me all the time that I am getting terribly stupid. . . . I make no noticeable progress." To her cousin: "My dream, for the moment, is to have a corner of my own where I can live with my father." And to Joseph again: "My soul, too, is worn out." Yet she was still sending money to Bronya and still, instinctively, putting the remainder aside; she hardly had enough to spare for the stamp.

In 1888 her father was appointed director of a reform school near Warsaw, a post and a place he did not like, but it meant a larger income—and the possibility of saving for Marya's own education. She herself left Szczuki, and became governess with a rich Warsaw family for a year. Then in 1890, Bronya, now engaged to a Polish fellow student, wrote from Paris, offering her sister a home for the following year.

But it was nearly five years since the great plan had been formed. It had grown increasingly unreal with time. "I dreamed

---

[2] **A city north of Warsaw where she worked. [Ed. note]**

150   *Success: A Search for Values*

of Paris as of redemption," she wrote to her sister, "but the hope of going there left me a long time ago. . . . I believe our plan of living together next year is close to [Father's] heart, and he clings to it; I want to give him a little happiness in his old age. On the other hand, my heart breaks when I think of ruining my abilities, which must have been worth, anyhow, something."

But, living in Warsaw with her father, she was able to rejoin the "floating university." And it was access to a laboratory run by another cousin — the first laboratory she had ever entered — which suddenly rekindled her ambition. "I had little time for work in this laboratory," she wrote in later life. "I could generally get there only in the evening after dinner, or on Sunday, and I was left to myself. I tried to reproduce various experiments described in the treatises on physics or chemistry. . . . I developed my taste for experimental research during these first trials." Behind the simple sentences one can detect the formidable sense of purpose which did not then and was never afterwards to allow her to waste a single second.

Yet before confirming that she would go to her sister in Paris she arranged to meet her former suitor in the September of 1891. Whatever she may still have hoped, the meeting was their last. Within a month, the carefully hoarded savings had been spent on a third-class railway ticket, her mattress and bedclothes were sent on ahead, a passport was obtained and, equipped with food and drink for the three days' journey, Marya Sklodowska was on her way to the Sorbonne. She was almost 24.

She had given up all thoughts of marriage; she made no attempt to make friends with her fellow students, and even, after a few months, because their family and social life were too much of a distraction, left her sister's house for a student lodging. And there she embraced poverty.

Her savings were enough for her university fees and her barest expenses, but not for rent, heating and food as well. She remembered once piling all her possessions, including the single chair, onto her bed in order to keep warm. She worked till 2 in the morning. And she starved.

The girl who had been plump at 13 and still solid at 23 lost weight — alarmingly. Occasionally she fainted. When she collapsed at a lecture, her sister and brother-in-law found out that she had eaten only a bunch of radishes and half a pound of cherries the previous day. There was only a packet of tea in her room. "Embraced" poverty: the word is hardly too strong.

But nothing prevented her working. She had already decided to try for not only one master's degree but two — in physics and mathematics; and in 1893, less than two years after her

Personal Success 151

arrival in Paris, she came out first in the Licence ès Sciences Physiques. She returned home to Poland for the summer, to be fattened up and feted by her family, and to worry about money. Then she was awarded a scholarship—enough to live on, in her economical manner, for over a year. (She later returned those 600 rubles to finance some other poor student.) In the summer of 1894 she was second in the Licence ès Sciences Mathématiques. She was still planning, once she had got her teaching qualifications, to return to her cousin's laboratory in Warsaw, when she met Pierre Curie.

Early in 1894 she was deep in her first research commission (the fee for which was to help repay her scholarship), and Polish friends suggested she might welcome the advice of a certain French physicist. They were both invited to dine.

Pierre Curie was at that time 35. He was not well-known in France, but his work had already attracted the attention of the British scientist Lord Kelvin. (The Curies were always more honored abroad than in France.) . . . When he met Marie he was immersed in the problems of magnetism.

He belonged to the same kind of family, the same intellectual middle class of late 19th-century Europe, high thinking and plain living; his father was a doctor. He was, if anything, even more austere and scrupulous than Marie, every bit as indifferent to the things of this world. Neither of them ever noticed what they ate or what they wore. Their courtship was slow and decorous. By the summer Pierre had proposed, but Marie could not bring herself to change her long-formed plans to spend her life in Poland. She seems, indeed, to have been almost angered by this new distraction, or so he suggests. Like her, he was an admirable letter writer; all that was most delightful in him emerged in the letters which pursued her around Poland that summer. . . .

But it was not until July, a year after he first proposed, that she suddenly agreed. . . .

There was no ring at the wedding, no religious ceremony, no reception. She did, however, agree not to make do with one of the dresses she had brought from Poland years before, and accepted the present of a dress from her brother-in-law's mother; it was navy blue. The honeymoon was spent on bicycles. It was the start of a momentous union.

They were united not only by their passion for science but by likes and dislikes, their distaste for the trivial, their indifference to personal comfort, their love of the countryside. . . . she, in her moving account of her husband's life, says he never knew how to be angry. Among friends his habitual reserve, wrote Marie

Curie, gave way to an openness in which confidence flowered. "His tenderness was the most exquisite of gifts, sure and secure, full of gentleness and solicitude. It was good to be enveloped in it, it was cruel to lose it. . . ." She bloomed with marriage; at 30, newly a mother, she looked 20. He wrote letters to her: "My dear little child whom I love." When he died, after 11 years of marriage, she froze. She never spoke of him to their children, hardly to anyone else. Only when alone with a piece of paper could she unburden herself without reserve, in the plain, direct prose that often made what she wrote a work of art.

Her orderliness, by now ingrained, spilled over into her marriage. She learned to cook, annotating her cookbook with the results of her efforts as if they were laboratory experiments. In the first of the great years, 1898, she was writing in the margin of a recipe for gooseberry jelly: "I took 8 lb. of fruit and the same weight in crystallized sugar. After boiling for 10 minutes, I passed the mixture through a rather fine sieve. I obtained 14 pots of very good jelly, not transparent, which 'took' perfectly."

She learned to shop and not only kept daily accounts of every *sou* she spent but transferred the results to monthly account books, everything itemized. Soon she was keeping a diary of her daughter's progress—weight, teeth, walking and talking—as accurate as one of her laboratory notebooks. It was the same automatic, disciplined habit which, in middle age, led her to measure, every spring, the diameter of the lime trees which she had planted in front of her beloved laboratory. But there were notes of more moment in the *carnets de travail*.

The year after her marriage Marie Curie spent working for her fellowship in secondary education; once more she came out top. Then she became pregnant. She suffered acutely from sickness, and found working (for a monograph on the magnetization of steel) very difficult. She had recovered enough to go on another bicycling holiday with her husband in her eighth month, but it was too much for her. Her daughter Irène was born safely in September, 1897 (the proud parents spent 3 francs—itemized under "unusual expenses"—on champagne), but Marie's health was undermined; there was even talk of TB. Nevertheless, by the end of 1897 she had finished her monograph and had embarked on a new piece of research for her doctor's degree. The subject of that research was an investigation into the source of energy which enabled salts of uranium to make an impression, as of light, on a photographic plate kept in darkness.

This was the phenomenon which had been remarked a year

Personal Success   153

earlier by the physicist Henri Becquerel and to which Marie Curie
was shortly to give the name radioactivity. It is no small part of
genius to scent, unerringly, the area of investigation which will
prove most fruitful; not to waste time on peripheral trivia but to
aim directly at one point in a wall of ignorance which will bring
the whole wall tumbling. In this sense Marie Curie could indeed
be said to have walked through walls.

Her husband undoubtedly helped her choose her field of
research; but it was she who, in the icy lumber room at the School
of Physics which she had been lent, intuitively realized early in
1898 that the mysterious rays were not necessarily a property of
uranium alone. She thereupon measured for radiation all known
chemical bodies, using, as in the earlier experiments, the elec-
trical measuring equipment devised by Pierre and his brother.
She soon found that thorium emitted the same rays. She then
applied her tests to all the geological mineral samples in the col-
lection at the School of Physics — and found that certain of the
minerals were far more radioactive than the amount of uranium
or thorium they contained could possibly justify. She became con-
vinced, within a few months of starting her research, that radioactivity pointed to the existence of a totally new element, so far
undetected by chemical analysis. On April 12, 1898, she announced in the Proceedings of the Academy of Science its probable presence in pitch-blende ores.

This was an immensely important result. It remained to
track down the element itself. Pierre — temporarily, as he thought
— deserted his crystallography research to help his wife; they
thought the new element would be about one part in every hundred of the pitchblende. In fact, the search was to last four years,
for radium was only one-*millionth* part of the ore; and long before they found it they discovered another element, polonium
(named in honor of Poland). They were to find other forms of
radioactive elements.

They had to obtain huge quantities of pitchblende, which,
since it contained the valuable uranium salts used in glassmak-
ing, was prohibitively expensive. Happily they calculated, cor-
rectly, that the elusive element they were searching for would
survive the uranium-extraction treatment, and would be found
in the unregarded residues. But they had to pay for these waste
products (though they were given one ton free), and their trans-
port from the uranium mines of St. Joachimsthal in Austria out
of Pierre's salary.

They needed somewhere to house their ore and to submit it

154   *Success: A Search for Values*

to the arduous chemical experiments which would eventually break it down into its component parts; and a place to measure the radioactivity of those parts to an incredible degree of accuracy. They finally found, at the School of Physics, a big shed with a leaking roof, no ventilation, no proper floor, a single inadequate iron stove. It was icy in winter, suffocating in summer. There they worked for four years, he engaged in examining radium's properties, she in trying to extract the pure element.

"It was in this miserable old shed," she wrote, "that the best and happiest years of our life were spent, entirely consecrated to work. I sometimes passed the whole day stirring a boiling mass with an iron rod nearly as big as myself. In the evening I was broken with fatigue. . . . [Yet] in spite of the difficulties of our working conditions, we felt very happy. . . ." During the whole of 1899 — though they visited Poland, whose language Pierre had struggled to learn to please his wife — they did not go once to the theater. Even in her student days Marie had sometimes scraped together time and money enough to do that.

Nothing of her work escapes into her letters; it was beyond the comprehension of all but her fellow scientists. These, however, were beginning to take great interest in the progress reports which the Curies were publishing. They acquired professional helpers, though a proper laboratory was to remain a dream for another 15 years. The tests and measurements grew increasingly delicate — and increasingly endangered by the dust and dirt and the radioactivity itself, which got into everything.

In all, she submitted eight tons of pitchblende to her herculean "cooking." After 45 months, they had yielded a decigram of pure radium. Marie announced that its atomic weight was 225 (it was soon discovered to be 226). Radium officially existed.

"This work," wrote Marie Curie later, "was the subject of my doctor's thesis." She had not been paid a penny for it; no doctorate was ever harder earned. News of his daughter's success brought intense happiness to the last weeks of the father she had left behind in Warsaw, who died in May, 1902.

Success, however, went hand in hand with setbacks. After the birth of Irène the Curies had to employ a nurse and a servant, and Pierre's salary as a university teacher was no longer enough. He failed to be appointed to the professorships he wanted, which would have meant more money and, almost more precious, more time for research. Instead, he had to take extra teaching work, while Marie joined the staff of a girls' college at Sèvres, which involved a journey by train to the suburbs two or three times a week, and homework to correct in the evenings. And they still

Personal Success   155

had to work in their miserable shed. Marie said later that radium could have been discovered in two years instead of five. . . .

It was not only work and poverty and tragedy they had to contend with, but the actual results of their researches. Radium's "burning" effect had rapidly led to the discovery that it could be used for the treatment of tumors and certain cancers. At once this gave the Curies' work a great human importance. Nothing could have given either of them greater pleasure.

The Curies had decided, right at the start, that they would not patent the extraction process Marie had devised; others might make money out of its manufacture, but not they. They always published their researches freely, and in the years between 1899 and 1904 they alone or with collaborators published 32 scientific reports. But they were also constantly asked for advice by other scientists and by industrialists who wished to extract radium for medical purposes. It all took time.

The real burden, however, was fame. The first honors came from Britain. In November, 1903, they were awarded the Davy Medal. But the following month, with Henri Becquerel, whose researches had inspired their own, they received from Sweden the Nobel Prize for physics. This was a sensation: Marie Curie was the first great woman scientist, and public recognition of this kind brought her instant—and unwelcome—celebrity.

They were too ill to attend the prize-giving. Marie wrote to her brother in December: "We are inundated with letters and with visits from photographers and journalists. One would like to dig into the ground somewhere to find a little peace. . . . With much effort we have avoided the banquets people wanted to organize in our honor. We refuse with the energy of despair. . . ." In February: "Our life has been altogether spoiled by honors and fame." And in March: ". . . I hardly reply to these letters, but I lose time by reading them." . . .

Their lives had changed forever. Marie never again found the anonymity in which, for so long, she had been happy. . . . When the two scientists went on holiday, they would register at hotels under false names. If strangers asked Marie if she were Madame Curie, she would deny it, driven to lie after half a lifetime devoted to the truth, as she had been driven to lie in childhood. . . . Her second child, Eve, was born in December, 1904. Marie, who had longed for caviar while she was bearing her, started teaching at Sèvres again eight weeks later.

Gradually, however, they came to terms, not with their celebrity but with their success. They almost relaxed. The delayed visit to Sweden, 18 months after the Nobel Prize had been awarded to them, proved an unexpected pleasure. In 1899 they never went once to the theater; now they began to go quite often. . . .

The 70,000 gold francs that came with the Nobel Prize had enabled Pierre Curie to give up some of his teaching, and the Curies were able to hire a proper laboratory assistant. But a considerable sum was lent to Marie's sister Bronya and her husband, who were founding a sanatorium in Austrian Poland; there were presents to buy and a bathroom was built.

Then, at long last, Pierre Curie received a professorship. There was still no laboratory, but there was a little more working space and three assistants. And his *chef d'atelier* was to be in name as well as in fact his wife. At the end of 1904, for the first time, Marie Curie was paid a salary as a scientist.

Pierre Curie was to hold his professorship for less than 18 months. On the afternoon of April 19, 1906, he was run over in the streets of Paris by a wagon loaded down with military uniforms. The mainspring went out of her life. . . .

Three weeks after his death, having refused a state pension, Marie Curie was offered her husband's professorship. At 38, she was the first woman to hold a chair at the Sorbonne. The day after the announcement she was confiding to her diary: "My little Pierre, I want to tell you that the laburnum is in flower, the wisteria, the hawthorn and the iris are beginning—you would have loved all that. I want to tell you, too, that I have been named to your chair, and that there have been some imbeciles to congratulate me on it. I want to tell you that I no longer love the sun or the flowers. The sight of them makes me suffer. I feel better on dark days, like the day of your death, and if I have not learned to hate fine weather it is because my children have need of it." When she took over his course that autumn, she began her first lecture at the very point where he had ended his last.

Her life was over, she felt, but she survived him by nearly 30 years. There were, indeed, other triumphs, some happiness, and always the work she loved. She recovered her phenomenal energy, could drive herself to the limits of her strength as before; even the gaiety re-emerged, to charm her assistants and her pupils, laughing *de bon coeur,* according to one of them. Even before she at long last got her proper laboratory at the Institut du Radium in the rue Pierre Curie, she made her little team international; apart from votes for women, international peace and cooperation was her only political commitment. Her former staff remembers the great interest she took in their lives—*"avec beau-*

Personal Success 157

coup de discrétion mais beaucoup de chaleur." Once she refused
to go to a scientific gathering with the great Jean Perrin; she preferred to attend the marriage of the son of one of her staff. "You
waste your time!" he exclaimed. "Less than you!" she replied.
"I can read up the speeches later." . . .

Her work, however, continued. She purified, for the first and
last time, radium metal (before it had been salts of radium); she
established the first international standard by which newly ex-
tracted radium could be measured; there was another Nobel
Prize (in chemistry, for her discovery of radium) in 1911 (the
money went into war bonds, which she knew would lose their
value); and in July, 1914, she got the laboratory Pierre had longed
for. She had insisted on a garden, and planted the rambler roses
herself. A month later war broke out.

During the war she organized mobile X-ray equipment for
the French Army. She had become something of a "fixer." She
demanded private cars from rich women, learned to drive herself in order to dispense with a chauffeur on her journeys to the
front, took Irène with her as her assistant, and trained 150 other
technicians in radiology. Her "radiological cars" became known
as *petits curies;* there were to be 20 of them. She also installed
some 200 radiological rooms in army hospitals, and was disap-
pointed not to be offered the Legion of Honor as a soldier (she refused the ordinary cross). By her efforts, over a million soldiers
were X-rayed at the front.

After the war, in her fifties, she grew more serene, but never
lost her energy. She even took up skiing, was still skating six
months before her death, and prided herself on her swimming.
There were to be happy holidays in Larcouest, in Brittany; there
were to be two great journeys to the United States to collect
grams of radium donated to her by the women of America; there
were visits to Rio de Janeiro, Spain, Czechoslovakia, England,
Holland, Italy, Belgium, Poland. She no longer had any material
worries: France had awarded her a pension in 1923 . . . and there
was also an American annuity. She built holiday houses at Larcouest and Cavalaire, on the Riviera, and gardened enthusiastically everywhere. There was, above all, intense joy in the success
of Irène and her husband, Frédéric Joliot, in their discovery of
artificial radioactivity a few months before her death, for which
they were soon to be awarded the Nobel Prize in chemistry—the
prize Marie had won 23 years earlier.

Marie Curie would have been delighted to know that the
young people's discovery was, through cobalt bombs, to contrib-

158   *Success: A Search for Values*

ute even more effectively to the treatment of cancer than her
own; and interested, certainly, that the fuller understanding of
the phenomenon of radioactivity would lead to the carbon 14
method of dating archeological remains. She would have been
far less happy about the other consequences of the investigation
of radioactivity, the mushroom growths at Hiroshima and Naga-
saki. But in 1934, when she finally succumbed to a lifetime of
ailments, only the younger generation of scientists was beginning to speculate on the possibilities of nuclear energy released
by man.

[SEE EXERCISE ON PAGE 347]

A wise man will make more opportunities than he finds.

                                                              BACON

Personal Success   159

The Iliad and The Odyssey *are generally considered to be the foundations of Western literature. Both poems are believed to have been written by Homer in Greece about 850* B.C. *The excerpt that follows is a prose translation.*

The Iliad tells about the tenth year of a war between the people of the city of Troy and a group of Greek kings and other noted warriors. This famous war started when the Trojan prince Paris stole Helen from her husband, a Greek king.

Achilles is the leader of his own army fighting on the side of the Greeks. He is a great warrior, son of a semi-goddess, and one of the chief characters in The Iliad. *In this passage, which occurs near the end of the book, he confronts Hector, brother of Paris, and the noblest and best Trojan warrior, in single combat, and defeats him. This act ends the war.*

The characters in The Iliad *are not "real" in the sense that you might expect those in a modern novel to be like people you know. Instead, the men are godlike, and, surprisingly, the gods (who play an important part in the story) are often manlike.*

Names and terms in this passage that may be unfamiliar to you are identified in brackets in this account of how Achilles overwhelms Hector—with help from the goddess Athene.

From "The Wrath
of Achilles" in *The Iliad*
*of Homer**

Translated by I. A. Richards

. . . Achilles came near in his waving helmet, with his great Pelean spear [Peleus was the father of Achilles] lifted; and suddenly fear moved Hector and away from the gates under the walls of Troy he ran, with swift-footed Achilles after him. Past the lookout station, and by the wind-waved fig tree away from the wall by the wagon road they went, and past the two springs which feed eddying Xanthus [a river]. One runs with warm water and a smoke goes up from it as if from a fire, the other even in sum-

---

* Reprinted from *The Iliad of Homer*, translated by I. A. Richards. By permission of W. W. Norton & Company, Inc. Copyright 1950 by W. W. Norton & Company, Inc.

mer is cold as snow or ice. And near them are the wide stone basins where the wives and daughters of the Trojans washed their clothes of old in the time of peace, before the Greeks came to Troyland. By these they ran — a good man in front but a far stronger man at his heels. And the prize they ran for was no bull's skin, or common prize for the swift-footed, but the life of horse-taming Hector.

And all the gods looked on. Then the father of gods and men [Zeus] said: "My heart sorrows for Hector, who has burned many thighs of oxen [a sacrifice] on the crests of Ida [a mountain sacred to the gods] and in the city. Now think and take counsel, gods. Are we to save him from death or now at last kill him, a good man though he is, at Achilles' hands?"

Then the goddess, flashing-eyed Athene [on the side of the Greeks], said: "Father, Lord of the bright lightning and the dark cloud, what are you saying? Would you save from death a mortal man whose hour has long been fixed by fate? Do as you will, but know that we other gods are not all with you in this."

And in answer Zeus ["father of gods" and their own king] said: "Take heart, my child. I am not as serious as I seem. Do as your pleasure is and hold back no longer." And down from Olympus [mountain where the gods lived] Athene went.

Three times round Troy Hector and Achilles ran. Whenever Hector made for the Dardanian [Trojan] gates to the cover of the walls, where the Trojans could help him by throwing, Achilles would head him off and turn him back toward the plain, keeping on the city side. They ran as in a dream where one man cannot escape or overtake another. And how could Hector have escaped so far, if Apollo [a god on the side of the Trojans], for the last time, had not kept up his strength and made swift his knees? And Achilles signaled to the other Greeks not to throw their spears at Hector. Three times round Troy they went, but when they came the fourth time to the springs, Zeus lifted up his golden balance and Hector's fate went down; and Phoebus Apollo left him.

Then Athene came to Achilles and said: "Stand and take breath while I go and make Hector fight with you man to man." And Achilles signaled to the other Greeks not to throw their spears at Hector. Three times round Troy they went, but when they came

"Dear brother," she said, "now let us two meet Achilles' attack together." And Hector answered: "Deïphobus, you were always dearest to me of my brothers, but now I honor you in my heart even more. You, only, have had the courage to come out here to help me while the others stay inside."

And bright-eyed Athene said: "Truly, my brother, they did all they could, with their prayers, to keep me back — so much they fear Achilles — but now let us fight."

Personal Success   161

With such words Athene tricked him; and Hector, coming near to Achilles, said: "I will run from you no longer, Achilles, but kill you now or be killed. And let this be our agreement before all the gods as witnesses: if Zeus lets me outlive you and take your life, I will give your body back to the Greeks, after taking your armor. And you will do the same."

But with an angry look Achilles answered: "Talk not to me of agreements, Hector. Between lions and men there is no swearing of oaths. How can wolves and sheep be of one mind? They must hate one another all through. No more of this, but fight your best. For now Pallas Athene will overcome you by my spear. Now you must pay for all my sorrows for my friends you have killed."

He lifted his far-shadowing spear as he spoke and threw. Hector watched its coming and bent low so that it went over him and fixed itself in the earth. But Athene took it out and gave it back to Achilles without Hector's seeing her. And Hector cried: "So you did not know from Zeus the hour of my death, O godlike Achilles! Did you think your false tongue would make me afraid? Now escape my spear if you can."

And he lifted his far-shadowing spear and threw it and hit Achilles' shield, but the shield turned it back. And Hector saw and cried to Deïphobus loudly for a long spear. But there was no man there. Then Hector knew all in his heart and said: "Alas! Now they have brought me to my death. I thought Deïphobus was with me, but he is inside the walls and that was Athene who tricked me. Now death is very near me and there is no way of escape. This from of old was the pleasure of Zeus and his son, Apollo, who helped me before, but now my fate has come upon me. At least let me die fighting, to be honored by later men who hear of this."

And he took his sharp sword that hung by his side, a great sword and strong, and sprang on Achilles like an eagle which falls from a cloud on some lamb or hare. But Achilles ran upon him, his heart raging, his breast covered by his shield and the gold feathers on his four-horned helmet waving. As a star comes out among the stars of night, the star of evening, the most beautiful of the stars of heaven, even so came the light from the bronze of his spear as he lifted it in his right hand looking for the place most open for the blow. Now Hector's body was covered with bronze armor, the beautiful armor he had taken from great Patroclus [a close friend of Achilles] when he killed him; but there was an opening where the collarbones come into the neck; and there, as he came on, Achilles let drive with his spear and straight through the neck went the point. But the bronze-weighted spear did not cut the windpipe, so that Hector still had his voice. Then as he fell in the dust, Achilles gloried over him: "You

162   *Success: A Search for Values*

thought, Hector, you would be safe when you took that armor
from Patroclus. Little you thought, you fool, of me, far away
among my ships. But now, stronger far, I have come from them
and loosed your knees. The Greeks will give him [Patroclus] his
funeral but throw you to the dogs and birds."

Then Hector, as the breath went from him, prayed: "By
your life and knees and parents take the bronze and gold and all
the gifts my father and mother will offer you and send my body
back so that the Trojans and the Trojans' wives may give me to
the fire after my death."

But with an angry look Achilles answered: "Pray me not,
dog, by knees or parents. O that I could make myself cut up your
flesh and eat it raw myself, for what you have done. There is no
man living who can keep the dogs from your head, Hector—no,
not though they paid me your weight in gold."

And dying Hector answered: "I know you for what you are,
and knew it before; the heart in your breast is of iron. See that I
do not bring the anger of the gods down upon you on the day
when Paris and Apollo kill you, strong though you are, at the
Scaean gate."

He ended and death overtook him and his spirit went from
him down to the house of Hades, crying out sadly against its fate.
And after his death Achilles said to him: "Lie dead there; I am
ready for my own death whenever Zeus and the other immortals
send it."

He pulled his spear out and put it aside and took the armor
from Hector's body. And the other Greeks ran up to wonder at
Hector's beauty. And all who came near wounded him with their
spears. And one would say looking at another: "Hector is softer
now to handle than when he burned the ships with fire." And
when Achilles had taken off the armor, he stood and said to the
Greeks: "Let us see what the Trojans are minded to do now that
the gods have let us overcome this man who has done us more
damage than all the rest together. But what am I thinking of?
Patroclus still waits at the ships for his funeral. How can I forget him while I live on and my knees are quick! Even if in the
house of Hades dead men forget their friends, even there I will
not forget him. But come, sons of the Greeks, let us go back to
the ships singing our song of glory and taking this man with us.
For we have won great glory. We have killed highborn Hector to
whom the Trojans throughout their city prayed as to a god."

[SEE EXERCISE ON PAGE 353]

Personal Success

Picasso, Pablo. *Horse's Head. Study for Guernica*, 2 May, 1937. Oil on canvas, 25½″ x 36¼″. On extended loan to The Museum of Modern Art, New York, from the artist, M. Picasso.

Picasso, Pablo. *Mother with Dead Child on Ladder. Study for Guernica*, 10 May, 1937. Color crayon and pencil on white paper, 17⅞″ x 9½″. On extended loan to The Museum of Modern Art, New York, from the artist, M. Picasso.

Picasso, Pablo. *Composition Study for Guernica*, 1 May, 1937. Pencil on gesso, 21 1/8″ x 25 1/2″. On extended loan to The Museum of Modern Art, New York, from the artist, M. Picasso.

Picasso, Pablo. *Composition Study for Guernica*, 9 May, 1937. Pencil on white paper, 9 1/2″ x 17 7/8″. On extended loan to The Museum of Modern Art, New York, from the artist, M. Picasso.

Picasso, Pablo. *Guernica* (mural). 1937. Oil on canvas, 11′6″ x 25′8″. On extended loan to The Museum of Modern Art, New York, from the artist, M. Picasso.

166 *Success: A Search for Values*

A significant step in American politics occurred in November 1967 when a black man was elected mayor of one of the country's largest cities. Carl Stokes of Cleveland has had many difficulties since taking office, not the least of which was serious rioting in ghetto areas the following summer. But to many people, both black and white, the election of Stokes indicates that black power comes in many ways and in many forms — and for many purposes.

ELECTIONS*

THE REAL BLACK POWER

"Hey! We got ourselves a mayor!" cried a white college student from New York. "We did it! We did it!" exulted a middle-aged Negro man. "Amen, amen," murmured an elderly Negro woman, tears starting from her eyes. It was 3:02 a.m. at a downtown hotel, and Cleveland, the nation's tenth biggest city, had just chosen as its mayor Carl Burton Stokes, great-grandson of a slave, over Seth Taft, grandson of a President.

With his swearing-in this week in the city council chamber, sinewy, stage-handsome Stokes becomes the first Negro elected to head any major U.S. city. He brings to the job not only political experience and ability but also grace, pugnacity and energy neatly packaged in a 6-ft., 175-lb. frame. In all, he is quite a change from the routine succession of organization men he succeeds. "This is not a Carl Stokes victory," he said when the results were in, "not a vote for a man but a vote for a program, for a visionary dream of what our city can

* Excerpts reprinted from "The Real Black Power," *Time*, November 17, 1967 by permission of Carl Stokes and Time, Inc. Copyright Time Inc. 1967.

become." He added softly: "I can say to you that never before have I ever known the full meaning of the words 'God Bless America.' " . . .

SHARING WITH RATS. In Cleveland, the excitement started for Carl Stokes even before his two-year term began. The tension of election night gave way to apprehension as the county elections board discovered sizable errors in the initial count, then whittled his lead practically to the vanishing point. It was in keeping with the roller-coaster life that Cleveland's new mayor has led for most of his 40 years.

Stokes was born in the Cleveland slum called Central. His handsome father, a laundry worker, died when Carl was a year old, leaving his son no legacy but looks. For the next eleven years, Carl, his older brother Louis and their mother shared one bed and one bedroom with the rats. While Mrs. Stokes, now 65, worked as a maid by day, their grandmother reared the boys. But Mother Stokes managed to get across one important message: "Study, so you'll be somebody."

Carl and Louis studied, though Carl, at least, suffered some ambiva-

Personal Success 167

lence. He would smuggle books home from the library under his clothes. "Reading was against the mores," he explains. "I couldn't let the other boys know." And in the Depression-era slums, he thought more about Joe Louis than Booker T. Washington. "All of us looked on boxing as a way of life," he says. "You had to fight." At 17 he dropped out of high school and soon found himself in the Army. His military career in Europe as the war was ending was more athletic than heroic. He continued to box, won the table-tennis championship of the European theater. He came home with corporal's stripes and a renewed determination to go back to his books.

PISTOL WHIPPING. Carl completed high school, enrolled under the G.I. bill as a psychology major at West Virginia State, but after a year went back home to Western Reserve University. He was still undecided as to a career — psychology and the ministry were possibilities — when in 1948 he became chauffeur to a political organizer in Frank Lausche's gubernatorial campaign. After Lausche won, Stokes was offered a state job and chose to be a liquor inspector. He was a tough one. In his first case, a lone foray against an unlicensed saloon, the tough barkeep and customers laughed in his scrawny face (he then weighed only 150 lbs.). Stokes pistol-whipped the bartender into submission. Later, in a shoot-out with some bootleggers, one of Stokes's colleagues was wounded while Stokes gunned down two men. Before long he had the second highest record of arrests among 85 inspectors.

By this time he had decided on law as a career. He went first to the Uni-

versity of Minnesota, where he earned a B.S. in law and the university's billiards championship, while working as a dining-car waiter; then to the Cleveland-Marshall Law School at night, where he obtained an L.L.B. while serving as a court probation officer during the day. He had married while he was a liquor inspector, but the marriage ended in divorce in 1956. In 1958 he married Shirley Edwards, an attractive Fisk University graduate in library science. They have a boy and a girl: Carl Jr., 9, and Cordi, 6.

On the day he passed the Ohio bar examination in 1957, Stokes resigned his court job and went into law practice with his brother. A year later Mayor Anthony Celebrezze appointed him an assistant proscecutor under City Law Director Ralph Locher. The next step, in 1962, was election to the state legislature, where he quickly established himself as a prolific, catholic lawmaker. He helped draft legislation establishing a state department of urban affairs, wrote a new mental-health services act, helped enact stiffer traffic regulations, promoted a gun-control bill, worked for tougher air-pollution controls, and was the only Democrat to sponsor a bill giving the Governor power to send the National Guard into a city before a riot situation gets out of hand. . . .

Certainly Stokes, with his expensively tailored, double-breasted pinstripe suits, monogrammed (CBS) shirts and Antonio y Cleopatra cigars, is no leveler. His children go to private schools. And now that he is king of Cleveland's mountain, he can be expected to work from the top to exise the civic decay that has retarded Cleveland's progress.

[SEE EXERCISE ON PAGE 359]

168   *Success: A Search for Values*

There was wild rejoicing in Cuba on January 1, 1959. The hated dictator Batista had been deposed by a band of patriots after a long, difficult, mostly guerrilla war. Fidel Castro was the adored one, the liberator, the man who made Cuba free again. His success brought boundless joy all over the island.

Then came rumors, loudly denied, that Castro had Communist leanings. Still uglier stories continued: Castro had planned all along to make his island into a Communist base in the Western hemisphere. The truth of these stories gradually became apparent. Castro had scored a second success.

These excerpts from Castro's own speeches show the change from denial to acceptance of a philosophy of government contrary to one most Americans believe in.

From *Fidel Castro Speaks**

Translated by Paul E. Sigmund

ON MAY 8, 1959[1]

. . . Can our Revolution be accused of being Communist? Can the ideals of our Revolution be confused? Have we not spoken with sufficient clarity on the doctrine of the 26th of July Movement? Are our purposes not clearly defined? Then why are these fears and fantasies pursued? Are they not trying to create obstacles for the path of our Revolution? If our ideas are very clear, if the majority of the people are behind those ideas, and we are all at the command of that movement and that Revolution, do the people not trust us? Can someone perhaps maintain that we have ever lied to the people? Can anyone think that we have

---

* Excerpts reprinted from "Fidel Castro Speaks" in *The Ideologies of the Developing Nations*, rev. ed., edited by Paul Sigmund. Reprinted by permission of Frederick A. Praeger, Inc.

[1] Excerpts from a speech delivered by Castro in the Plaza Civica, Havana; translated by Paul E. Sigmund from the text in *Guia del Pensamiento Politico Economico de Fidel* (Havana: Diario Libre, 1959).

Personal Success   169

lacked courage to speak to the people? Can anyone think that we lack the necessary sincerity to speak what we think to the people? Can anyone perhaps think that we are hypocrites or cowards? Then why do we say that our Revolution is not Communist? Why, when we prove that our ideals are different from Communist doctrine, that the Revolution is not Communist or capitalist, that it is a revolution of its own . . . that it has its own ideology – entirely its own – which has a Cuban basis and is entirely Cuban, entirely Latin American, why then, do they start to accuse our Revolution of being something it is not? It is necessary to explain for once that if our ideas were Communist, we would say so here, and if our ideas were capitalist, we would say so here. . . .

FROM SPEECHES BETWEEN SEPTEMBER 30, 1965 AND OCTOBER 2, 1965

When the time comes to defend the institutions of our Revolution, we can discuss them in any university or intellectual center in the world and prove that we have a very superior governmental system, a much more democratic governmental system, a government henceforth by one class, that of the workers. When all the citizens are workers, then it is a government of the whole people. To achieve this we must keep this objective before us and struggle unceasingly to establish this society – the Communist society. . . .

We are fighting for a higher type of society, the Communist society. This name has been calumniated by the exploiters in the capitalist society, and even before capitalism – in the period of slavery, in the period of feudalism, and even in the period of the bourgeois revolutions – it has been a name which the exploiters, those who live by the sweat and labor of other men and other peoples, have tried to blot out.

When we say a Communist society, we are speaking of a higher type of society, a thousand times more just and perfect than that rotten bourgeois imperialist society which discriminates against men and sacrifices them, which condemns women to prostitution and children to misery, which shows no mercy and has no ideal but the worship of riches and money.

We are fighting for a new higher type of society which no nation today has achieved and I think we can compete in this

170   *Success: A Search for Values*

effort to try to be among the first to achieve these more advanced forms of human society. If we pursue this objective, we should raise up the ideals of the Revolution for men to see, expressed in the name of the Party so that the members of our Party may always keep in mind what those objectives are and how we must try to achieve them—objectives which I am sure our people will achieve among the first in the world.

And therefore to adopt a name which implies both the absolute unity of all the people and at the same time expresses the final goals of our Revolution, we have suggested the name of the Communist Party of Cuba. . . .[2]

[SEE EXERCISE ON PAGE 363]

Nothing is enough to the man for whom enough is too little.

EPICURUS

He that fails in his endeavors after wealth or power will not long retain either honesty or courage.

DR. JOHNSON

[2] Excerpts from speeches by Fidel Castro at the first meeting of the Central Committee of the Communist Party of Cuba, September 30, 1965 to October 2, 1965; translated by Paul E. Sigmund from *Granma*, October 10, 1965.

Personal Success 171

> *Real people in a not quite possible situation is the stuff
> from which fantasy is made. Although not quite science
> fiction, this story nevertheless is real only in its implica-
> tions. For sometimes it is possible to be "too successful."*

The Wonderful Dog Suit*

Donald Hall

Lester was terribly intelligent and only nine years old. He
was especially good at mathematics. "Hey, Lester," his father
would say to him, "if $X^2 - Y (32 X) + \frac{X}{y} \div 14Y^3$, then $\sqrt{XY} = ?$"
Lester would come back with an answer, quick as Jackie Robin-
son.

So when he graduated into the fifth grade at the head of his
class, his Uncle Fred gave him a dog suit. It was the best dog
suit you ever saw, and it fitted Lester perfectly. The minute he
put it on you'd swear it wasn't Lester at all but some big fat
mongrel.

Lester worked over his dog act until he was very good. He
taught himself to shake hands, roll over, play dead and everything. Then he learned how to bury a bone, lift a leg against a
bush and chase cars. When he was perfect, he showed his parents and they were impressed. "You are a *Wunderkind*, Lester,"
said his father.

"Bow wow," said Lester.

Now when his parents had company, they asked Lester to
get into his dog suit and fool everybody. He imitated a dog's
nyeh-nyeh-nyeh-nyeh-nyeh so that grown-up ladies would clap
their hands and exclaim, "Oh, listen! He's trying to talk." He
frisked and romped and they rubbed his ears. Then he would
unzip his dog suit and step out of it, and everyone would be very
surprised.

He liked his dog suit so much that he no longer studied all
the time. "Lester is more of a normal boy now," said his mother
sadly. He took to putting on his dog suit after school and going

---

* **Reprinted from "The Wonderful Dog Suit" in** *The Carleton Miscellany,* **by permission of
the author.**

172   *Success: A Search for Values*

out to play with the kids in the park. He chased balls or sticks for them. Sometimes he played tag or ran around the bases or wrestled. It was a lot of fun for Lester, who had never belonged to a group before. The kids thought he was a smart dog and petted him all the time.

One day in the park Lester heard some kids talking about him.

"Hey, this mutt doesn't belong to nobody," said one.

"What do you want, a reward?" his companion answered.

"Nah, I'm going to take him home."

Lester thought it would be great fun to surprise the kid and his family when they took him home, so he went along. He played all the way, pretending he saw cats and things, and when he got to the kid's slum-clearance project, it was someplace he had never seen before. He was lost.

The kid took him upstairs and into a kitchen. "Hey, Ma," he said. "I brought home a mutt."

"You get that frigging mutt out of here before I cut you open," said the kid's mother absentmindedly. Lester slunk off into another room with his tail between his legs. In the other room there was a man drinking out of a bottle who kicked Lester in the side.

Lester went out into the hall. He decided he didn't like it here and that he ought to get out of his dog suit.

But the zipper was stuck!

He tried and tried, but he couldn't make it budge. What could he do? Maybe if he went home his Uncle Fred could take him back to the factory. Anyway his mother could always call the fire department. But he didn't know how to get home. He would have to ask the kid and his mother for directions.

He padded back to the kitchen. He laughed to himself as he thought how surprised they would be to hear him talk! As he came into the room he heard the mother say, "Okay, okay, okay. But he's got to eat garbage and nothing but garbage."

He said, "I realize this will come as a shock to you, but I am not a dog at all. I am a boy named Lester and I live at 2331 Hummingbird Crescent and I am entering the fifth grade next autumn. Uncle Fred gave me this dog suit but the zipper is unfortunately stuck. May I inquire directions to my house? I want to see my mother and father again. $X^2 - \sqrt{4Y}\left(\dfrac{3Y}{X}\right) = 7$."

The mother clapped her hands together and said, "Listen, he's trying to talk!"

[SEE EXERCISE ON PAGE 367]

Personal Success   173

> *Another boy genius is described in the article that follows.*
> *The story is about a real person and the information is*
> *factual.*

A Bachelor at 16*

Don Zagier, a short (5 ft. 4 in.), amiable youth, graduated last week at 16. That may sound only mildly interesting and not at all rare until it is said that Don's diploma was not from high school but rather from M.I.T.—and that he picked up not one, but two bachelor of science degrees.

Don, whose mother is a psychiatrist and whose father is dean of instruction at The American College of Switzerland, is not the customary introverted boy genius. He enjoys skiing and bridge, makes friends easily, dates a 20-year-old coed. Like most students, he prefers eleventh-hour cramming to term-long study. But he is bright, fast, hates to go to bed before five in the morning, and is in a very big hurry to succeed academically.

How did Don do it? I.Q. tests put him high in the genius category, but his grades were mediocre until his interest was aroused. He was so bored by his fifth-grade schoolwork in Stockton, Calif., where his father then taught at the University of the Pacific, that concerned school officials gave him a battery of psychological tests, then decided to let him skip the sixth grade. His marks climbed, and he was jumped past the ninth and eleventh grades. He went to summer school, took eight semesters of Berkeley math and humanities courses by mail, graduated from high school at 13.

Don was accepted by M.I.T. after scoring a perfect 800 in English and advanced-math achievement tests; instead of beginning that September, he decided to take a year's preparation at England's exclusive Winchester College. He spent his spare time studying M.I.T. textbooks, then took tests in virtually all of the university's freshman courses (including calculus, physics and chemistry), and passed them all. That permitted him to substitute more advanced courses in his first year at M.I.T.

---

* **Reprinted from *Time*, June 14, 1968 by permission of Time Inc. Copyright Time Inc. 1968.**

174   *Success: A Search for Values*

In his third semester, he stepped up the pace, took twelve courses instead of the usual four. By maintaining high course loads, he not only earned the required 360 credits for his math degree in just two years, but an extra 90 for a physics degree as well. And he did so without scheduling any classes before 11 a.m., so he could sleep late. Don will enter graduate study next fall at Oxford under Theoretical Mathematician Michael F. Atiyah. When math is really understood, Don says, "it becomes art, and you realize that you are seeing beauty."

[SEE EXERCISE ON PAGE 371]

. . . Real success . . . finds its essence in the growth and flowering of the person. The individual who achieves it comes to know, in place of the values of the market place and the glassy glitter of the symbols of success, such personal satisfactions as the joy of living, warm relationships with others, a feeling of productive aliveness.

For real success is not an outward show but an inward feeling. It begins inside, and probably its first inkling is the feeling, even the knowledge, that one is worth while. That's quite a discovery. Regardless of how the rest of the world may value us, there is no fooling the inner Bureau of Standards. We know when we feel adequate and when we don't (and if the prevalent neuroses of our time were listed, the inadequate feeling would rank high). Success is the opposite pole; it is a glow inside, a warmth that speaks to us with the language of comfort and satisfaction. With it comes the ability to work with a greater feeling of giving and less feeling of taking, and the courage to do the kind of work we really want to do (and to do it with more love and less fear), and a greater response to nature, stemming from a feeling of belonging to the universe, an inner quality of freedom and repose instead of tension and entrapment, a feeling of growth and growingness rather than stasis and decline.*

HOWARD WHITMAN

* **From** *Success Is Within You* **by Howard Whitman. Copyright © 1956 by Howard Whitman. Reprinted by permission of Doubleday & Company, Inc.**

Personal Success 175

The story of Pygmalion is not a new one. It was told long before the Roman poet Ovid (who lived from 43 B.C. to A.D. 17 or 18) recorded it, and the story has appeared in many guises since then.

Pygmalion was a gifted sculptor, but a woman hater who resolved never to marry. He did, however, work very hard at making a statue of a perfect woman; and when it was completed he fell passionately in love with his creation, lavishing on it fine clothes and other gifts. When Venus, the goddess of love, discovered the situation, she caused the statue to come to life. Pygmalion named his lady-love Galatea and, so the story goes, Venus herself attended their wedding.

The Pygmalion of George Bernard Shaw's play (and of My Fair Lady, *the musical and the movie based on it) is another kind of sculptor: a man who molds people rather than clay or marble. Professor Henry Higgins is a British speech teacher who takes pride in the fact that he can change anyone's dialect so that the speaker could pass as a member of "high society." Higgins makes a bet with his friend Pickering that he can make Eliza, a lowly flower seller whom he chooses at random, into a "lady" and introduce her to society without anyone ever guessing who she really is. He proposes to do this by dressing her in the right clothes, teaching her proper manners, and primarily by changing her way of speaking.*

This portion of the play from the end of Act III shows Professor Higgins' success. Or is it Eliza's success?

From *Pygmalion* (end of Act III)*

George Bernard Shaw

Clearly Eliza will not pass as a duchess yet; and Higgin's bet remains unknown. But the six months are not yet exhausted and just in time Eliza does actually pass as a princess. For a glimpse of how she did it imagine an Embassy in London one summer evening after dark. The hall door has an awning and a carpet across the sidewalk to the kerb, because a grand reception is in progress. A small crowd is lined up to see the guests arrive.

A Rolls-Royce car drives up. Pickering in evening dress, with

---

* Reprinted by permission of The Public Trustee and The Society of Authors.

176 *Success: A Search for Values*

*medals and orders, alights, and hands out Eliza, in opera cloak, even-
ing dress, diamonds, fan, flowers and all accessories. Higgins follows.
The car drives off; and the three go up the steps and into the house,
the door opening for them as they approach.*

*Inside the house they find themselves in a spacious hall from
which the grand staircase rises. On the left are the arrangements for
the gentlemen's cloaks. The male guests are depositing their hats and
wraps there.*

*On the right is a door leading to the ladies' cloakroom. Ladies are
going in cloaked and coming out in splendor. Pickering whispers to
Eliza and points out the ladies' room. She goes into it. Higgins and
Pickering take off their overcoats and take tickets for them from the
attendant.*

*One of the guests, occupied in the same way, has his back turned.
Having taken his ticket, he turns round and reveals himself as an important looking young man with an astonishingly hairy face. He has
an enormous moustache, flowing out into luxuriant whiskers. Waves
of hair cluster on his brow. His hair is cropped closely at the back, and
glows with oil. Otherwise he is very smart. He wears several worthless
orders. He is evidently a foreigner, guessable as a whiskered Pandour
from Hungary; but in spite of the ferocity of his moustache he is
amiable and genially voluble.*

*Recognizing Higgins, he flings his arms wide apart and ap-
proaches him enthusiastically.*

WHISKERS.   Maestro, maestro [*he embraces Higgins and kisses
him on both cheeks*]. You remember me?

HIGGINS.   No I don't. Who the devil are you?

WHISKERS.   I am your pupil: your first pupil, your best and
greatest pupil. I am little Nepommuck, the marvellous boy.
I have made your name famous throughout Europe. You
teach me phonetic. You cannot forget ME.

HIGGINS.   Why don't you shave?

NEPOMMUCK.   I have not your imposing appearance, your chin,
your brow. Nobody notice me when I shave. Now I am famous: they call me Hairy Faced Dick.

HIGGINS.   And what are you doing here among all these swells?

NEPOMMUCK.   I am interpreter. I speak 32 languages. I am in-
dispensable at these international parties. You are great
cockney specialist: you place a man anywhere in London
the moment he open his mouth. I place any man in Europe.
*A footman hurries down the grand staircase and comes to
Nepommuck.*

FOOTMAN.   You are wanted upstairs. Her Excellency cannot
understand the Greek gentleman.

NEPOMMUCK.   Thank you, yes, immediately.
The footman goes and is lost in the crowd.

Personal Success   177

NEPOMMUCK [*to Higgins*] This Greek diplomatist pretends he
    cannot speak nor understand English. He cannot deceive
    me. He is the son of a Clerkenwell watchmaker. He speaks
    English so villainously that he dare not utter a word of it
    without betraying his origin. I help him to pretend; but I
    make him pay through the nose. I make them all pay. Ha ha!
    [*He hurries upstairs*].
PICKERING. Is this fellow really an expert? Can he find out
    Eliza and blackmail her?
HIGGINS. We shall see. If he finds her out I lose my bet.
    Eliza comes from the cloakroom and joins them.
PICKERING. Well, Eliza, now for it. Are you ready?
LIZA. Are you nervous, Colonel?
PICKERING. Frightfully. I feel exactly as I felt before my first
    battle. It's the first time that frightens.
LIZA. It is not the first time for me, Colonel. I have done this
    fifty times—hundreds of times—in my little piggery in Angel
    Court in my day-dreams. I am in a dream now. Promise me
    not to let Professor Higgins wake me; for if he does I shall
    forget everything and talk as I used to in Drury Lane.
PICKERING. Not a word, Higgins. [*To Eliza*] Now, ready?
LIZA. Ready.
PICKERING. Go.
    They mount the stairs, Higgins last. Pickering whispers
    to the footman on the first landing.
FIRST LANDING FOOTMAN. Miss Doolittle, Colonel Pickering, Pro-
    fessor Higgins.
SECOND LANDING FOOTMAN. Miss Doolittle, Colonel Pickering,
    Professor Higgins.
    At the top of the staircase the Ambassador and his wife,
    with Nepommuck at her elbow, are receiving.
HOSTESS [*taking Eliza's hand*] How d'ye do?
HOST [*same play*] How d'ye do? How d'ye do, Pickering?
LIZA [*with a beautiful gravity that awes her hostess*] How do
    you do? [*She passes on to the drawingroom*].
HOSTESS. Is that your adopted daughter, Colonel Pickering?
    She will make a sensation.
PICKERING. Most kind of you to invite her for me. [*He passes on*].
HOSTESS [*to Nepommuck*] Find out all about her.
NEPOMMUCK [*bowing*] Excellency—[*he goes into the crowd*].
HOST. How d'ye do, Higgins? You have a rival here tonight. He
    introduced himself as your pupil. Is he any good?
HIGGINS. He can learn a language in a fortnight—knows dozens
    of them. A sure mark of a fool. As a phonetician, no good
    whatever.

178   *Success: A Search for Values*

HOSTESS.   How d'ye do, Professor?

HIGGINS.   How do you do? Fearful bore for you this sort of thing. Forgive my part in it. [*He passes on*].

In the drawingroom and its suite of salons the reception is in full swing. Eliza passes through. She is so intent on her ordeal that she walks like a somnambulist in a desert instead of a debutante in a fashionable crowd. They stop talking to look at her, admiring her dress, her jewels, and her strangely attractive self. Some of the younger ones at the back stand on their chairs to see.

The Host and Hostess come in from the staircase and mingle with their guests. Higgins, gloomy and contemptuous of the whole business, comes into the group where they are chatting.

HOSTESS.   Ah, here is Professor Higgins: he will tell us. Tell us all about the wonderful young lady, Professor.

HIGGINS [*almost morosely*]   What wonderful young lady?

HOSTESS.   You know very well. They tell me there has been nothing like her in London since people stood on their chairs to look at Mrs. Langtry.

Nepommuck joins the group, full of news.

HOSTESS.   Ah, here you are at last, Nepommuck. Have you found out all about the Doolittle lady?

NEPOMMUCK.   I have found out all about her. She is a fraud.

HOSTESS.   A fraud! Oh no.

NEPOMMUCK.   YES, yes. She cannot deceive me. Her name cannot be Doolittle.

HIGGINS.   Why?

NEPOMMUCK.   Because Doolittle is an English name. And she is not English.

HOSTESS.   Oh, nonsense! She speaks English perfectly.

NEPOMMUCK.   Too perfectly. Can you shew me any English woman who speaks English as it should be spoken? Only foreigners who have been taught to speak it speak it well.

HOSTESS.   Certainly she terrified me by the way she said How d'ye do. I had a schoolmistress who talked like that; and I was mortally afraid of her. But if she is not English what is she?

NEPOMMUCK.   Hungarian.

ALL THE REST.   Hungarian!

NEPOMMUCK.   Hungarian. And of royal blood. I am Hungarian. My blood is royal.

HIGGINS.   Did you speak to her in Hungarian?

NEPOMMUCK.   I did. She was very clever. She said "Please speak to me in Enlgish: I do not understand French." French! She pretend not to know the difference between Hungarian and French. Impossible: she knows both.

Personal Success   179

HIGGINS.   And the blood royal? How did you find that out?

NEPOMMUCK.   Instinct, maestro, instinct. Only the Magyar races can produce that air of the divine right, those resolute eyes. She is a princess.

HOST.   What do you say, Professor?

HIGGINS.   I say an ordinary London girl out of the gutter and taught to speak by an expert. I place her in Drury Lane.

NEPOMMUCK.   Ha ha ha! Oh, maestro, maestro, you are mad on the subject of cockney dialects. The London gutter is the whole world for you.

HIGGINS [*to the Hostess*]   What does your Excellency say?

HOSTESS.   Oh, of course I agree with Nepommuck. She must be a princess at least.

HOST.   Not necessarily legitimate, of course. Morganatic perhaps. But that is undoubtedly her class.

HIGGINS.   I stick to my opinion.

HOSTESS.   Oh, you are incorrigible.

The group breaks up, leaving Higgins isolated. Pickering joins him.

PICKERING.   Where is Eliza? We must keep an eye on her.

Eliza joins them.

LIZA.   I don't think I can bear much more. The people all stare so at me. An old lady has just told me that I speak exactly like Queen Victoria. I am sorry if I have lost your bet. I have done my best; but nothing can make me the same as these people.

PICKERING.   You have not lost it, my dear. You have won it ten times over.

HIGGINS.   Let us get out of this. I have had enough of chattering to these fools.

PICKERING.   Eliza is tired; and I am hungry. Let us clear out and have supper somewhere.

[SEE EXERCISE ON PAGE 375]

180   *Success: A Search for Values*

The day the mouse roared.

You're in school for 12 years. But most of you will never make a team. Why? Because you're too light. Because you're a girl. Because you work after school and can't practice. Whatever the reason, it's a fact: the same kids make all the teams.

Today you can stand up and do something about it. There's a new kind of team at school. The President's All America Team. And everybody has the same chance to make it. Don't let the name scare you into thinking it's difficult. It's easy if you're in shape. Impossible if you're not. Every boy and girl 10 to 17 can try out. This is a test of all-around ability (not how good you are in one sport).

It's a test of strength, speed and endurance. You have to run, jump, sit-up, pull-up and throw a softball. Big guys have no advantage over little guys. Boys have no advantage over girls. This is the youngest, smallest, lightest, newest, strongest team in America. Last year, 50,000 kids made the team and won an award and a badge from the President. Can you make the President's All America Team? You'll never know unless you try out. So do it. And don't worry about your size, sex or shape. After all, David beat Goliath. Delilah took away Samson's strength. And you can be the mouse that roared.

For information, write: President's Council on Physical Fitness, Washington, D.C. 20201.

PUBLISHED IN THE PUBLIC'S INTEREST BY READER'S DIGEST

Reproduced by permission of V. L. Nicholson for The President's Council on Physical Fitness & Sports, and Papert, Koenig, Lois, Inc.

Personal Success 181

This chapter (it is the second of six), from a book, The Pearl *marks a beginning and an end for Kino and his little family. Like everyone who searches long for something highly desired—a cure for a disease, a long-lost relative, a better future, or a great pearl—Kino is both pleased and fearful when his hope is fulfilled.*

There is more than just the finding of the pearl in this chapter. It is a portrait of gentle people and their way of life. It also contains a sensitive description of the sea from which comes much of the life of these people.

Chapter II from *The Pearl**

John Steinbeck

The town lay on a broad estuary, its old yellow plastered buildings hugging the beach. And on the beach the white and blue canoes that came from Nayarit were drawn up, canoes preserved for generations by a hard shell-like waterproof plaster whose making was a secret of the fishing people. They were high and graceful canoes with curving bow and stern and a braced section midships where a mast could be stepped to carry a small lateen sail.

The beach was yellow sand, but at the water's edge a rubble of shell and algae took its place. Fiddler crabs bubbled and sputtered in their holes in the sand, and in the shallows little lobsters popped in and out of their tiny homes in the rubble and sand. The sea bottom was rich with crawling and swimming and growing things. The brown algae waved in the gentle currents and the green eel grass swayed and little sea horses clung to its stems. Spotted botete, the poison fish, lay on the bottom in the eel-grass beds, and the bright-colored swimming crabs scampered over them.

On the beach the hungry dogs and the hungry pigs of the town searched endlessly for any dead fish or sea bird that might have floated in on a rising tide.

Although the morning was young, the hazy mirage was up.

---

* From *The Pearl* by John Steinbeck. Copyright 1945 by John Steinbeck. Reprinted by permission of The Viking Press, Inc.

182   *Success: A Search for Values*

The uncertain air that magnified some things and blotted out others hung over the whole Gulf so that all sights were unreal and vision could not be trusted; so that sea and land had the sharp clarities and the vagueness of a dream. Thus it might be that the people of the Gulf trust things of the spirit and things of the imagination, but they do not trust their eyes to show them distance or clear outline or any optical exactness. Across the estuary from the town one section of mangroves stood clear and telescopically defined, while another mangrove clump was a hazy black-green blob. Part of the far shore disappeared into a shimmer that looked like water. There was no certainty in seeing, no proof that what you saw was there or was not there. And the people of the Gulf expected all places were that way, and it was not strange to them. A copper haze hung over the water, and the hot morning sun beat on it and made it vibrate blindingly.

The brush houses of the fishing people were back from the beach on the right-hand side of the town, and the canoes were drawn up in front of this area.

Kino and Juana came slowly down to the beach and to Kino's canoe, which was the one thing of value he owned in the world. It was very old. Kino's grandfather had brought it from Nayarit, and he had given it to Kino's father, and so it had come to Kino. It was at once property and source of food, for a man with a boat can guarantee a woman that she will eat something. It is the bulwark against starvation. And every year Kino refinished his canoe with the hard shell-like plaster by the secret method that had also come to him from his father. Now he came to the canoe and touched the bow tenderly as he always did. He laid his diving rock and his basket and the two ropes in the sand by the canoe. And he folded his blanket and laid it in the bow.

Juana laid Coyotito on the blanket, and she placed her shawl over him so that the hot sun could not shine on him. He was quiet now, but the swelling on his shoulder had continued up his neck and under his ear and his face was puffed and feverish. Juana went to the water and waded in. She gathered some brown seaweed and made a flat damp poultice of it, and this she applied to the baby's swollen shoulder, which was as good a remedy as any and probably better than the doctor could have done. But the remedy lacked his authority because it was simple and didn't cost anything. The stomach cramps had not come to Coyotito. Perhaps Juana had sucked out the poison in time, but she had not sucked out her worry over her first-born. She had not prayed directly for the recovery of the baby — she had prayed that they might find a pearl with which to hire the doctor to cure the baby,

Personal Success

for the minds of people are as unsubstantial as the mirage of the Gulf.

Now Kino and Juana slid the canoe down the beach to the water, and when the bow floated, Juana climbed in, while Kino pushed the stern in and waded beside it until it floated lightly and trembled on the little breaking waves. Then in co-ordination Juana and Kino drove their double-bladed paddles into the sea, and the canoe creased the water and hissed with speed. The other pearlers were gone out long since. In a few moments Kino could see them clustered in the haze, riding over the oyster bed.

Light filtered down through the water to the bed where the frilly pearl oysters lay fastened to the rubbly bottom, a bottom strewn with shells of broken, opened oysters. This was the bed that had raised the King of Spain to be a great power in Europe in past years, had helped to pay for his wars, and had decorated the churches for his soul's sake. The gray oysters with ruffles like skirts on the shells, the barnacle-crusted oysters with little bits of weed clinging to the skirts and small crabs climbing over them. An accident could happen to these oysters, a grain of sand could lie in the folds of muscle and irritate the flesh until in self-protection the flesh coated the grain with a layer of smooth cement. But once started, the flesh continued to coat the foreign body until it fell free in some tidal flurry or until the oyster was destroyed. For centuries men had dived down and torn the oysters from the beds and ripped them open, looking for the coated grains of sand. Swarms of fish lived near the bed to live near the oysters thrown back by the searching men and to nibble at the shining inner shells. But the pearls were accidents, and the finding of one was luck, a little pat on the back by God or the gods or both.

Kino had two ropes, one tied to a heavy stone and one to a basket. He stripped off his shirt and trousers and laid his hat in the bottom of the canoe. The water was oily smooth. He took his rock in one hand and his basket in the other, and he slipped feet first over the side and the rock carried him to the bottom. The bubbles rose behind him until the water cleared and he could see. Above, the surface of the water was an undulating mirror of brightness, and he could see the bottoms of the canoes sticking through it.

Kino moved cautiously so that the water would not be obscured with mud or sand. He hooked his foot in the loop on his rock and his hands worked quickly, tearing the oysters loose, some singly, others in clusters. He laid them in his basket. In some places the oysters clung to one another so that they came free in lumps.

184   *Success: A Search for Values*

Now, Kino's people had sung of everything that happened or existed. They had made songs to the fishes, to the sea in anger and to the sea in calm, to the light and the dark and the sun and the moon, and the songs were all in Kino and in his people – every song that had ever been made, even the ones forgotten. And as he filled his basket the song was in Kino, and the beat of the song was his pounding heart as it ate the oxygen from his held breath, and the melody of the song was the gray-green water and the little scuttling animals and the clouds of fish that flitted by and were gone. But in the song there was a secret little inner song, hardly perceptible, but always there, sweet and secret and clinging, almost hiding in the counter-melody and this was the Song of the Pearl That Might Be, for every shell thrown in the basket might contain a pearl. Chance was against it, but luck and the gods might be for it. And in the canoe above him Kino knew that Juana was making the magic of prayer, her face set rigid and her muscles hard to force the luck, to tear the luck out of the god's hands, for she needed the luck for the swollen shoulder of Coyotito. And because the need was great and the desire was great, the little secret melody of the pearl that might be was stronger this morning. Whole phrases of it came clearly and softly into the Song of the Undersea.

Kino, in his pride and youth and strength, could remain down over two minutes without strain, so that he worked deliberately, selecting the largest shells. Because they were disturbed, the oyster shells were tightly closed. A little to his right a hummock of rubbly rock stuck up, covered with young oysters not ready to take. Kino moved next to the hummock, and then, beside it, under a little overhang, he saw a very large oyster lying by itself, not covered with its clinging brothers. The shell was partly open, for the overhang protected this ancient oyster, and in the lip-like muscle Kino saw a ghostly gleam, and then the shell closed down. His heart beat out a heavy rhythm and the melody of the maybe pearl shrilled in his ears. Slowly he forced the oyster loose and held it tightly against his breast. He kicked his foot free from the rock loop, and his body rose to the surface and his black hair gleamed in the sunlight. He reached over the side of the canoe and laid the oyster in the bottom.

Then Juana steadied the boat while he climbed in. His eyes were shining with excitement, but in decency he pulled up his rock, and then he pulled up his basket of oysters and lifted them in. Juana sensed his excitement, and she pretended to look away. It is not good to want a thing too much. It sometimes drives the luck away. You must want it just enough, and you must be very

Personal Success   185

tactful with God or the gods. But Juana stopped breathing. Very deliberately Kino opened his short strong knife. He looked speculatively at the basket. Perhaps it would be better to open *the* oyster last. He took a small oyster from the basket, cut the muscle, searched the folds of flesh, and threw it in the water. Then he seemed to see the great oyster for the first time. He squatted in the bottom of the canoe, picked up the shell and examined it. The flutes were shining black to brown, and only a few small barnacles adhered to the shell. Now Kino was reluctant to open it. What he had seen, he knew, might be a reflection, a piece of flat shell accidentally drifted in or a complete illusion. In this Gulf of uncertain light there were more illusions than realities.

But Juana's eyes were on him and she could not wait. She put her hand on Coyotito's covered head. "Open it," she said softly.

Kino deftly slipped his knife into the edge of the shell. Through the knife he could feel the muscle tighten hard. He worked the blade lever-wise and the closing muscle parted and the shell fell apart. The lip-like flesh writhed up and then subsided. Kino lifted the flesh, and there it lay, the great pearl, perfect as the moon. It captured the light and refined it and gave it back in silver incandescence. It was as large as a sea-gull's egg. It was the greatest pearl in the world.

Juana caught her breath and moaned a little. And to Kino the secret melody of the maybe pearl broke clear and beautiful, rich and warm and lovely, glowing and gloating and triumphant. In the surface of the great pearl he could see dream forms. He picked the pearl from the dying flesh and held it in his palm, and he turned it over and saw that its curve was perfect. Juana came near to stare at it in his hand, and it was the hand he had smashed against the doctor's gate, and the torn flesh of the knuckles was turned grayish white by the sea water.

Instinctively Juana went to Coyotito where he lay on his father's blanket. She lifted the poultice of seaweed and looked at the shoulder. "Kino," she cried shrilly.

He looked past his pearl, and he saw that the swelling was going out of the baby's shoulder, the poison was receding from its body. Then Kino's fist closed over the pearl and his emotion broke over him. He put back his head and howled. His eyes rolled up and he screamed and his body was rigid. The men in the other canoes looked up, startled, and then they dug their paddles into the sea and raced toward Kino's canoe.

[SEE EXERCISE ON PAGE 379]

186 *Success: A Search for Values*

One of the results of the Watts riot in 1965 was the estab-lishment of a Writer's Workshop. It is a group that helps young writers by teaching them their craft, and many of its members have published their plays, stories, and poems. The author of this poem is a member of that workshop.

*Existence**

Guadalupe de Saavedra

> Grin, fight, kick, joke —
>> It's the only way to fly.
> Smile, stab, pat, strike
>> Before he looks my way.
> Cry, stick, tear, steal —
>> The means are justified.
> Crush, rise, heel crack
>> It's grown too big
>> And it must die.
>
> How else could be successful
>> A person such as I?

[SEE EXERCISE ON PAGE 385]

---

* "Existence" by Guadalupe de Saavedra reprinted by permission of The World Publishing Company from *From the Ashes* by Budd Shulberg. An NAL book. Copyright © 1967 by The New American Library, Inc.

Personal Success   187

> *Once there was an old man who read too many books about the past and so imagined himself a daring knight whose mission it was to right the wrongs of the world. He persuaded a peasant to join him as squire, a man of no formal education but of considerable common sense. Together they roamed the countryside of Spain, forever mistaking people, confusing situations, and mixing things up more than they straightened things out.*
>
> *The men, of course, are Don Quixote and Sancho Panza, created by Cervantes and first known to readers in 1605. They have been acknowledged universally as more than just two fictional misfits, for in each of them is a little of all of us. The hit musical play* Man of La Mancha *attests to their present appeal.*
>
> *Sancho's goal in life was to govern his own island, and an elaborate practical joke gave him that opportunity. In this passage, Don Quixote, who imagines himself a very wise person, advises Sancho Panza about how to govern both himself and his "island."*

From *Don Quixote of La Mancha**

Miguel de Cervantes Saavedra
Translated by Walter Starkie

"First of all, O my son, fear God, for to fear Him is wisdom, and if you are wise you cannot err.

"Secondly, consider what you are, and try to know yourself, which is the most difficult study in the world. From knowing yourself you will learn not to puff yourself up like the frog that wished to rival the ox; . . .

". . . Show pride, Sancho, in your humble origins, and do not scorn to say that you spring from labouring men, for, when men see that you are not ashamed, none will try to make you so; and consider it more deserving to be humble and virtuous than proud and sinful. . . .

---

* **Excerpts reprinted from Chapter X, Part 2 from** *Don Quixote of La Mancha,* **by Miguel de Cervantes Saavedra, translated by Walter Starkie. Reprinted by permission of Macmillan & Co. Ltd.**

188   *Success: A Search for Values*

"Remember, Sancho, if you make virtue your rule in life, and pride yourself on acting always in accordance with such a precept, you will have no cause to envy princes and lords, for blood is inherited, but virtue is acquired, and virtue in itself is worth more than noble birth. Seeing that this is so, if, by chance, one of your poor relations comes to visit you in your island, do not reject or affront him, but, on the contrary, welcome and entertain him; for this way you will please God, who insists that none of the beings created by Him should be scorned. . . .

"Let the tears of the poor find more compassion, but not more justice, from you than the pleadings of the wealthy.

"Be equally anxious to sift out the truth from among the offers and bribes of the rich and the sobs and entreaties of the poor. . . .

"When a beautiful woman appears before you to demand justice, blind your eyes to her tears and deafen your ears to her lamentations and give deep thought to her claim, otherwise you may risk losing your judgment in the one and your integrity in the other.

"When you have to punish a man, do not revile him, for the penalty the unhappy man has to suffer is sufficient without the addition of abusive language.

"When a criminal is brought before you, treat him as a man subject to the frailties and depravities of human nature, and as far as you can, without injuring the opposite party, show pity and clemency, for though one attribute of God is as glorious as another, His mercy shines more brightly in our eyes than His justice.

"If you follow these precepts, Sancho, your days will be long and your renown eternal, your rewards will be without number, and your happiness unimaginable. You shall marry your children to your heart's content, and they and your grandchildren shall receive titles. You will live peaceful days cherished by all men, and when, after a gentle, ripe old age, Death steals upon you, your grandchildren's children with their tender and pious hands shall close your eyes."

Sancho listened most attentively to his master's instructions, and tried his best to commit them to memory, that he might hereby be enabled to support the burden of government and acquit himself honourably. Don Quixote continued as follows: "Now let us consider the regulation of your own person and your domestic concerns. In the first place, Sancho, I want you to be clean in your person. Keep your finger-nails pared, and do not allow them to grow as some do, who in their ignorance imagine that long

Personal Success   189

nails embellish their hands, whereas such long finger-nails are rather the claws of a lizard-hunting kestrel. Do not wear your clothes baggy and unbuttoned, Sancho, for a slovenly dress is proof of a careless mind; . . .

"Investigate carefully the income of your office, and if you can afford to give liveries [uniforms] to your servants, supply them with garments that are decent and durable rather than garish and gaudy; and give what you save in this way to the poor. . . .

"Do not eat either garlic or onions, lest the stench of your breath betray your humble birth.

"Walk slowly and gravely; speak with deliberation, but not so as to give the impression that you are listening to yourself, for all affectation is hateful.

"Eat little at dinner, and still less at supper, for the health of the whole body is forged in the stomach.

"Drink with moderation, for drunkenness neither keeps a secret nor observes a promise.

"Be careful, Sancho, not to chew on both sides of your mouth at once, and do not on any account eruct in company."

"Eruct," quoth Sancho, "I don't know what you mean by that."

"To eruct," said Don Quixote, "means to belch, but since this is one of the most beastly words in the Castilian language, though a most significant one, polite people, instead of saying 'belch', make use of the word 'eruct' which comes from Latin, and instead of 'belchings' they say 'eructations.' And though some do not understand these terms, it does not much matter, for in time use and custom will make their meanings familiar to all, and it is by such means that languages are enriched."

"'Pon my word, master," said Sancho, "I shall make a special point of remembering your advice about not belching, for, to tell you the honest truth, I'm mighty given to it."

"Eructing, Sancho, not belching," said Don Quixote.

"From now on," replied Sancho, "I'll say eructing, and please God I'll never forget it."

"Furthermore, Sancho, you must not overload your conversation with such a glut of proverbs, for though proverbs are concise and pithy sentences, you so often drag them in by the hair, that they seem to be maxims of folly rather than of wisdom."

"God alone can remedy that," answered Sancho, "for I know more proverbs than would fill a book, and when I talk, they crowd so thick and fast into my mouth that they struggle which shall get out first. And the tongue starts firing off the first that comes,

190   *Success: A Search for Values*

haphazard, no matter if it's to the point or no. However, in future I'll take good care not to let any fly save 'tis beneficial to the dignity of my place, for 'where there's plenty the guests can't be empty'; and 'he that cuts doesn't deal'; and 'he's safe as a house who rings the bells'; and 'he's no fool who can spend and spare.'"

"There, there you are, Sancho!" said Don Quixote, "on you go, threading, tacking and stitching together proverb after proverb 'til nobody can make head or tail of you! With you 'tis a case of 'my mother whips me yet I spin the top!' Here I am warning you not to make such an extravagant use of proverbs, and you then foist upon me a whole litany of old saws that have as much to do with our present business as 'over the hills of Ubeda.' Mind, Sancho, I do not condemn a proverb when it is seasonably applied, but to be for ever stringing proverbs together without rhyme or reason makes your conversation tasteless and vulgar.

"When you ride on horseback, do not throw your body back over the crupper [a part of the back of a saddle]; nor keep your legs stiff and straddling from the horse's belly; nor yet so loose, as if you were still riding Dapple [Sancho's donkey]. Remember that the air of sitting a horse distinguishes a gentleman from a groom.

"Be moderate in your sleep; for he who rises not with the sun enjoys not the day; and remember, Sancho, that diligence is the mother of good fortune, and sloth, her adversary, never accomplished a good wish.

"There is one final piece of advice which I wish to give you; though it has nought to do with the adornment of your body, I would have you remember it carefully. It is this . . . Never allow yourself to discuss lineage, or the pre-eminence of families, for if you compare them, one is sure to be better than the other, and he whose claim you have rejected will hate you, and he who is preferred will not reward you.

"Now with regard to your dress, you should wear breeches and hose, a long coat, and a cloak somewhat longer; as for wide-kneed breeches or trunk-hose, do not think of them: they are not becoming either to gentlemen or governors.

"This is all the advice I think of giving you for the present. As time goes on, if you let me know the state of your affairs, I shall give you further instructions as the occasions warrant. . . ."

[SEE EXERCISE ON PAGE 287]

Success is something you can't leave a son

In today's complex and specialized world, success depends more and more on whether he gets a college education.

But he may not be able to get one unless the nation's colleges can answer some serious questions: How to cope with rapidly increasing student enrollments? How to keep the quality of education constantly improving with more modern laboratories, better libraries, new classrooms? How to attract able new faculty members?

Your support will help colleges answer these questions . . . help them make your son ready for his world.

Give to the college of your choice.

COUNCIL FOR
FINANCIAL AID TO
EDUCATION

advertising contributed
for the public good

192   Success: A Search for Values

The cartoons of Jules Feiffer are often biting comments on contemporary society. Here is a familiar situation: the boy reads a homework assignment to his father. However, Feiffer's boy is really reading much more than a sixth-grade composition, and the father is doing more than just listening to a son's ideas.

From *The Explainers* by Jules Feiffer. Copyright © 1960 by Jules Feiffer. Used by permission of McGraw-Hill Book Company.

[SEE EXERCISE ON PAGE 393]

When She Lost Pounds, Fat Friends Left at Same Time*

By ANN LANDERS

DEAR ANN:

I got tired of hearing people say, "You have such a pretty face — if you lost some weight you'd be beautiful." So I went to my family doctor and asked him to put me on a strict diet. I shed 40 pounds in seven months.

So what am I writing about? Well, since I've lost weight I've also lost my fat girl friends. I shared my diet with them and kept urging them to stick with it but they didn't have the willpower.

At first they seemed thrilled about my weight loss but as I began to look better they became cooler and cooler. The real break came when I started to date some very attractive men. It's hard for me to believe that my friends are jealous yet I don't know how else to figure it. Do you?

—THE NEW ME

Success can be awfully hard to take — particularly somebody else's. Those dames were not friends. They were merely acquaintances with whom you once shared a common misery. You've lost nothing of value.

* Ann Landers reprinted by permission Publishers — Hall Syndicate.

Personal Success 195

> *"They laughed when I sat down to play . . ." That was the headline on one of the most famous advertisements ever run. It convinced thousands of people that they could be the life of the party, the surprise success among their friends, by learning to play the piano quickly and expertly. People who can play musical instruments, tell jokes, or do imitations are often social successes. So are those who can do clever tricks or stump others by faultlessly reeling off tongue-twisters.*

*Tongue Twisters**

SHIFTLESS SHEEP

Silly Sally swiftly shooed seven silly sheep.
The seven silly sheep Silly Sally shooed
shilly-shallied south.
These sheep shouldn't sleep in a shack;
sheep should sleep in a shed.

FISH TALE

A fresh young fisher named Fisher
Once fished for a fish in a fissure.
The fish with a grin
Pulled the fisherman in,
And they're fishing the fissure for Fisher.

THE BANKRUPT PROMOTER

Bill had a billboard. Bill also had a board bill.
The board bill bored Bill, so that Bill sold the billboard
to pay the board bill. After Bill
sold the billboard to pay the board bill, the board bill
no longer bored Bill. But though he had no board bill,
neither did he have his billboard!

* **From *The Big Book of Tongue Twisters and Double Talk* by Arnold Arnold. © Copyright 1964 by Manuscript Press, Inc. Reprinted by permission of Random House, Inc.**

In dreams there is success, too. Perhaps it can come in even greater measure than is possible in the world of reality.

Dream Variation*

Langston Hughes

To fling my arms wide
In some place of the sun,
To whirl and to dance
Til the white day is done.
Then rest at cool evening
Beneath a tall tree
While night comes on gently,
    Dark like me,—
That is my dream!

To fling my arms wide
In the face of the sun,
Dance! whirl! whirl!
Till the quick day is done.
Rest at pale evening . . .
A tall, slim tree . . .
Night coming tenderly
    Black like me.

---

* Copyright 1926 by Alfred A. Knopf, Inc. and renewed 1954 by Langston Hughes. Reprinted from *Selected Poems* by Langston Hughes by permission of the publisher.

Personal Success 197

The special qualities of an entertainer that make him a top box office draw vary for each individual, and the same apparent combination that works for one person does not always work for another. Stars have generally been "loners," known as themselves alone. Even when musical groups have great popularity, for example, fans often regard the members individually and have special favorites within the group.

James Brown's stardom is unique, and it is enormous if measured by two currently popular yardsticks: the ability to fill Yankee Stadium with screaming (and paying) fans, and the ability to sell such quantities of records that almost every release results in a million-copy gold record reward.

James Brown also has been successful at something no performer ever before has been called upon to demonstrate: keeping people at home watching him on television instead of rioting in the streets.

For James Brown, like all great entertainers, has developed a special, highly individualized style. Some analyze it as a compound of social status wish fulfillment and a frankly sexual evocation. Others prefer not to analyze his appeal but simply to enjoy and respond to it.

*James Brown Sells His Soul**

Mel Ziegler

James Brown has done everything for soul but create it. There was a pilgrimage to Africa just to find it, and performances for the troops in Vietnam to share it. He has studied it, analyzed it, tested it, packaged it, and marketed it. He has given it style and personified its rhythm. He is an architect of its vocabulary, a supreme purveyor of its message. It has come with him from a shabby Georgia Baptist church and followed him onto stereo tape decks. He has brought it out of Harlem's Apollo Theater and put it into Yankee Stadium. He is its prize salesman, and the soul he sells reaps him nearly $3 million a year.

There are other soul heroes, the late Otis Redding, Aretha

---

* Reprinted from *Tropic* magazine (August 18, 1968) by permission of the author.

Franklin, Ray Charles and Wilson Pickett among them. But James Brown warms the throne. He is the King of Soul, Soul Brother Number One. Mr. Dynamite.

Soul Business Number One is James Brown Enterprises, which includes the Georgia radio station where as a youth he shined shoes, another radio station, a record production company, a publishing company, a road show, and acres of choice New York real estate. JBE grosses more than $20 million annually. It supports the entourage of 40 persons who travel with Brown for an average of 320 performances a year, appearances so rigorous that "The King" loses up to seven pounds each time he performs. His Soul Court includes a valet, a man who sleeps in an adjoining hotel room just to answer his telephone calls, a woman who plays mother, three more personal aides, a 21-piece orchestra including two drummers who just stand-by, stage hands, and a crew of five to handle the books.

James Brown's soul business is a trust in which millions of Black Americans have invested. They have bought most of the 50 million James Brown records, and last year alone they dominated crowds three million strong who turned out to see the King of Soul perform live. In return, Black America has made its own Horatio Alger.

The King zips from one frenzied stockholder's meeting to the next, night after night, in his $618,000 Lear jet, soon to be traded for a $2 million Jet Star. At each stop, advance men stake out the largest performing arena, plaster the town with posters and invade the pop music radio waves with heralding proclamations on the coming of Soul Brother Number One. Brown, who has described himself as "75 per cent businessman and 25 per cent talent," rarely fritters a day away from the crowds.

He has a mansion in St. Albans, Queens, with "J.B." monogrammed onto the front lawn, emblazoned on the chimney and etched into the furnishings, but he is rarely there for more than a month a year. In the garage are a Rolls-Royce, two Cadillacs, a Toronado, a Rambler and a Lincoln. Two large rooms are cluttered with nothing but hundreds of suits and shoes.

James Brown has built this empire on soul. Soul. To White America, soul is little more than the primitive screeching from the car radio when the teenage daughter is along. But to Black Americans, soul is the catchword of the new racial narcissism, something that elates them and ignites them, something they have for no other reason but for the color of their skin. Something all their own; something only a pariah Whitey can have — yet only if he waxes black, and only if he plays in reverse the same debas-

Personal Success   199

ing color game Negroes have had to play for two hundred years.

"Soul is sass, man. Soul is arrogance. Soul is walkin' down the street in a way that says, 'This is me muh! Soul is the nigger whore comin' along . . . ja . . . ja . . . ja, and walkin' like she's sayin', 'Here it is, baby. Come an' git it.' Soul is bein' true to yourself, to what is you. Now, hold on: soul is . . . that . . . uninhibited . . . no extremely uninhibited self . . . expression that goes into practically every Negro endeavor. That's soul. And there's a swagger in it, man. It's exhibitionism, and it's effortless. Effortless. You don't need to put it on; it just comes out," writes black author Claude Brown, himself a soul man.

The King of Soul grew up in Augusta, Ga. "I was nine before I got my first pair of underwear from a store. All my clothes were made from sacks and things like that," Brown recalls. He quit school after the seventh grade, and worked shining shoes and picking cotton to help his family meet its $7 monthly rent. He would sing gospel songs in those days—for a price—to local National Guard troops. But the pennies this brought him could not satiate an obsessive business ambition: Brown spent nearly four years in a reform school for stealing. Afterwards, he formed a trio and played at local engagements. By 1956, he had cut a record in a Macon radio station. Forty-three records (average sales each: one million) and a dozen years later, Brown is a millionaire. He is a soul millionaire who refuses to forget Georgia.

"Sheee . . .," said Brown. "Soul is when a man do everything he can and come up second. Soul is when a man make a hundred dollars a week and it cost him a hundred and ten to live. Soul is when a man got to bear other people's burdens. Soul is when a man is nothin' because he's black." . . .

The eyes in the slight, five-foot-six, 135 pound, frame commanding the microphone emit intense alertness. His body vibrates, and the lyrics move between screeches and grunts, mumbling under the band's clamor.

The King's gyrations are clipped, sometimes brutal, always with a suggestion of the primitive.

James Brown's face mirrors the faces in the crowd—except that the eyes looking out at him are half shut in self-induced agony. Faces wrinkle in tormented joy. Soul brothers mouth lyrics the white ear cannot understand. Only a few, scattered white people are among the crowd, almost all of them in button-down collars and stylish miniskirts. They dominate the $5 box seats. In the bleachers above them, 12,000 blacks ($.99 children, $3 adults) are brewing bugaloo from their seats. Some cannot restrain themselves, and bound from the stands into the aisles, dancing. Two girls in matching iridescent white and pink polka dot dresses stand on their seats and shimmy erotically to the rhythm. They have no words for soul. It is something between them and the King, something private. A white policeman looks on, puzzled.

The suggestion of rain looms. A drop. Two drops. The electronic equipment on the field is covered, but The King, in a frenetic dance, is still belting his soul into the microphone. The band continues to play behind him. The white people in the box seats cup their palms upward for early warning of the two more drops which will send them to cover. "Oh dear," says a blonde white girl, draping her long hair over the back of her chair, "I just set it, too". The sky bursts.

The Negroes in the bleachers dance down into the box seats the whites are abandoning. The King's hair flattens under the wetness; a dripping shirt grips his chest. The rain seems to inspire him. He is in a wild, drilling twirl, whipping the microphone from right hand to left, and back. With a swift, slippery ditch, The King collapses onto the grass. A bellowing "Oooooh" rings from the stands.

An aide rushes out with a sequined blue cape, which he drapes over The King's hunched back. He helps Brown up and guides him off the field. The crowd screams. Halfway off the field, Brown casts the cape off and rushes back to seize the microphone. The band starts up again and The King screeches his soul sound even louder, whips his body into another frenzy. Again, he collapses.

Again, a cape, this time red. Again, the feigned exit. Again, the triumphant return. Again, the shrieking of the crowd. Again, the collapse. The crowd begins to dribble on to the field.

The King does it again, from cape to collapse. The crowd is over the fence and storming toward him, through a barrier of policemen. The cape again, and he is off the field, into the dugout, and back in the dressing room.

Twenty-two thousand feet below, the lakes of Central Florida sew blue polka dots into the green quilt. A James Brown tape blares through the Lear jet's stereo. The King is shuffling his feet over the fire-red carpet to its rhythm, his eyes absorbed in his wife's heart-shaped diamond. With his fingers, Brown eats the hot sauce, soggy french fries, gripping a cold hamburger in his other hand. The comedian who performs with his show has a standard joke: "The soul brother got a jet because he couldn't get on the back of a bus."

Personal Success 201

"A lot of the things I got I got because it makes my people feel good to see me with them," he is saying. "Because it's an unusual thing to see a black man with a Rolls-Royce. Anything I want I get. This is what our people really dig. 'We may not be able to get it,' they say, 'but a soul brother got it, and it's not impossible.'"

This is the James Brown brand of soul. Beneath the frantic gyrations and the undistinguished lyrics, lies a message: I got soul and you got soul. I made it and so can you. Just work hard like I did.

It's the Protestant ethic, over-hauled and with a color job.

"It's trust and confidence," said Brown. "James Brown is somebody. They believe in James Brown. James Brown ain't never gonna turn his back on his people."

Dr. Martin Luther King is dead in Memphis. First Malcolm X, then Kennedy, now King. Washington is under siege. In scenes reminiscent of a Latin-American military coup, armed troops stand guard at the political bastions of America. At his own expense, James Brown has cancelled performances and flown into the ravaged capital city. He is broadcasting a television message to his people, a message which will be rebroadcast time and again in the coming days, as the white man in desperation surrenders his expensive airwaves to a black man of whom he knows virtually nothing.

"I am not a speechmaker. I am not a writer. But I can tell you what's happening," Brown begins, and then launches into a capsule account of his own rags-to-riches story, embroidering it for the black ear. Dramatically, he concludes:

"I am not what we call around the country a man who would do anything anybody says . . . take sides. I am not what a black man describes as a Tom. I am a man. Nobody can buy me. I do what I want. I say what I want because this is America. A man can get ahead here. Through you, I got ahead. I've been able to say what I want to say. I say to you . . . get off the streets, go home. Take your families home. Turn on your television, listen to your radio or listen to some James Brown records. But get off the streets."

Ketchup oozes from the hamburger and onto James Brown's silver supershirt, a long-sleeved satin garment with a stand-up collar and ruffles in the front and at the cuffs. His wife dips a napkin into water and rubs the stain out. Suddenly, she is thrown back into her seat as the plane whips through air turbulence.

202 *Success: A Search for Values*

"Madison Square Garden called me today," said Brown, with a mouth full of hamburger, to Ben Bart at the conclusion of their airborne business conference.

"Yeah, how much?" asked Bart.

"Ninety-seven thousand. They said it would be good for $97,000," said Brown.

"They're crazy," said Bart, who obviously figured the show was worth more for a stand in New York during Christmas week.

Bart had sauntered aboard the plane in Miami, unshaven, in red felt bedroom slippers, and a flowered shirt (resembling pajama tops) open at the collar, like a man off to the drugstore for a cigar. He is a huge and flabby man, with white hair, and his belly uncomfortably jammed behind Brown's airplane dinner table. It was a dozen years ago when Bart, as he put it, "saw the act," in Macon, Ga., hitched on as Brown's manager and brought the Georgia bootblack to the gold-studded Kingdom of Soul.

Now Bart is only a "business associate." Brown, who is his own manager, still retains much affection for Bart, even though the two are so opposite in terms of physical habit and grace. (Brown didn't even offer Bart a hamburger, because he knew that his former manager is not a man to eat hamburgers.) The clinical efficiency with which James Brown Enterprises operates is The King's inheritance from Bart.

JBE is a business, and it is run like one. The King addresses his subordinates as "Mister" and, in turn, demands that they call him "Mr. Brown." Those who work beneath him are cautioned to keep up the corporate image. Brown imposes heavy fines on them for cursing, drinking, and unkempt physical appearance.

The jet whirred to the end of the runway and deposited Brown in a group of waiting fans, among them a trio of young Negroes who had come to seek the Soul Brother's aid in raising money for the construction of an Orlando youth center.

BROWN: Ain't no time to do nothin'. We're here for the show, and we're leavin' right after it. That's a drag. Wish you got to me earlier.

SPOKESMAN: We felt it was time for us to do something. Our parents didn't do nothin'.

BROWN: I got you. I'm a black man. Mine didn't do nothin' either. My father was afraid, you know. He say, 'sheeee, sheeee.' I say to him, 'sheeee, wha', Dad? I been hearin' that every day for twenty years. We gotta do somethin'.'

The youths politely suggested that The King make an announcement at the show that evening, urging contributions. Brown replied, "I got you, man. I'm black. Be only too happy to do it."

Personal Success　　　　203

James Brown never made that announcement.

No doubt, he forgot. But the Soul Brother has a highly developed business acumen which won't let him forget when it pays not to. He doesn't forget Georgia, because amid the thrust of the Negro revolution in this country, the prototype of a brother who made it and kept his soul sells records. He recorded a song entitled "Don't Be A Dropout," hoping publicly that it would be an inspiration to Negro children, yet knowing well that more than a million of them would have a dollar out of their pockets for it. At his own expense, he has printed thousands of "Stay in School" buttons which are distributed as a bonus at performances, where the "Official James Brown Program" brings in $1.50.

With considerably less fanfare than Bob Hope, and with only the barest cooperation from USO, Brown was the first of his race to perform in Vietnam. He complained bitterly before departing, and when he came back, that black soldiers were not getting the black performers they would like to see. Yet, when some representatives from a group of Negro Vietnam veterans approached him for help after one of his performances, he turned them down.

"Soul is when a man is true to himself," Brown has said, and because he is a businessman true to his business, his people forgive him easily. . . .

Another night, another show. This time the crowd, teased by the cape and the collapse, chases The King around the periphery of the Orlando Sports Stadium to a trailer, serving as his dressing room. Safely there, his aides undress him, comb out his hair and set it in rollers.

Outside, the guards at the door tell a disc jockey from Nashville that Mr. Brown will have no guests. James Brown himself had invited the disc jockey to the dressing room, because when James Brown was 20-years-old and a nobody, this disc jockey promoted the show. That was when the soul man made $100 before he paid the band and the rent.

Now James Brown is 35 years old and somebody, and he is on the inside of an air-conditioned trailer with a half dozen helpers picking up after him, and the disc jockey who knew him when he was nobody is outside swatting the bugs off his complaining wife and their crying infant.

It is 3 a.m. He will wait. The show is over, and Ben Bart is in a small room with his glasses on counting out the gate receipts, and James Brown has forgotten about his friend, the disc jockey from Nashville.

[SEE EXERCISE ON PAGE 397]

204   *Success: A Search for Values*

Mohandas K. Gandhi was born in 1869. His country, India, was part of the British Empire then, and though he worked long and hard for its independence, he was killed by an assassin's bullet shortly before his dream became a reality.

A lawyer by training, a political leader and social reformer, he is probably best known in this country for his policy of nonviolent resistance first undertaken in the 1920s in order to oppose British policies in India. Gandhi was revered in his lifetime almost as a saint, and all the world was shocked by his unexpected death.

Jawaharlal Nehru, 20 years younger than Gandhi, had long worked with him for Indian independence and participated in his campaigns of passive resistance. As Prime Minister of India, he made this radio speech a few hours after Gandhi's death.

Nehru Speaks to Mourning Millions a Few Hours after the Murder of Gandhi*

(JANUARY 30, 1948)

Friends and comrades, the light has gone out of our lives and there is darkness everywhere. I do not know what to tell you and how to say it. Our beloved leader, Bapu as we called him, the father of the nation, is no more. Perhaps I am wrong to say that. Nevertheless, we will not see him again as we have seen him for these many years. We will not run to him for advice and seek solace from him, and that is a terrible blow, not to me only, but to millions and millions in this country, and it is a little difficult to soften the blow by any other advice that I or anyone else can give you.

The light has gone out, I said, and yet I was wrong. For the light that shone in this country was no ordinary light. The light

---

* Copyright © 1941, 1942, 1945, 1946, 1948 by The John Day Co., Inc. Reprinted from *Nehru on Ghandi* by Jawaharlal Nehru by permission of The John Day Company, Inc., publisher.

Personal Success 205

that has illumined this country for these many years will illumine this country for many more years, and a thousand years later that light will still be seen in this country and the world will see it and it will give solace to innumerable hearts. For that light represented the living truth . . . the eternal truths, reminding us of the right path, drawing us from error, taking this ancient country to freedom.

All this has happened when there was so much more for him to do. We could never think that he was unnecessary or that he had done his task. But now, particularly, when we are faced with so many difficulties, his not being with us is a blow most terrible to bear.

A madman has put an end to his life, for I can only call him mad who did it, and yet there has been enough of poison spread in this country during the past years and months, and this poison has had effect on people's minds. We must face this poison, we must root out this poison, and we must face all the perils that encompass us and face them not madly or badly but rather in the way that our beloved teacher taught us to face them. The first thing to remember now is that no one of us dare misbehave because we are angry. We have to behave like strong and determined people, determined to face all the perils that surround us, determined to carry out the mandate that our great teacher and our great leader has given us, remembering always that if, as I believe, his spirit looks upon us and sees us, nothing would displease his soul so much as to see that we have indulged in any small behavior or any violence.

So we must not do that. But that does not mean that we should be weak, but rather that we should in strength and in unity face all the troubles that are in front of us. We must hold together, and all our petty troubles and difficulties and conflicts must be ended in the face of this great disaster. A great disaster is a symbol to us to remember all the big things of life and forget the small things, of which we have thought too much.

It was proposed by some friends that Mahatmaji's body should be embalmed for a few days to enable millions of people to pay their last homage to him. But it was his wish, repeatedly expressed, that no such thing should happen, that this should not be done, that he was entirely opposed to any embalming of his body.

Tomorrow should be a day of fasting and prayer for all of us. Those who live elsewhere out of Delhi and in other parts of India will no doubt also take such part as they can in this last homage. For them also let this be a day of fasting and prayer.

And at the appointed time for cremation, that is, four P.M. tomorrow afternoon, people should go to the river or to the sea and offer prayers there. And while we pray, the greatest prayer that we can offer is to take a pledge to dedicate ourselves to the truth and to the cause for which this great countryman of ours lived and for which he has died.

[SEE EXERCISE ON PAGE 401]

"The odd thing about assassins, Dr. King, is that they think they've killed you."

Copyright © 1968 *Chicago Sun Times*. Reproduced by courtesy of Wil-Jo Associates, Inc. and Bill Mauldin.

Personal Success   207

> *The nonviolent beliefs of Gandhi were also the code of*
> *Martin Luther King, Jr. Standing on the steps of the Lincoln*
> *Memorial in Washington, D.C. on August 28, 1963, Dr. King*
> *addressed the 200,000 people who had come from all over*
> *the country in peaceful support of his plea for civil rights.*
> *This portion of his speech is probably among the most fa-*
> *mous words he ever spoke, and the last line is engraved on*
> *his tomb.*

From *I Have a Dream**

Martin Luther King, Jr.

. . . I say to you today, my friends, that in spite of the difficulties and frustrations of the moment I still have a dream. It is a dream deeply rooted in the American dream.

I have a dream that one day this nation will rise up and live out the true meaning of its creed: "We hold these truths to be self-evident; that all men are created equal."

I have a dream that one day on the red hills of Georgia the sons of former slaves and the sons of former slaveowners will be able to sit down together at the table of brotherhood.

I have a dream that one day even the state of Mississippi, a desert state sweltering with the heat of injustice and oppression, will be transformed into an oasis of freedom and justice.

I have a dream that my four little children will one day live in a nation where they will not be judged by the color of their skin but by the content of their character.

I have a dream today.

I have a dream that one day the state of Alabama, whose governor's lips are presently dripping with the words of interposition and nullification, will be transformed into a situation where little black boys and black girls will be able to join hands with little white boys and white girls and walk together as sisters and brothers.

I have a dream today.

I have a dream that one day every valley shall be exalted,

* Reprinted by permission of Joan Daves. Copyright © 1963 by Martin Luther King, Jr.

208   *Success: A Search for Values*

every hill and mountain shall be made low, the rough places
will be made plain, and the crooked places will be made straight,
and the glory of the Lord shall be revealed, and all flesh shall
see it together.

This is our hope. This is the faith with which I return to the
South. With this faith we will be able to hew out of the mountain
of despair a stone of hope. With this faith we will be able to trans-
form the jangling discords of our nation into a beautiful symphony of brotherhood. With this faith we will be able to work together, to pray together, to struggle together, to go to jail together,
to stand up for freedom together, knowing that we will be free
one day.

This will be the day when all of God's children will be able
to sing with new meaning

> My country, 'tis of thee,
> Sweet land of liberty,
>   Of thee I sing:
> Land where my fathers died,
> Land of the pilgrims' pride,
> From every mountain-side
>   Let freedom ring.

And if America is to be a great nation this must become true.
So let freedom ring from the prodigious hilltops of New Hampshire. Let freedom ring from the mighty mountains of New York.
Let freedom ring from the heightening Alleghenies of Pennsylvania!

Let freedom ring from the snowcapped Rockies of Colorado!

Let freedom ring from the curvacious peaks of California!

But not only that; let freedom ring from Stone Mountain of
Georgia!

Let freedom ring from Lookout Mountain of Tennessee!

Let freedom ring from every hill and molehill of Mississippi.
From every mountainside, let freedom ring.

When we let freedom ring, when we let it ring from every
village and every hamlet, from every state and every city, we will
be able to speed up that day when all of God's children, black
men and white men, Jews and Gentiles, Protestants and Catholics, will be able to join hands and sing in the words of the old
Negro spiritual, "Free at last! free at last! thank God almighty,
we are free at last!"

[SEE EXERCISE ON PAGE 405]

Personal Success 209

*If there is any one thing to be learned from the many ex-
amples in this book, it may be that success does not come
easily. If it is possible to sum up the continued pursuit of
success, however, this poem is such a summary.*

I May, I Might, I Must*

Marianne Moore

If you will tell me why the fen [*a marshland*]
appears impassable, I then
Will tell you why I think that I
can get across it if I try.

* From *The Complete Poems of Marianne Moore*. All rights reserved. Reprinted by permission of The Viking Press, Inc.

Exercises

NAME _____

$500,000 Thaws
Peggy's Icy Outlook

EXERCISE [*Article on Page 10*]

FOR UNDERSTANDING

1.   As a news story, this is supposed to be straightforward writing without prejudice on the part of the writer. Is it? In the appropriate columns, write quotations from the article that seem to be slanted either for or against Miss Fleming.

For Miss Fleming   Against Miss Fleming

_____   _____

_____   _____

_____   _____

_____   _____

_____   _____

_____   _____

What conclusion can you draw about the prejudice in the article?

_____

_____

2.   What play on words does the headline use?

_____

Can you think of another headline for this story that is either

clever or "straight"? _____

_____

213

NAME _____

$500,000 Thaws
Peggy's Icy Outlook

3. List at least three words or phrases of description that give information that would lead the reader to believe Peggy Fleming could "take on the aura of movie or theater celebrities."

a. _____

b. _____

c. _____

FOR DISCUSSION

1. Certain sports traditionally have been the stronghold of amateurs; others of professionals. What is the difference between amateurism and professionalism in sports?

"Amateur" Sports	"Professional" Sports
_____	_____
_____	_____
_____	_____
_____	_____

What Makes an Amateur	What Makes a Professional
_____	_____
_____	_____
_____	_____
_____	_____
_____	_____

NAME _____

$500,000 Thaws
Peggy's Icy Outlook

2.   How close to professionalism is the college student who accepts an athletic scholarship?

_____ not at all a professional

_____ something like a professional

_____ mostly a professional

Give reasons for your choice.

_____

_____

Is it ethical for schools to offer such scholarships? Give reasons.

Yes   No

_____   _____

_____   _____

_____   _____

_____   _____

3.   Do you know any athletes who plan to be professionals in their field?
_____ No   _____ Yes   (List names.)

_____

_____

What are their reasons for this goal?   _____

_____

4.   There is a widespread belief that some countries subsidize their amateur athletes. If this is true, what do such countries

215

NAME _____

$500,000 Thaws
Peggy's Icy Outlook

gain by making a good showing in the Olympics? _____

_____

If this kind of athletic subsidization is a fact, would it be better for all countries to treat their representatives in the same way?

Yes   No

_____   _____

_____   _____

_____   _____

_____   _____

5.   In some countries, all students in colleges are paid by the government, thus creating academic rather than athletic subsidies. Can you see any effect this might have on the future leadership of the country? List at least three.

a. _____

b. _____

c. _____

What is your reaction to the suggestion that such payment be made to U.S. college students?

_____ for   _____ against   _____ undecided

_____ partly for, partly against

Give reasons for your choice. _____

_____

_____

NAME _____

$500,000 Thaws
Peggy's Icy Outlook

FOR WRITING

1. Write a news story about an individual (not a team) winner in an athletic event you have witnessed at one time. Try to be as objective as possible.

Person involved: _____

Event: _____

Time and place: _____

Details about winner: _____

Details about situation: _____

_____

Your reaction to person or event: _____

_____

2. Imagine you are a representative of one of the rival professional ice shows bidding against the Ice Follies for Miss Fleming's services. Compose a telegram (no word limit) that you would send making her an offer and giving information that would lead her to join your show. Be as imaginative as you wish with the terms and other inducements.

Financial terms: _____

_____

Other inducements: _____

_____

_____

_____

217

NAME _____

$500,000 Thaws
Peggy's Icy Outlook

ESSAY

_____

_____

_____

_____

_____

_____

_____

_____

_____

_____

_____

_____

_____

_____

_____

_____

_____

_____

_____

_____

NAME _____

Harry

EXERCISE [*Story on Page 11*]

FOR UNDERSTANDING

1.   In the left-hand column, list the business ventures Harry is involved in. (Follow the order in the story.) On the appropriate line in the right-hand column, list the subsidiary or "sideline" benefits he gained from these ventures.

Businesses   Sideline Benefits

_____

_____

_____   _____

_____

_____   _____

_____   _____

_____

2.   What evidence is there in the story to show that Harry is

clever with words?   _____

_____

_____

_____

_____

Give one quotation that shows Harry as a clever talker.

219

NAME _____

Harry

(Page: ____) _____

_____

3.   List four clues in the story that show that Harry did not live within the past two or three years.

    a. (Page: ____) _____

    b. (Page: ____) _____

    c. (Page: ____) _____

    d. (Page: ____) _____

4.   Saroyan deliberately uses most of the story to stress Harry's money-making ability, and most of the anecdotes about him are humorous. What does Saroyan accomplish by making these choices in the telling of his story?

_____

_____

_____

_____

_____

5.   List three things Saroyan actually tells you about the kind of person Harry is, in addition to his ability to make money.

    a. (Page: ____) _____

    b. (Page: ____) _____

    c. (Page: ____) _____

6.   The story is told by someone who knows Harry. What passages indicate the storyteller's attitude toward Harry?

NAME _____

Harry

_____

_____

_____

How would you summarize this attitude? _____

_____

_____

FOR DISCUSSION

1. ". . . a real American go-getter" is the concluding phrase of this story. Do you accept this picture of Harry as that of the American go-getter?

Definition of go-getter: _____

My ideas of an American go-getter: _____

_____   _____

_____   _____

_____   _____

2. The last three paragraphs of the story show how Harry is remembered by the townspeople. Would you be satisfied with the kind of remembrance about yourself that the townspeople have about Harry? Explain your answer.

What I would like to have people remember about me: _____

_____   _____

_____   _____

_____   _____

221

NAME _____

Harry

3.   Saroyan writes that no one ever criticized Harry for his business methods. Do you think Harry was an ethical man?

Definition of "ethical": _____

Characteristics of an ethical businessman: (List.)

_____   _____

_____   _____

_____   _____

_____   _____

4.   Saroyan writes that ". . . a lot of unconventional things began to happen" after Harry sold magazine subscriptions to a number of women in town. After he sold magazines, the "neighborhood was getting to be slightly immoral" and after Harry sold used cars several girls "had babies and didn't know who the other parent was. . . ." Do you think this relation between cause and effect, suggested by the author, is accurate? _____ Yes _____ No

Reason for choice: _____

_____

_____

_____

Cite an activity which is a cause and an effect that you believe go together. (Exclude the sciences.)

Cause   Effect

_____   _____

Cite a cause and an effect that you believe *do not* go together.

Cause   Effect

_____   _____

222

NAME _____

Harry

5. Without trying to psychoanalyze Harry, discuss his apparently continual desire to make money as an end in itself rather than as a means to achieving another goal.

_____

_____

_____

FOR WRITING

1. Which of Harry's money-making schemes most impress you? Why?

Harry's scheme: _____

Reasons I am impressed by it: _____

_____

_____

_____

2. Write another sequence to the story showing another successful venture Harry might have had. You may make the story more up-to-date by including something connected with television, portable hair dryers, rockets, or any other device or idea not available to Harry in his own time.

Subject of new sequence: _____

What Harry did: _____

_____

_____

_____

_____

223

NAME _____

Harry

Result of Harry's activity: _____

_____

3. Write an essay pointing out what you believe admirable about Harry. Or, write an essay showing what you believe is *not* admirable about him. Use only the information Saroyan gives in the story about the character.

Harry's Admirable Qualities	Evidence in Story
_____	_____
_____	_____
_____	_____
_____	_____

Qualities *not* Admirable	Evidence in Story
_____	_____
_____	_____
_____	_____

4. Certain magazines often print brief stories with titles such as "The Most Unforgettable Character I Ever Met." Write such a character sketch about someone you have actually known.

Person: _____

_____

224

NAME _____

Harry

Description of person: _____

_____

_____

_____

_____

_____

_____

Reasons he is "unforgettable": _____

_____

_____

_____

_____

_____

_____

_____

_____

NAME _____

Harry

ESSAY

NAME _____

Ruler of the Queen's
Navee

EXERCISE [*Poem on Page* 22]

FOR UNDERSTANDING

1.   Some of the British terms in the poem may be unfamiliar.
From the context (or from a book, if necessary), "translate" the
following terms into American equivalents:

Articled clerk: _____

_____

Pass-examination: _____

_____

Pocket borough: _____

_____

2.   What personal qualities enabled Sir Joseph to make the following advances?

From office boy to junior clerk? _____

_____

From junior clerk to articled clerk? _____

_____

From articled clerk to junior partnership? _____

_____

From attorney to Member of Parliament (the British equivalent of

227

NAME _____

Ruler of the Queen's
Navee

the United States Congress)? _____

_____

From Parliament to Ruler of the Queen's Navee [Navy]?

_____

3.   The form of this poem is easy to follow: each stanza has four lines in an *a a b b* rhyme scheme, but each stanza ends in the same two-line couplet. What does this repeated rhyme scheme accomplish?

_____

_____

_____

4.   Based on the form and information of the poem, how well prepared are you for the advice contained in the last two lines?

_____ ready   _____ almost ready   _____ not ready

Give two reasons for your choice.   _____

_____

_____

What other concluding advice could you offer to replace the final couplet (not necessarily in rhyme)?

_____

_____

_____

_____

NAME _____

Ruler of the Queen's
Navee

FOR DISCUSSION

1.   Do you think Sir Joseph is an opportunist?

Definition of an opportunist: _____

_____

Do you consider his behavior good or bad, or a combination of the two?

Good   Bad

_____   _____

_____   _____

_____   _____

2.   What training ground *is* available to people interested in political or governmental jobs in this country?

People   Places   Others

_____   _____   _____

_____   _____   _____

_____   _____   _____

_____   _____   _____

_____   _____   _____

3.   Does Sir Joseph's statement that while he was in Parliament he "never thought of thinking for myself at all" strike you as sad? true of your opinion of politicians? _____ funny because

it is in the poem? _____ something else? _____

229

NAME _____

Ruler of the Queen's
Navee

4. Compare your opinion of the credibility of Sir Joseph's rise to eminence with that of Harry's success in the Saroyan story. Is one more satirical than the other?

Sir Joseph's Rise   Harry's Rise

_____   _____

_____   _____

_____   _____

_____   _____

_____   _____

Definition of "satirical" in the question: _____

_____

My opinion about whether one is more satirical than the other:

_____

_____

_____

5. Give at least one reason, based on the content, for saying that the written form of each rise to fame — one poetic and one prosaic — is most suitable for that particular story.

Poetry suitable for Sir Joseph because: _____

_____

Prose suitable for Harry because: _____

_____

230

NAME _____

Ruler of the Queen's
Navee

FOR WRITING

1. W. S. Gilbert chose to treat a serious subject (a man's advancement to a high position in government) in a humorous way. Write the same material in a serious fashion, as if it were the biography of Sir Joseph Porter. (Create whatever details you feel are needed.)

Place and date of birth: _____

Parentage: _____

Schooling: _____

Work experience: _____

_____

Personal qualities: _____

_____

Other information: _____

_____

_____

2. Describe an incident in your life as a result of which you accomplished something you wanted to do.

The accomplishment: _____

Time and place: _____

The situation: _____

Other people involved: _____

NAME _____

Ruler of the Queen's
Navee

Reason you wanted to do this: _____

_____

3.   Write an imaginary, humorous story of a man or woman's attainment of a high position in a field other than government or politics. Some suggestions are: a school principal, a bartender, a dress designer, an inventor.

Job or field of success: _____

How he (or she) got there: (List.) _____

_____

_____

_____

_____

_____

NAME _____

You Got to Be a Hero

EXERCISE [*Article on Page 24*]

FOR UNDERSTANDING

1. What is the Hero sandwich described in the article?

(Page: ____) _____

_____

Does it have another name in your part of the country, or is this the first time that you have heard about this particular food?

_____

_____

2. The author writes that Marotta's place of business "isn't a private restaurant; it's an institution." What is the difference between the two?

A Private Restaurant   An Institution

_____   _____

_____   _____

_____   _____

Why does the author call The House of 1000 and 1 Italian Delights "an institution"? _____

_____

3. Note at least four passages in the article that describe Tony Marotta's attitude toward work.

a. (Page: ____) _____

233

NAME _____

You Got to Be a Hero

    b. (Page: ____) _____

    c. (Page: ____) _____

    d. (Page: ____) _____

4.   The article begins with a description of Mr. Marotta visiting his childhood home in Italy and ends with a description of him in his Long Island home. Give one reason the author could have had for choosing these opening and closing descriptions.

_____

_____

5.   List at least three details the author gives about Mr. Marotta's business.

    a. (Page: ____) _____

    b. (Page: ____) _____

    c. (Page: ____) _____

The author obviously thinks such details are necessary. Do you? For example, why should he describe in detail the contents of Marotta's Special on page 26 (the star sandwich on the menu) and then repeat the ingredients near the end of the article on page 29?

_____

_____

_____

_____

6.   List at least four items of information the article gives about Mr. Marotta as an individual.

NAME _____

You Got to Be a Hero

a. (Page: ____) _____

b. (Page: ____) _____

c. (Page: ____) _____

d. (Page: ____) _____

FOR DISCUSSION

1. Compare the "Great American Dream" of success (evidenced by Anthony Marotta) with your idea of what the term means.

My idea of the term: (List.) _____

_____

_____

_____

Mr. Marotta's idea of the term: (List.) _____

_____

_____

_____

In what ways are they the same? _____

_____

In what ways are they different? _____

_____

235

NAME _____

You Got to Be a Hero

2.   Discuss the values that seem to be important to Mr. Marotta. Are they the same as the values important to you?

Mr. Marotta's values: (List.) _____

_____

_____

_____

My values: (List.) _____

_____

_____

_____

3.   By many standards, Mr. Marotta would seem to be successful; that is, he has a going business, an expensive house, and he is able to take a trip to Europe. Is he successful by *your* standards?

My standards of success: (List.) _____

_____

_____

_____

_____

4.   Assuming that the word "hero" in the title is used ambiguously, in what way is (or is not) Mr. Marotta a hero?

Qualities of a Hero   Qualities of Mr. Marotta

_____   _____

_____   _____

236

NAME _____

You Got to Be a Hero

_____   _____

_____   _____

_____   _____

FOR WRITING

1.   Although the article gives some information about Tony Marotta (see Ques. 6 of "For Understanding"), it does not tell you many other things about the man. Write an essay telling what else you would like to know about Tony Marotta and why.

Other Information
Desired   Reasons

_____   _____

_____   _____

_____   _____

_____   _____

_____   _____

_____   _____

2.   If you know someone who emigrated to the United States, write a brief theme telling why he came here. Or, write a brief theme telling what he has achieved here.

Person who emigrated: _____

His reasons for coming: _____

_____

NAME _____

You Got to Be a Hero

How expectations have been fulfilled: _____

_____

or

His achievements: _____

_____

_____

_____

3.   The Hero sandwich is described in great detail in this article. Write an essay describing in detail a meal you enjoyed. Try to include as many sensory details as possible.

Meal I enjoyed: _____
                              (breakfast, lunch, etc.)

Time and place: _____

Who was there: _____

What was served: _____

_____

_____

_____

What it looked like: _____

_____

_____

_____

NAME _____

You Got to Be a Hero

How it smelled: _____

_____

_____

_____

4.   This article explains how to make a Hero sandwich. Explain how to prepare some other food, such as scrambled eggs, a cake, and so on. (If you do not know how to cook anything, give instructions for making something else, such as a dog house, a clay ashtray, a model car, and so forth.)

Food (or object): _____

Ingredients (or materials) required: _____

_____

_____

_____

_____

_____

Order and method of use: _____

_____

_____

_____

_____

_____

_____

NAME _____

You Got to Be a Hero

ESSAY

NAME _____

Success Rushed Up
to Pat Palmer

EXERCISE [*Article on Page 31*]

FOR UNDERSTANDING

1.   In what ways can Miss Palmer's business success be attrib-

uted to luck? _____

_____

In what ways can Miss Palmer's business success be attributed

to special knowledge? _____

_____

In what ways can Miss Palmer's business success be attributed

to perseverence? _____

_____

2.   Which single aspect of Miss Palmer's rise in business does

the article focus on? _____

What kind of information does the article leave out? _____

_____

_____

3.   The last sentence of the article refers to Miss Palmer's business in cities outside New York. What would be the effect upon
the focal point or main idea of the article if the last sentence were
to be developed and the reader was given more detailed information about that aspect of Miss Palmer's business? _____

_____

241

NAME _____

Success Rushed Up
to Pat Palmer

4.   Identify the celebrities who Miss Palmer numbers among her clients?

Name   Reason for Prominence

_____   _____

_____   _____

_____   _____

_____   _____

_____   _____

_____   _____

_____   _____

5.   List at least three items of personal information (that is, items that probably you would not find in an official biography) that this article gives about Miss Palmer:

a. _____

b. _____

c. _____

6.   List at least four items of "public" information under each column heading (that is, information that might be given in a biographical press release):

Family   Early Life   Business

_____   _____   _____

_____   _____   _____

242

NAME _____

Success Rushed Up
to Pat Palmer

_____   _____   _____

_____   _____   _____

FOR DISCUSSION

1.   If someone wanted to "learn a lesson" from this article, although there is no reason to read it for that purpose alone, the lesson might be that success can be achieved by paying attention to people as individuals. Can this "lesson" be applied in some way to your own contacts with people in school, in the

family, at work, and so on? How? _____

_____

_____

_____

_____

2.   How important do you think it is for people to be recognized as individuals? If you think it is important, can you offer specific suggestions for improvement in school, social, or business situations?

Importance: _____

_____

Situation: _____

Suggestions: _____

_____

_____

_____

243

NAME _____

Success Rushed Up
to Pat Palmer

3. What is your opinion of Miss Palmer's apparent desire to change her vocation? Do you think she should have pursued her original ideas? Why or why not?

My opinion about the switch: _____

_____

_____

She should _____ should not _____ have changed because:

_____

_____

4. In what ways is Pat Palmer like Anthony Marotta? In what ways is she different?

Like	Different
_____	_____
_____	_____
_____	_____
_____	_____

5. If "Pat Palmer" were a man, rather than a woman, and if she were 49 rather than 29, do you think your feelings would be different from what they were when you read the article?

_____ Different   _____ The same

Reasons: _____

_____

_____

244

NAME _____

Success Rushed Up
to Pat Palmer

FOR WRITING

1. Write an imaginary newspaper article describing your own
success in some venture: business, sports, community activity,
and so forth. Make it imaginary if you wish, and as wild as you
wish. You do not even have to be able to do some of the things you
write about. (For example, you can make yourself a ski champion
even if you have never seen snow, or a singer even if you cannot
carry a tune.)

Successful venture: _____

Time and place: _____

Other people involved: _____

How success was achieved: _____

_____

_____

_____

_____

2. Tell in essay form about an incident or occasion which
started in one way, or for one purpose, and ended quite differently or unexpectedly.

Incident: _____

Time and place: _____

Original planned outcome: _____

_____

Actual outcome: _____

245

NAME _____

Success Rushed Up
to Pat Palmer

Your reaction to the outcome: _____

_____

_____

_____

3.   Imagine that you want Miss Palmer to find you an apartment in a city in the United States. Write her a letter giving the requirements you expect. Pretend that the rental price is of no concern to you; let your imagination go.

Apartment requirements: _____

_____

_____

_____

_____

_____

_____

SUGGESTED ACTIVITY *for*
"Richest of the American Rich," page 34

Choose one of the names on the list and find out something about the person through library research.

Or, choose one of the businesses noted and gather information about it through library research.

246

NAME _____

*Eight Days to
Foreclosure . . .*

EXERCISE [*Article on Page 39*]

FOR UNDERSTANDING

1.   List at least three cliches the writer of this article uses.
(You may include quotations.)

     a. _____

     b. _____

     c. _____

2.   List what you learn about the people, the situation, and the
silver market in this article.

People

_____   _____

_____   _____

_____   _____

_____   _____

_____   _____

Situation   Silver Market

_____   _____

_____   _____

_____   _____

_____   _____

_____   _____

247

NAME _____

*Eight Days to
Foreclosure . . .*

What would account for the greater amount of information about the people than about the situation or the silver market?

_____

3.   In the last paragraph, Ernie Escapule is quoted as speaking of ". . . a yacht, and big house and . . . some of the real luxuries of life." Would you be willing to guess what some of those luxuries might be, knowing what you do about the people on the basis of this article?

_____ Yes   _____ No

If "Yes," list here: _____

_____

_____

_____

_____

FOR DISCUSSION

1.   How authentic do the quotations attributed to the Escapules sound? What is the basis for your belief?

Authenticity: _____

_____

Reasons for choice: _____

_____

_____

_____

NAME _____

Eight Days to
Foreclosure . . .

2.   Discuss the interest some people have and some people do not have in this kind of news story. What personal traits would account for either the interest or disinterest?

Interest   Disinterest

_____   _____

_____   _____

_____   _____

3.   Discuss ways in which the urge to find gold or silver might be the same or different from the urge to fulfill other goals.

Gold or Silver   Other Goals

_____   _____

_____   _____

_____   _____

_____   _____

FOR WRITING

1.   Write an imaginary interview with someone who has just achieved something he set out to do.

Person being interviewed: _____

_____

His goal: _____

_____

249

NAME _____

*Eight Days to
Foreclosure . . .*

Information you want from him: (List.) _____

_____

_____

_____

_____

_____

2. Write a theme telling why you would or would not want to meet the Escapule family.

_____ Would   _____ Would not

Reasons: (List.) _____

_____

_____

_____

_____

NAME _____

If at First You Don't
Succeed . . . Skip It

EXERCISE [*Article on Page 41*]

FOR UNDERSTANDING

1.   Why is it necessary to print the disclaimer that this story is

not true?   _____

_____

2.   List at least ten cliches concerning success the article contains.

a.   _____   f.   _____

b.   _____   g.   _____

c.   _____   h.   _____

d.   _____   i.   _____

e.   _____   j.   _____

3.   Were you surprised by the ending?

_____ Yes   _____ No

Is there anything in the article that prepared you for the ending?

_____

_____

_____

FOR DISCUSSION

1.   Discuss some of the "how to succeed" articles or books you
have read. How realistic do they seem to be? Have you tried to

251

NAME _____

If at First You Don't
Succeed . . . Skip It

follow any of the advice? If so, what has been the outcome?

Books or articles read: _____

_____

_____

_____

My estimate of their personal value: _____

_____

_____

_____

2. What is your attitude toward the executive about whom the article is written? Do you feel sorry for him? Do you think he should be ridiculed?

My attitude: _____

_____

_____

_____

FOR WRITING

1. Write a theme describing what you imagine a day in the life of this executive (as described in the article) would be like.

List, in order, his daily activities:

_____

_____

NAME _____

If at First You Don't
Succeed . . . Skip It

_____

_____

_____

_____

_____

2.   Choose an occupation you would like to have. Then imagine
that the man in this article (he is not given a specific business)
is your boss. Write an essay describing what you think it would
be like to work for him.

Occupation: _____

Demands made on you: (List.) _____

_____

_____

_____

_____

Your reactions to this boss: (List.) _____

_____

_____

_____

_____

3.   Write an essay explaining what you think you could learn
from working for the man described in the article.

NAME _____

If at First You Don't
Succeed . . . Skip It

What I could learn: (List.) _____

_____

_____

_____

_____

_____

NAME _____

*How Savitri Retrieved
Her Husband from Death*

EXERCISE [Story on Page 45]

FOR UNDERSTANDING

1. The Indian names in this story are unusual. In order to keep people straight, identify the following:

Asvapati: _____

Savitri: _____

Satyavan: _____

Dumyatsen: _____

Narada: _____

Yama: _____

2. List three customs or traditions followed by the people that make it obvious that this is not an American story.

a. (Page: _____) _____

b. (Page: _____) _____

c. (Page: _____) _____

3. Yama should be a fearsome figure to Savitri because of his eminence. How do you account for the fact that the woman is not afraid of the god? Refer to passages in the story.

a. (Page: _____) _____

b. (Page: _____) _____

c. (Page: _____) _____

255

NAME _____

How Savitri Retrieved
Her Husband from Death

4.   Why would Yama grant special favors to Savitri?

_____

_____

Is this action godlike or manlike? Explain.

_____

_____

5.   List, in order, the favors Yama granted Savitri.

a. (Page: _____) _____

b. (Page: _____) _____

c. (Page: _____) _____

d. (Page: _____) _____

e. (Page: _____) _____

Can you make a judgment about the importance of the favors

based on their progression? _____

_____

Can you suggest another order that would be acceptable in this
story?

_____ Yes   _____ No

If "Yes", write it here: _____

_____

_____

256

NAME _____

*How Savitri Retrieved
Her Husband from Death*

FOR DISCUSSION

1. How believable is the accomplishment of goals through conversation? In this case, it is a personal goal. Is there a time when talk about group or community (or national) goals should cease and other action should begin?

My ideas about success through talking: _____

_____

_____

Situations calling for other action: _____

_____

_____

2. On what basis does Savitri become admirable? Check one.

Because she married the man she wanted? _____

Because she was a good wife? _____

Because she had the courage to face Yama? _____

Because she outwitted someone "above" herself? _____

What would your opinion be if the story had been different with

respect to any one of the previous questions? _____

_____

_____

3. If the story had been told in such a way that Savitri wanted to save her husband and her father-in-law's kingdom in order to

257

NAME _____

How Savitri Retrieved
Her Husband from Death

become queen herself, what changes would need to be made?
Would you then feel she was also successful, although in a different way?

Changes in story: (List.) _____

_____

_____

_____

My attitude toward Savitri: _____

_____

_____

_____

FOR WRITING

1. Pretend you are Savitri writing a message to her father,
Asvapati, telling him how she overcame the terrible prophecy
about her husband. Add details about personal feelings, sur-
rounding countryside, fatigue, or hunger omitted in the story.

What happened: (List.) _____

_____

_____

Personal feeling: (List.) _____

_____

_____

NAME _____

How Savitri Retrieved
Her Husband from Death

Countryside: (Describe.) _____

_____

_____

Other details: _____

_____

_____

2.   Pretend you are Satyavan writing the story of how he became king as he might want to have it recorded in the history
books of his country.

Events leading to kingship: (List.) _____

_____

_____

_____

Other People Involved   Part They Played

_____   _____

_____   _____

_____   _____

_____   _____

3.   If you have ever "talked your way out of" a difficult situation,
write a paper telling about the event. The situation might be the
time you did not get a traffic ticket, the day you persuaded a
teacher to change a grade, or the day you overcame the wrath of
a friend's father, and so on.

259

NAME _____

How Savitri Retrieved
Her Husband from Death

Situation: _____

Reason it was a difficult one: _____

_____

How you talked your way out of the situation: _____

_____

_____

_____

_____

_____

NAME _____

Richard Cory

EXERCISE [*Poem on Page 49*]

FOR UNDERSTANDING

1. List at least five words or phrases the poet uses to show that Richard Cory was a person greatly admired in his town.

    a. _____

    b. _____

    c. _____

    d. _____

    e. _____

2. List the words that appear in the poem that *you* would *not* use to describe someone.

_____   _____

_____   _____

_____   _____

3. The poem states that Richard Cory was "richer than a king." List at least three words associated with kings and two associated with riches.

Kings   Riches

_____   _____

_____   _____

_____   _____

NAME _____

Richard Cory

4.   What effect is achieved for you by the poet having Richard Cory shoot himself on a "calm summer night"?

_____

What effect would have been achieved if it had happened in another time or at another season?

_____

FOR DISCUSSION

1.   How "public" do you think the lives of public officials ought to be? Of movie or television personalities? Of school teachers and administrators? Give reasons for your choices.

_____

_____

_____

2.   How can dissatisfactions and frustrations be directed to useful rather than to destructive ends? (You may want to talk in terms of a specific dissatisfaction rather than use the word in a general sense.)

What Needs Channeling	Ways to Make Frustrations Useful
_____	_____
_____	_____
_____	_____
_____	_____

NAME _____

Richard Cory

FOR WRITING

1.   Write a theme telling about some of the things the towns-people might not have known about Richard Cory.

The "unknowns": (List.) _____

_____

_____

_____

_____

2.   Write a descriptive sketch of someone sitting next to you in class. Then give it to that person and let him add to it the things he wishes you had known about him before you wrote the theme.

NAME _____

Richard Cory

ESSAY

NAME _____

Ozymandias
and *Ozymandias Revisited*

EXERCISE [*Poems on Pages 50 and 51*]

FOR UNDERSTANDING

1.   Shelley tells of an actual statue of Ramses (Ozymandias), although not the ones at Abu Simbel. What three words or phrases in the poem describe what the man in the statue really looked like?

a. _____

b. _____

c. _____

2.   Cite at least three words or phrases (stated or implied) that give evidence that the Ozymandias Shelley wrote about was an important person, both to himself and to other people.

a. _____

b. _____

c. _____

3.   The last three lines of Shelley's poem are quite different from the first eleven lines. What feeling does the author intend

to convey by making this change?   _____

_____

4.   The last three lines of Bishop's poem are also quite different from the first eleven lines. What feeling does the poet intend to

convey by this change?   _____

_____

265

NAME _____

Ozymandias
and *Ozymandias Revisited*

5. Show how the last three lines of each poem indicate the different attitudes of the two poets.

Shelley's Attitude   Bishop's Attitude

_____   _____

_____   _____

FOR DISCUSSION

1. The first eleven lines of Bishop's poem are identical to those written by Shelley. Is this plagiarism? Explain your answer.

Definition of "plagiarism": _____

_____

Bishop's poem _____ is _____ is not plagiarism.

Reasons for my choice: (List.) _____

_____

_____

2. Which ending is more satisfying to you? Why?

_____ Shelley's ending   _____ Bishop's ending

Reasons for choice: _____

_____

3. People often build "monuments" to themselves, not necessarily in the form of stone statues. What forms do such monuments take? What is your opinion of those you can list?

266

NAME _____

Ozymandias
and *Ozymandias Revisited*

"Monuments" I am aware of: (List.) _____

_____

_____

_____

My opinion of this practice: _____

_____

_____

_____

FOR WRITING

1. Write three new last lines to "Ozymandias," but keep the proper rhyme scheme (*a b a*).

_____

_____

_____

2. Try to do what Morris Bishop did. Find a poem in which the thought is completed in the last few lines (a Shakespearean sonnet would be easy to work with); then change the last lines so that the main thought is interpreted in a new way.
3. Write a serious story, in prose, that ends in a surprising way.
4. Tell about something you did that seemed successful at the time but did not seem successful later because of some reason (such as a different time, varying circumstances, different people). Then make a judgment about the value of your original success.

267

NAME _____

Ozymandias
and *Ozymandias Revisited*

Situation: _____

Change: _____

_____

Reason for change: _____

_____

_____

Opinion of original success after comparison: _____

_____

_____

_____

_____

SUGGESTED ACTIVITY

Use the resources of a library to find out more about Ramses II and then consider the poems again in the light of your new knowledge.

NAME _____

The Overshoe

EXERCISE [*Story on Page 58*]

FOR UNDERSTANDING

1. At what two points could the story have ended?

    a. On page _____ with the line ending ". . . _____."

    b. On page _____ with the line ending ". . . _____."

If the story had stopped at either of these places, how would the total effect upon the reader have differed?

_____

_____

2. What does the storyteller probably mean by the final sentence ("Let posterity admire it [the overshoe].")?

_____

_____

3. Under what circumstances would a man be likely to say that his overshoes were "practically new . . . only the third

season"? _____

_____

_____

4. Which line first indicated to you that this was going to be a

"light" story? Write it here: _____

_____

269

NAME _____

The Overshoe

5.   Cite two phrases or passages in which the word order or word usage is not the kind you usually expect from the sort of short stories you have read before.

a.   (Page: _____) _____

b.   (Page: _____) _____

FOR DISCUSSION

1.   Does the man in the story go through more "red tape" in recovering his lost overshoe than seems to be necessary?

_____ Yes   _____ No

If your answer is "yes," suggest ways in which the service could have been quicker or more effective.

Suggestions: (List.) _____

_____

_____

_____

2.   What kind of business would have such an efficient lost-and-found service? What kind of people would need to subscribe to or buy from that business?

Kind of Business   Kind of People

_____   _____

_____   _____

_____   _____

NAME _____

The Overshoe

3. Who is most successful in this story: the man or the trolley company?

_____ Man   _____ Trolley company

Reasons for choice: (List.) _____

_____

_____

_____

FOR WRITING

1. The newspaper sometimes carries stories about strange things left on subways, buses, trains, or other public conveyances. Even the lost-and-found department of a school or store often has an unusual assortment. Obtain such a list, choose one item on it, and write a story describing the circumstances under which it might have been lost — either accidentally or deliberately.

2. Describe a success, or failure, you have had in retrieving something from a lost-and-found department or from a friend who had one of your possessions.

What was lost: _____

Who had it: _____

How I found out where it was: _____

_____

How I retrieved it: _____

_____

_____

271

NAME _____

The Overshoe

3.   Choose something (not an object) that you have wanted, but which you were prevented from getting because of an unwritten rule or custom. Write an essay arguing that the rule or custom should be changed and give reasons for the change you propose.

What I wanted: _____

Why _____ rule _____ custom   should be changed: (List.)

_____

_____

_____

_____

NAME _____

Robot at M.I.T. . . .

EXERCISE [*Article on Page 61*]

FOR UNDERSTANDING

1. Machines have been constructed to do many unusual jobs for men. What information in the first paragraph seems so unusual to you that this particular "arm-and-eye assembly" or robot

should be newsworthy? _____

_____

List at least two specific pieces of information found later in the article that reinforce your suppositions about the first sentence.

    a. (Paragraph: _____) _____

    b. (Paragraph: _____) _____

2. Explain why each of the following familiar words are enclosed in quotation marks in this article:

    a. "Brain" (paragraph 2): _____

    b. "Sees" (paragraph 2): _____

    c. "Eye" (paragraph 4): _____

    d. "Sees" (paragraph 5): _____

    e. "Informs" (paragraph 5): _____

    f. "Know" (paragraph 9): _____

NAME _____

Robot at M.I.T. . . .

FOR DISCUSSION

1. What jobs would you like to see machines do. Why?

Jobs	Reason
_____	_____
_____	_____
_____	_____
_____	_____

2. Choose a familiar mechanical device in the home (a television set, a toaster, a radio) and discuss what changes in living would be necessary if it were to disappear tomorrow.
Then . . .
Choose a larger device (but not a form of transportation) and one outside the home (welding equipment, road-surfacing machinery, and so on), and discuss what changes in living or in familiar activities would be required if it should disappear tomorrow.

3. How important is pure research, as differentiated from practical research? Do government and industry get their money's worth from the large sums they spend on pure research? Should such money be channeled into more "practical" projects?

Definition of pure research: _____

_____

Definition of practical research: _____

_____

Advantages of Pure Research	Advantages of Practical Research
_____	_____
_____	_____

274

NAME _____

Robot at M.I.T. . . .

FOR WRITING

1. This article describes how something works. Choose a simple object you are familiar with and describe how it works.

Object: _____

Its parts: _____

_____

_____

_____

_____

How the parts operate: _____

_____

_____

_____

2. Choose some activity in which group work is preferable (but not necessary) to individual work. Tell why the group is preferable.

Group activity: _____

Reasons it is preferable: _____

_____

_____

_____

_____

NAME _____

Robot at M.I.T. . . .

ESSAY

NAME _____

Tactical Missiles:
A Report from General
Dynamics

EXERCISE *[Advertisement on Page 64]*

FOR UNDERSTANDING

1.   This advertisement appeared in a magazine addressed to general readers. Each of the subheads in the ad is printed below. If you can find any words in the advertising copy under each that you consider to be special vocabulary words or dependent on scientific knowledge, write them under the appropriate subhead here.

Evening the Odds
Against Surprise Attack

The Bullet That Gets
a Second Chance

_____   _____

_____   _____

_____   _____

Terrier   Tartar   Redeye

_____   _____   _____

_____   _____   _____

_____   _____   _____

What conclusion can you draw from this close look at the language or vocabulary of the advertisement? _____

_____

_____

2.   Write a one-sentence summary of each section next to the subheads printed below.

277

NAME _____

Tactical Missiles:
A Report from General
Dynamics

Evening the odds against surprise attack: _____

_____

_____

The bullet that gets a second chance: _____

_____

_____

Terrier: _____

_____

Tartar: _____

_____

Redeye: _____

_____

3.   If space were no consideration in the ad, what questions would you like to have answered in each section?

Subhead   Questions

Evening the odds against
      surprise attack: _____

                             _____

                             _____

                             _____

278

NAME _____

Tactical Missiles:
A Report from General
Dynamics

The bullet that gets a

second chance: _____

_____

Terrier: _____

_____

_____

Tartar: _____

_____

_____

Redeye: _____

_____

_____

FOR DISCUSSION

1. If you have ever used any of these weapons as a serviceman, discuss some of their characteristics not described in the advertisement. How much of the success of these weapons depends upon the men who use them?

_____

_____

_____

_____

NAME _____

Tactical Missiles:
A Report from General
Dynamics

2.   Many people feel that corporations, such as General Dynamics, should devote themselves to peaceful rather than to military developments. What is your own attitude toward the often-stated necessity for developing military "hardware"?

_____

_____

_____

_____

_____

FOR WRITING

1.   Choose one of the illustrations in this ad, and write a description of it, as if you were describing it to a blind person. Be as detailed as possible, based on what you see and what you read in the ad.

Picture: _____

Details to note: (List.) _____

_____

_____

_____

_____

2.   Write a description of a simple object, from a picture or from memory. Tell what it looks like, how it works, and what its purpose is.

280

NAME _____

Tactical Missiles:
A Report from General
Dynamics

Object: _____

What it looks like: (List.) _____

_____

_____

_____

_____

How it works: _____

_____

_____

_____

Its purpose: _____

_____

_____

ESSAY

_____

_____

_____

_____

_____

_____

NAME _____

Tactical Missiles:
A Report from General
Dynamics

NAME _____

As U.S. Speeds Up the Space Race;
Historic Voices . . .; How U.S. Astronaut "Walked" . . .

EXERCISE [*Articles Begin on Page 66*]

FOR UNDERSTANDING

1.   List the passages or phrases that make you think the introductory part of the first article is unbiased reporting.

_____

_____

_____

_____

List those passages or phrases that make you think the article is pro-American.

_____

_____

_____

2.   In the transcript of the conversation, list three passages that are scientific and serious.

a. _____

b. _____

c. _____

List six passages that are informal.

a. _____

b. _____

283

NAME _____

As U.S. Speeds Up the Space Race;
Historic Voices . . .; How U.S. Astronaut "Walked" . . .

c. _____

d. _____

e. _____

f. _____

List three passages that reveal a friendship among the three men.

a. _____

b. _____

c. _____

3.   In the description of the spacewalk ("How a U.S. Astronaut . . . ," page 68), show how the four divisions of this explanation follow a time sequence.

_____

_____

_____

4.   List at least three passages from "How a U.S. Astronaut Walked . . . " that could be called "human interest."

a. _____

b. _____

c. _____

List at least four passages that are scientific.

a. _____

b. _____

284

NAME _____

As U.S. Speeds Up the Space Race;
Historic Voices . . .; How U.S. Astronaut "Walked" . . .

c. _____

d. _____

FOR DISCUSSION

1. Is it really necessary to spend billions of dollars on space exploration?

_____ Yes   _____ No

Reasons for choice: (List.) _____

_____

_____

_____

2. What scientific feats, if any, impress you more than the spacewalk described in these three articles?

Feat	Reason
_____	_____
_____	_____
_____	_____
_____	_____

3. Since many people work on each space exploration project, should any way be devised to give them all special credit? Or, are they all simply people doing their jobs?

My opinion is: _____

_____

NAME _____

As U.S. Speeds Up the Space Race;
Historic Voices . . .; How U.S. Astronaut "Walked" . . .

FOR WRITING

1.   Listen to and record the conversation of one of your acquaintances who has accomplished something he wanted to achieve: a certain score in bowling, a grade in school, a date with someone, and so on. Then select those passages that were very personal, that reveal something about the person accomplishing the goal, and tell how they are or are not characteristic of this person.

2.   Select something a friend wants to do but which you do not approve of or agree with. Write a paper arguing your point of view.

My friend wants to: _____

I disagree (or disapprove) because: (List.) _____

_____

_____

_____

_____

3.   There are probably many things you have watched people do but have never done yourself, such as changing a tire, scrambling eggs, putting on makeup, and so on. Write a theme telling how to do one of these things you have watched, but have never done.

I have never _____ myself.

But by watching, I know that in order to do this I would need: (List.)

_____

_____

_____

286

NAME _____

As U.S. Speeds Up the Space Race;
Historic Voices . . .; How U.S. Astronaut "Walked" . . .

The order of doing this is: (List.)

_____

_____

_____

_____

_____

ESSAY

_____

_____

_____

_____

_____

_____

_____

_____

_____

_____

_____

NAME _____

As U.S. Speeds Up the Space Race;
Historic Voices . . .; How U.S. Astronaut "Walked" . . .

NAME _____

from *The Bernal Diaz Chronicles*

EXERCISE *[Article on Page 70]*

FOR UNDERSTANDING

1.   What does Bernal Diaz mean when he writes that he will tell the truth "without flattering certain captains or putting down others"?

_____

_____

Why is it important for him to establish this fact early in his narrative? (Remember that he was not a nobleman or a commander, but an ordinary soldier.)

_____

_____

2.   Cite at least three passages that show how Bernal Diaz regards Cortes.

   a.   (Page: _____) _____

   b.   (Page: _____) _____

   c.   (Page: _____) _____

3.   Cite at least three passages that show how Bernal Diaz regards Montezuma.

   a.   (Page: _____) _____

   b.   (Page: _____) _____

   c.   (Page: _____) _____

289

NAME _____

from *The Bernal Diaz Chronicles*

4.   What kind of "pictures of all the battles" had Montezuma received?

_____

_____

5.   Point out at least two passages that show how Montezuma and Cortes regarded one another.

   a.   (Page: ____)   _____

   b.   (Page: ____)   _____

6.   What evidence is there that Cortes will accomplish his dual objective of acquiring riches while disseminating his religion?

   Evidence: (page: ____)   _____

   Evidence: (page: ____)   _____

   Evidence: (page: ____)   _____

7.   Point out at least four words or phrases that help you "see" the scene Bernal Diaz describes.

   a.   _____

   b.   _____

   c.   _____

   d.   _____

FOR DISCUSSION

1.   On the basis of knowledge about what happened between the Spaniards and the Indians of Mexico, with which group does your sympathy lie?

   ____   Spaniards   ____   Indians

290

NAME _____

from *The Bernal Diaz Chronicles*

Reasons for choice: (List.)

_____

_____

_____

_____

2.   Do you find any parallels between the Spanish conquest of the New World and other "conquests" (not necessarily by armies) of one culture by another?

Spanish   Other Conquest

_____   _____

_____   _____

_____   _____

3.   Even today when the representative of opposing factions (gangs, countries, labor and management, political parties) meet, they observe certain customs or "courtesies." What are some of them you know of? Do you approve of these customs, or should people act as they feel?

291

NAME _____

from *The Bernal Diaz Chronicles*

Opposing Factions   Customs

_____   _____

_____   _____

_____   _____

_____   _____

My opinion about such actions: _____

_____

_____

_____

FOR WRITING

1.   Describe your first meeting with someone – a date, a teacher, an athletic coach, an employer, and so forth.

Person I met: _____

Time and place: _____

Situation: _____

_____

My impressions: _____

_____

_____

2.   In the passage you have read, Cortes explained to Montezuma something about Christianity, which he wanted the Aztec . . .

292

NAME _____

from *The Bernal Diaz Chronicles*

king to embrace. Write a paper explaining some attitude or idea you believe in and would like another person to feel the same about.

My attitude or idea: _____

Details about it: _____

_____

_____

_____

_____

Others should believe in it because: _____

_____

_____

_____

_____

3. Tell about a successful event in which you were a participant, but not a leader.

Event: _____

Time and place: _____

What was accomplished: _____

Who was leader: _____

Why it was successful: _____

_____

293

NAME _____

from *The Bernal Diaz Chronicles*

4.   What do you find most impressive about the meeting described by Bernal Diaz? Write a theme explaining why you made this choice.

I was most impressed by: _____

_____

Because: (List.) _____

_____

_____

5.   If you would like to have been with Cortes at this first meeting with Montezuma, write a paper giving your reasons. Then, tell what questions you would have liked to put to Montezuma and why.

Reasons I would have liked to be with Cortes: (List.)

_____

_____

_____

_____

I would have asked Montezuma:

Questions	Reasons for Interest
_____	_____
_____	_____
_____	_____
_____	_____

294

NAME _____

from *"Underwater Bonanza"* in *Pieces of Eight*

EXERCISE [Article on Page 75]

FOR UNDERSTANDING

1.   Cite eight words or phrases that mark this as especially informal, even colloquial, writing.

    a.   (Page: ____) _____

    b.   (Page: ____) _____

    c.   (Page: ____) _____

    d.   (Page: ____) _____

    e.   (Page: ____) _____

    f.   (Page: ____) _____

    g.   (Page: ____) _____

    h.   (Page: ____) _____

2.   What are "doubloons"? _____

How deep is a "fathom"? _____

3.   This is the kind of article that could be fiction in an adventure magazine (though it is not fiction). List at least three details that have probably been included to convince you that this is a true account.

    a.   (Page: ____) _____

    b.   (Page: ____) _____

    c.   (Page: ____) _____

4.   List the evidence contained in this passage that shows it is

NAME _____

from *"Underwater Bonanza"* in *Pieces of Eight*

part of a continuing story, or that the men had made treasure finds before.

    a. (Page: _____) _____

    b. (Page: _____) _____

    c. (Page: _____) _____

    d. (Page: _____) _____

5.   What effect is the last paragraph meant to have on your feelings about the discovery?

_____

_____

_____

_____

FOR DISCUSSION

1.   What advantages can you find to people making a great effort to recover such sunken ships as those described in the passage you just read? What advantages are there to leaving them alone?

          Recovering   Leaving Alone

_____   _____

_____   _____

_____   _____

_____   _____

NAME _____

from *"Underwater Bonanza"* in *Pieces of Eight*

2. The state of Florida lays claim to part of the treasure found in its offshore waters. Most countries lay claim to objects found by archaeological excavation on their lands. Do you believe this system is fair, or should the case of "finder's keepers . . ." apply?

Fair (List reasons.)   Unfair (List reasons.)

_____   _____

_____   _____

_____   _____

_____   _____

FOR WRITING

1. If you have ever gone skin diving, write an account of some special memory such as finding a certain kind of fish, seeing a spectacular reef, and so on. (If you have done some other kind of exploring – through a cave, an old building, an empty lot, and so on – write about some special memory concerning the event.)

The event: _____

Time and place: _____

Special find: _____

Reasons for it being special: _____

_____

_____

2. Pretend that you are a Spanish commander (such as one who might have been with Cortes). You have gathered a treasure and are sending it back to Spain. Write a letter to accompany the

NAME _____

from *"Underwater Bonanza"* in *Pieces of Eight*

treasure telling what is included in the shipment and how it is to be handled or distributed upon arrival. Be as fanciful as you wish.

Contents of shipment: (List.) _____

_____

_____

_____

_____

Method of handling or distribution: (List.) _____

_____

_____

_____

_____

_____

3.   Write directions for reaching one of the wrecks licensed to the Real Eight Corporation. Pretend that your departure point is some city either to the north or the south (not necessarily in Florida). Use the map on page 76 as required.

NAME _____

from *The Mouse That Roared*

EXERCISE [*Story on Page 80*]

FOR UNDERSTANDING

1. What is believable about this passage?

_____

_____

_____

What is unbelievable?

_____

_____

_____

2. Which four passages make it obvious that you are reading something meant to be humorous?

    a. (Page: _____) _____

    b. (Page: _____) _____

    c. (Page: _____) _____

    d. (Page: _____) _____

3. Cite three ways in which the author leads you to laugh at Dr. Kokintz?

    a. (Page: _____) _____

    b. (Page: _____) _____

    c. (Page: _____) _____

299

NAME _____

from *The Mouse That Roared*

Cite three ways in which you are led to laugh at Tully Bascomb.

    a. (Page: _____) _____

    b. (Page: _____) _____

    c. (Page: _____) _____

4.   Give at least three ways in which the author makes Dr. Kokintz believable.

    a. (Page: _____) _____

    b. (Page: _____) _____

    c. (Page: _____) _____

Give at least three ways in which the author makes Tully believable.

    a. (Page: _____) _____

    b. (Page: _____) _____

    c. (Page: _____) _____

5.   Find one passage that shows how Will (one of Tully's men) is different from Tully. What is the difference between them?

(Page: _____) _____

_____

6.   What do the characters mean when they say that the bomb and the sword are "peace weapons"? What is contradictory in the term?

    Explanation: _____

_____

NAME _____

from *The Mouse That Roared*

7. What is there in this chapter that indicates that it is part of a longer work and not complete in itself?

_____

_____

_____

FOR DISCUSSION

1. Satire is a method of pointing out the faults of a society by mockery or by ridicule. How effective do you think satire is in writing, based on your own experience in reading it? How effective is satire in the mass media?

Effectiveness in writing: _____

_____

_____

_____

Effectiveness in the mass media: _____

_____

_____

2. If Dr. Kokintz were not a native of Grand Fenwick, how would this part of the story have been different?

_____

_____

301

NAME _____

from *The Mouse That Roared*

3. Why did the author of the novel make a wine the cause of the war Grand Fenwick declared on the United States? Do you know of other occasions (not necessarily of national importance) in which what began as a relatively unimportant incident led to a major event? Use both historical (or general) and personal examples.

Incident   Important Result

_____   _____

_____   _____

_____   _____

_____   _____

FOR WRITING

1. Without reading the book from which this chapter is taken, write about an event that could happen either before or after the portion you have just read. Use the same situation and any characters you want to, but you may invent additional characters or information in order to create your own story.
2. Write an imaginary letter that Tully could send back to the Duchess Gloriana XII telling about his successful invasion of the United States. Make your letter as detailed as you can by including street names, sights, sounds, times, and so on. (You need not be accurate about the real New York City, but you can make up whatever information you require.)
3. Often a personal accomplishment carries with it an unexpected reward, just as the invasion of the United States brought Tully the capture of Dr. Kokintz and his bomb. Write a theme telling of such a success you had that also had something unexpectedly good come with it.

The success: _____

The situation it was part of: _____

302

NAME _____

from *The Mouse That Roared*

The "bonus": _____

_____

_____

4.   Describe a situation in which you had difficulty believing
you were really involved, that is, which had some quality about
it that made you believe you were imagining your own partici-
pation.

The situation: _____

The time and place: _____

Other people involved: _____

_____

Why it seemed unreal: _____

_____

_____

_____

_____

_____

_____

_____

_____

_____

NAME _____

from *The Mouse That Roared*

ESSAY

NAME _____

Making Park Promise Good

EXERCISE [*Editorial on Page 85*]

FOR UNDERSTANDING

1.   Point out at least five words or phrases that reveal where the sympathy of the editorial writer lies.

a. _____

b. _____

c. _____

d. _____

e. _____

2.   Photographs usually do not accompany editorials. Why do you think this photograph did?

_____

_____

Why were the photo and article not printed on a regular news page?

_____

_____

FOR DISCUSSION

1.   Under what circumstances does overt action seem preferable to words in helping an individual achieve a goal? In helping a group?

305

NAME _____

Making Park Promise Good

_____

_____

_____

2.   If the park and pool were not built, what other action do you believe these people should have taken?

_____

_____

_____

FOR WRITING

1.   What one thing do you believe your home neighborhood needs most? Write a paper asking for it, and address your request to the authority that could fulfill the need.

My neighborhood most needs: _____

Who can fulfill request: _____

Reasons request should be granted: (List.) _____

_____

_____

_____

2.   Using the basic information or "facts" contained in this editorial, write one from an unsympathetic point of view.

_____

_____

NAME _____

from *"Where We Are Going"*
in *Where Do We Go From Here*

EXERCISE [*Article on Page 86*]

FOR UNDERSTANDING

1.   What stereotype is attacked here? _____

What method of attack is used? _____

_____

2.   As part of a chapter within a book, this passage has no title. What title would you give it?

_____

3.   Show the parallels Dr. King draws between what Jews have done and what Negroes can do.

Jews	Negroes
_____	_____
_____	_____
_____	_____

4.   Write a resume of this passage.

_____

_____

_____

_____

_____

_____

307

NAME _____

from *"Where We Are Going"*
in *Where Do We Go From Here*

FOR DISCUSSION

1.   What strengths among minority groups could you cite for
someone willing to learn from the past experience of others?

Group   Strengths

_____   _____

_____   _____

_____   _____

2.   If you are familiar with other ideas expressed by Dr. King,
discuss them in relation to this passage. Are they similar or different from what you have read here?
3.   Do Dr. King's aims, as expressed in this passage, coincide
with your own aims? Conflict with them?

Coincide (List.)   Conflict (List.)

_____   _____

_____   _____

_____   _____

_____   _____

4.   Is the course Dr. King suggests either too slow or too difficult
to suit you? Or do you find yourself agreeing with him?

_____   Too slow because: _____

_____   Too difficult because: _____

_____   Agreeable because: _____

308

NAME _____

from *"Where We Are Going"*
in *Where Do We Go From Here*

FOR WRITING

1.   This passage uses a specific example as an introduction to
the writer's larger idea. Write a theme about a belief you hold,
but lead the reader to it by telling something he will be familiar
with or by telling a specific incident that illustrates the belief
you are writing about.

My belief: _____

Illustrative incident: _____

OR   _____

Familiar idea: _____

_____

2.   The next to last paragraph of Dr. King's writing asks several
questions. Choose one of them and write an answer based on
your own knowledge and beliefs.

The question: _____

My answer: _____

_____

_____

3.   Write a theme pointing out the differences between two individuals (yourself and a relative, yourself and a friend, two
friends), but show how the two have worked together to accomplish a specific goal.

The two people are: _____

309

NAME _____

from *"Where We Are Going"*
in *Where Do We Go From Here*

Differences between

A (Name)_____   B (Name)_____

_____   _____

_____   _____

_____   _____

The goal accomplished: _____

How goal was achieved: _____

_____

4.   Dr. King wrote about both educational and social action. Express your interpretation of each of these terms by writing definitions of them. Begin by looking up each in a dictionary.

Dictionary definition of "education": _____

_____

Dictionary definition of "social action": _____

_____

_____

_____

5.   Write a paper illustrating your concept of a "conscious, alert, and informed" person. Make the theme as specific as possible by illustrating how that person would behave in a specific situation. Use either a real or an imaginary person and situation.

The situation: _____

How the person would behave: _____

310

NAME _____

Kindly Unhitch That Star,
Buddy

EXERCISE [*Poem on Page 93*]

FOR UNDERSTANDING

1.   What is the meaning of the expression "hitch your wagon

to a star"? _____

_____

2.   Discover the organization of ideas in this poem by seeing
how the sentence ideas are related. Next to each number, write
the principal thought of that sentence in the poem.

   Sen. 1: _____

   Sen. 2: _____

   Sen. 3: _____

   Sen. 4: _____

   Sen. 5: _____

   Sen. 6: _____

3.   List the five "coined" words in this poem. Next to each, write
its meaning.

   a. _____

   b. _____

   c. _____

   d. _____

   e. _____

311

NAME _____

Kindly Unhitch That Star,
Buddy

4.   This poem mentions eight ways people think they can achieve success. Write down five of them.

a. _____

b. _____

c. _____

d. _____

e. _____

FOR DISCUSSION

1.   Are there any methods of success sketched by Nash that you believe in to some degree? Discuss them and your attitude.

Nash's method: _____

_____

Why I believe in it: _____

_____

_____

2.   Do you know of any popular songs that deal with the kind of people or the subject matter of Mr. Nash's poem? If so, write out the words; then discuss how the songwriter makes his point. (Or, perhaps you know some jokes that deal with the same subject. Write them out and discuss them.)

FOR WRITING

1.   If you have ever known one type of person sketched poeti-

312

NAME _____

Kindly Unhitch That Star,
Buddy

cally by Mr. Nash, write a theme telling about that person, his idea of success, and how he tried to achieve it.

The person: _____

His idea of success: _____

_____

How he tried to achieve it: _____

_____

_____

My comments about the person: _____

_____

_____

_____

2.   In your own words, write a general statement about what Mr. Nash seems to be saying in his poem. Then write a theme agreeing or disagreeing with this statement.

Statement of the poem: _____

_____

I agree _____ disagree _____ with this statement because:

_____

_____

_____

_____

NAME _____

Kindly Unhitch That Star,
Buddy

ESSAY

NAME _____

The Ghost Horse

EXERCISE [*Article on Page 96*]

FOR UNDERSTANDING

1.   Show at least two pieces of evidence that indicate the person writing this is telling a true story.

a. (Page: ____) _____

b. (Page: ____) _____

Does the story anywhere *not* seem to be told by this same person?

Answer: _____

Evidence: _____

2.   What evidence is there that indicates that the Indians making this roundup are self-sufficient? _____
Give at least two indications that these people live close to the land.

a. (Page: ____) _____

b. (Page: ____) _____

3.   What indication is there that the people hold each other in

high regard? _____

Give at least three indications that the people have respect for the horses.

a. (Page: ____) _____

b. (Page: ____) _____

c. (Page: ____) _____

315

NAME _____

The Ghost Horse

4.   This narrative has several parts; it is thus similar to the acts

in a play. Point out how it falls into "acts." _____

_____

5.   Choose one paragraph and show how details make it seem
as if the reader is included in the story and is not just a disinterested spectator.

   The paragraph: ___ _____

   The details: (List.) _____

   _____

   _____

   _____

6.   What unexpected or surprising information did you gain

from reading this essay? (List.) _____

_____

_____

_____

_____

FOR DISCUSSION

1.   What is your feeling about the horse that got away: sympathy for or against the animal? Give reasons for your choice.

   For _____   Against _____   Reasons: (List.) _____

316

NAME _____

The Ghost Horse

_____

_____

_____

2.   Another kind of wild horse roundup is the subject of the film *The Misfits* by Arthur Miller. The screenplay of this is available in book form. Read the book and compare the attitude of the men in it to that of the Indians. Also, compare the way both groups of people conducted the roundup.

FOR WRITING

1.   Write a theme describing how to participate in some activity you are familiar with. Remember to use specific details to make the reader feel he belongs with you.

Activity: _____

What you do: _____

_____

_____

_____

2.   Write a theme describing a custom you are familiar with.

Custom: _____

Description of it: _____

_____

_____

NAME _____

The Ghost Horse

People involved: _____

_____

3.   What one thing was most unusual or surprising to you after reading this account of the roundup? Write a theme explaining your choice.

Most unusual or surprising: _____

What I really expected: _____

Reasons for choice: _____

_____

_____

4.   Assume you are preparing to interview Chief Buffalo Child Long Lance for a 15-minute television show. Prepare questions you would ask him in order to make an interesting show. Some questions may relate to the material he wrote about in "The Ghost Horse" but all of them need not.

_____

_____

_____

_____

_____

_____

_____

_____

_____

NAME _____

*The Notorious Jumping Frog
of Calaveras County*

EXERCISE [*Story on Page 105*]

FOR UNDERSTANDING

1.   What does Mark Twain accomplish by making this a story-within-a-story? _____

_____

2.   What information do you get about Simon Wheeler?

(Page: ____) _____

(Page: ____) _____

(Page: ____) _____

About the way he tells the story?

(Page: ____) _____

(Page: ____) _____

(Page: ____) _____

On the basis of this information, how would you characterize

Wheeler? _____

_____

_____

3.   Which is the main narrative or story? _____

_____

_____

319

NAME _____

*The Notorious Jumping Frog
of Calaveras County*

What other stories about Smiley are told: (List.) _____

_____

_____

_____

Why are the other stories included? _____

_____

_____

4.   What information do you get about Smiley?

(Page: _____) _____

(Page: _____) _____

(Page: _____) _____

(Page: _____) _____

On the basis of this, how would you characterize him? _____

_____

_____

5.   Why is the stranger who wins the bet from Smiley not identified?

_____

_____

_____

_____

320

NAME _____

*The Notorious Jumping Frog
of Calaveras County*

FOR DISCUSSION

1. Account for the popularity of this story.

_____

_____

_____

2. Do you feel sorry for Smiley? Explain your answer.

Yes _____   No _____   Reasons: (List.) _____

_____

_____

_____

3. Do you believe that the stranger cheated Smiley? Are there ever circumstances in which certain kinds of "cheating" are acceptable?

Stranger cheated _____   Stranger didn't cheat _____

Is cheating ever acceptable? Yes _____   No _____

If yes, under what circumstances: _____

_____

_____

For what purposes: _____

_____

If no, why not? (List.) _____

_____

321

NAME _____

The Notorious Jumping Frog
of Calaveras County

FOR WRITING

1.   Who do you think is the real "winner" in this story – Smiley, the stranger, Simon Wheeler, another person? Write a theme supporting your choice.

Winner: _____

Reasons for choice: (List.) _____

_____

_____

_____

_____

2.   Wheeler tells several stories about Smiley and his bets. Write an original story to add to the list. (Do not write in a dialect unless you wish to.)

Characteristics of the stories that must be imitated: (List.)

_____

_____

_____

_____

_____

3.   A news report of the 1968 frog-jumping contest at Angel's Camp is on page 111. Write the frog-jumping section of the Mark Twain story as if it were the same kind of newspaper article.

NAME _____

The Passionate Shepherd
to His Love and *The Nymph's Reply*

2.   What does it take to achieve that success? (List.)

_____

_____

_____

_____

3.   Are there any qualities about male-female relationships
that you wish existed, although they are not current or popular
today?

_____

_____

_____

_____

FOR WRITING

1.   Write an example of a young man of today persuading a girl
to go on a date (or choose any other allowable situation). Use
colloquial language rather than the more formal kind used in
class themes.

Situation: _____

Inducements	Her Answers
_____	_____
_____	_____
_____	_____
_____	_____

NAME _____

The Passionate Shepherd
to His Love and *The Nymph's Reply*

2.   Put either the Marlowe or the Raleigh poem into modern language. (Follow the rhyme only if you can with ease.)

NAME _____

Miniver Cheevy

EXERCISE [*Poem on Page 118*]

FOR UNDERSTANDING

1.   Two places and two people that may be unfamiliar to you are important in this poem. Write the identifications next to these terms:

Thebes: _____

Camelot: _____

Priam: _____

Medici: _____

2.   Why are the words "Romance" and "Art" (in the fourth

verse) capitalized? _____

_____

3.   List at least three past eras Miniver wished he had lived in.

a. _____

b. _____

c. _____

4.   List three things Miniver wished he had but which the poet indicated Miniver would not have known how to live with.

a. _____

b. _____

c. _____

327

NAME _____

Miniver Cheevy

5.   Write in one sentence the reason the poet gives for the fact

that Miniver Cheevy never amounts to anything.   _____

_____

_____

_____

FOR DISCUSSION

1.   If Miniver Cheevy had lived during one of the past eras he wished to, do you think he could have achieved his dreams of glory?

Yes ____   No ____

Reasons: (List.) _____

_____

_____

_____

2.   Do you believe that fate directs a person's life?

Yes ____   No ____

Examples to support belief: _____

_____

_____

_____

_____

NAME _____

Miniver Cheevy

3. Under what conditions do you think a person ought to be dissatisfied with his life? (List.)

_____

_____

_____

4. If someone is dissatisfied about himself or the way in which he lives, what do you think he ought to do about it? (List.)

_____

_____

_____

FOR WRITING

1. Choose a time during the past or in the future when you think it was, or will be, interesting to live. Write a theme explaining your choice.

Time: _____

What would be better: _____

_____

_____

What would be more desirable: _____

_____

_____

_____

NAME _____

Miniver Cheevy

Other reasons for choice: _____

_____

_____

2.   Write an imaginary letter to Miniver Cheevy telling why he should be satisfied to live now instead of in the past, as he wished.

Material progress: _____

_____

_____

Social progress: _____

_____

_____

Specifics: (health, food, clothes, and so on) _____

_____

_____

_____

3.   Write a humorous article directed to Miniver Cheevy and tell him what a day would be like if he lived in one of the past times mentioned in the poem. (Try to use accurate details, but make up whatever you need to.)

NAME _____

The Way Up to Heaven

EXERCISE [*Story on Page 121*]

FOR UNDERSTANDING

1. The tension between Mr. and Mrs. Foster is indicated in many of their actions. List 10 passages that show Mr. Foster's unhappiness with his marriage or his wife.

a. (Page: ____) _____

b. (Page: ____) _____

c. (Page: ____) _____

d. (Page: ____) _____

e. (Page: ____) _____

f. (Page: ____) _____

g. (Page: ____) _____

h. (Page: ____) _____

i. (Page: ____) _____

j. (Page: ____) _____

List six passages that show Mrs. Foster's unhappiness with her marriage or her husband.

a. (Page: ____) _____

b. (Page: ____) _____

c. (Page: ____) _____

d. (Page: ____) _____

331

NAME _____

The Way Up to Heaven

e. (Page: _____) _____

f. (Page: _____) _____

2. Time (including hours, dates, and so on) is an important element in this story. List at least 10 occasions during which time is mentioned or is important.

a. _____

b. _____

c. _____

d. _____

e. _____

f. _____

g. _____

h. _____

i. _____

j. _____

3. Cite at least three references to time or time elements in the portion of the story referring to Mrs. Foster's stay in France or her return to New York.

a. _____

b. _____

c. _____

4. The author, Roald Dahl, makes it very evident that Mrs. Foster is a changed woman after she leaves the front door and tells the chauffeur to drive her to the airport without her husband.

332

NAME _____

The Way Up to Heaven

In the spaces below, write ten phrases Mr. Dahl uses to show her changed look and attitude.

a. _____ f. _____

b. _____ g. _____

c. _____ h. _____

d. _____ i. _____

e. _____ j. _____

5. What is ironic about the ending of Mrs. Foster's weekly

letter home? _____

_____

6. If you were not already prepared for something extraordinary in the house when Mrs. Foster returns, the author makes certain you are by his description of the house when she enters (fifth paragraph from the end). List four elements that prepare you for the ending of the story.

   a. _____

   b. _____

   c. _____

   d. _____

7. "Elevator" is the last word in the story. Yet it is not even mentioned in Mrs. Foster's phone call in the previous paragraph. There are, however, several clues early in the story that the house has an elevator. Note at least two of them.

   a. _____

   b. _____

NAME _____

The Way Up to Heaven

FOR DISCUSSION

1. Should Mrs. Foster have left the house knowing, as she did, that her husband was stuck in the elevator? Could you act in the same way?

    She should _____ should not _____ have left.

    Reasons: (List.) _____

    _____

    Why I could _____ could not _____ act as Mrs. Foster

    did: (List.) _____

    _____

    _____

2. Do you think Mrs. Foster really triumphed over her husband? Would you call hers a "successful" venture?

    Yes _____ No _____

    What would make her successful: _____

    Reasons for your response: _____

    _____

3. Was it silly for Mrs. Foster to keep writing letters home every week when she knew her husband was not receiving them?

    Yes _____ No _____

    Other actions she could have taken: _____

    _____

NAME _____

The Way Up to Heaven

4.   What courses of action seem suitable in dealing with people you do not like? With customs or institutions you do not like?

With People   With Institutions

_____   _____

_____   _____

_____   _____

_____   _____

FOR WRITING

1.   Assume that you are a marriage counselor consulted by either Mr. or Mrs. Foster. Write your recommendations for your client.

Client: _____

Satisfactory parts of marriage: _____

_____

Recommended changes in action: _____

_____

Recommended changes in attitude: _____

_____

_____

2.   Based on what you know about the physical appearance and characteristics of Mr. and Mrs. Foster from the story, write a description of one of them.

335

NAME _____

The Way Up to Heaven

Subject of character sketch: _____

What he or she looks like: _____

_____

His or her characteristics: _____

_____

_____

3.   Find one word that you think best describes how you feel about either Mr. or Mrs. Foster (such as "admire," "sad," "unhappy," "disinterested," and so on). Write a theme explaining why you made this choice.

My attitude toward   Mr. _____   Mrs. _____   Foster

can best be described as _____

Because: (List.) _____

_____

_____

4.   Write an article consisting of suggestions to high school students about what makes a successful marriage. Base your ideas on your own observations of married people as well as on any reading you may have done on marriage. Write in the language you know teenagers will read.

Elements of successful marriage: (List.) _____

_____

_____

_____

336

NAME _____

The Verger

EXERCISE [*Story on Page 133*]

FOR UNDERSTANDING

1. List the jobs, in order, that Mr. Foreman held before becoming a verger.

a. _____   d. _____

b. _____   e. _____

c. _____   f. _____

         g. _____

2. What qualities of character does Mr. Foreman admire (and have)?

(Page: _____) _____

(Page: _____) _____

(Page: _____) _____

How do his former jobs prepare you to accept this kind of man?

_____

_____

3. Somerset Maugham has used specific phrases to make you feel sympathetic toward Albert Edward and unsympathetic toward the vicar before Albert Edward's dismissal. List as many as you can.

Albert Edward
(Sympathetic)   Vicar (Unsympathetic)

_____   _____

337

NAME _____

The Verger

_____   _____

_____   _____

_____   _____

_____   _____

_____   _____

4.   Name at least one thing about Mr. Foreman's way of running his business that leads you to believe this is not a story that takes place within the last two years.

_____

FOR DISCUSSION

1.   Do you think Mr. Foreman should have tried to keep his job at St. Peter's, Neville Square? What would have been the advantages of doing so? How important do you believe the security of such a job is?

      Keep job _____ not keep job _____

      Reasons: (List.) _____

      _____

      Advantages of keeping job: _____

      _____

      _____

      Definition of "job security": _____

      _____

338

NAME _____

The Verger

Importance of such security: _____

_____

_____

2.   Why does Maugham use so much of this story to describe in detail the obviously successful vicar and the two church-wardens?

_____

_____

3.   How much chance and how much hard work do you believe were responsible for Mr. Foreman's business success? How do you think each is responsible for *any* business success? For personal success?

	Chance	Hard Work
	_____	_____
For Mr. Foreman]	_____	_____
	_____	_____
	_____	_____
	_____	_____
For Anybody]	_____	_____
	_____	_____

4.   Discuss the saying "You never know when opportunity is knocking if you don't keep answering the door."

339

NAME _____

The Verger

Meaning: _____

Beliefs about saying: _____

_____

_____

5.   Does this story remind you in any way of "Harry," by William Saroyan (in Part I of this book)?

Yes ____   No ____   If yes, explain how:

   "The Verger"   "Harry"

_____   _____

_____   _____

_____   _____

FOR WRITING

1.   "The Verger" could have been a different story if Albert Edward were a habitual smoker and did not have to look for some cigarettes after being fired. Write another ending to this story that does not begin with the search for a tobacconist.
2.   Summarize this story in one sentence. Then write a theme pointing out the difference between your one-sentence summary and the way in which Maugham told the story of Albert Edward.

Summary: _____

_____

_____

_____

340

NAME _____

The Verger

3.　Albert Edward is described as an "unflappable" man; as the kind of man who never shows outwardly how he feels. Write a theme expressing your admiration, or lack of it, for this type of person.

I admire _____　do not admire _____　the "unflappable" man

Because (List.): _____

_____

_____

4.　Tell about an incident in your own life (or in the life of someone you know) in which what seemed to be a misfortune led to success in something else.

The time: _____

The place: _____

People involved: _____

Incident: _____

_____

Why it seemed a misfortune: _____

_____

_____

Why it turned into a success: _____

_____

_____

_____

341

NAME _____

from *Men Who Manage*

EXERCISE [*Article on Page 140*]

FOR UNDERSTANDING

1. Summarize briefly the attitude expressed by each of the four men quoted in these interviews.

L. Bierner: _____

_____

_____

H. Trimble: _____

_____

_____

J. Cunningham: _____

_____

_____

E. Stein: _____

_____

_____

2. Choose the statement of one man and write down at least six phrases or words from it that make you believe this is an actual quotation rather than something written by a professional author.

Speaker: _____

a. _____   b. _____

342

NAME _____

from *Men Who Manage*

c. _____   d. _____

e. _____   f. _____

3.   Point out at least three ways in which the statement of Mr. Stein (the only college graduate) differs from that of either Bierner, Trimble, or Cunningham.

Mr. Stein   Mr. _____

_____   _____

_____   _____

_____   _____

FOR DISCUSSION

1.   Since people reveal themselves when they talk, discuss what the four men indicate of themselves in these answers to the question posed.

Bierner	Trimble	Cunningham	Stein
_____	_____	_____	_____
_____	_____	_____	_____
_____	_____	_____	_____
_____	_____	_____	_____
_____	_____	_____	_____
_____	_____	_____	_____

2.   Which of these speakers might be voicing your own opinions about how to rise in a job you now hold or recently held? (If you

343

NAME _____

from Men Who Manage

have not worked, how do the opinions coincide with those you have?)

Speaker my beliefs are closest to: _____

Reason for similarity: _____

_____

_____

_____

3. Discuss the part you think each of the following ought to have in your attempt to reach goals that you have set for yourself: good looks, neat appearance, high morality, education, chance, knowing the right people, having clothes, having a car. Add others to the list.

My goals: (Be specific.) _____

Importance of items listed: _____

_____

_____

Other things that will help me: _____

_____

_____

FOR WRITING

1. Write a theme in answer to the question, "What are the things that enable students to be successful in this school?" Be as frank as those men whose answers in the interviews you have just read.

344

NAME _____

from Men Who Manage

Definition of success in this school: _____

_____

_____

Ways to achieve it: _____

_____

_____

_____

_____

2.   What job would you like to hold after completing courses at this or other schools? Imagine you are applying for that job and must answer the following question in essay form on the job application: "What are the qualities you think necessary for success in this job?"

Job: _____

Qualities for success: _____

_____

_____

_____

3.   Choose a person you know who is satisfied with his job. Write a description of him.

Subject of theme: _____

His job: _____

What he is like: _____

345

NAME _____

from *Men Who Manage*

_____

_____

_____

_____

Reasons for his satisfaction: _____

_____

_____

_____

_____

NAME _____

*The First Great Woman
Scientist . . . And Much More*

EXERCISE [Essay on Page 146]

FOR UNDERSTANDING

1.   What is the meaning of the words ". . . And Much More" in
the title of this article?

_____

2.   As a young girl Marie Curie is described, in paragraph 7, as
having a marvelous memory, the ability to concentrate, curiosity
and enthusiasm, and a close relationship with her family. Show
how each of these qualities was apparent in at least one way in
her adult life.

Youthful Quality   Way Apparent Later

Good memory: (Page: ____) _____

Ability to concentrate: (Page: ____) _____

Curiosity and enthusiasm: (Page: ____) _____

Closeness to family: (Page: ____) _____

3.   Cite at least five words or phrases in the article that make it
obvious that the author admires Marie Curie.

a. (Page: ____) _____

b. (Page: ____) _____

c. (Page: ____) _____

d. (Page: ____) _____

e. (Page: ____) _____

NAME _____

The First Great Woman
Scientist . . . And Much More

4.   Other words describing Marie Curie (in paragraph 11) indicate that she had "self-discipline, self-reliance, and . . . capacity
for taking pains. . . ." Give one example of each of these qualities
in the life of Marie Curie.

Quality	How Apparent

Self-discipline: (Page: ____) _____

Self-reliance: (Page: ____) _____

Takes pains: (Page: ____) _____

5.   Give at least two items of information contained within the
article that tell something about life in nineteenth century Poland.

a.   (Page: ____) _____

b.   (Page: ____) _____

6.   Summarize briefly the events leading to the discovery of

radium by the Curies. _____

_____

_____

_____

7.   What did "success" consist of for the Curies, according to

this article? _____

_____

_____

_____

NAME _____

*The First Great Woman
Scientist . . . And Much More*

8.   Which passages are mostly about Marie Curie as a scientist? (Give page numbers.)

From page _____   to page _____.

From page _____   to page _____.

From page _____   to page _____.

Which are mostly about her as a person? (Give page numbers.)

From page _____   to page _____.

From page _____   to page _____.

From page _____   to page _____.

FOR DISCUSSION

1.   Did anything seem unusual or unexpected about Marie Curie's work in World War I?

    Yes _____   No _____

    List reasons: _____

    _____

    _____

    _____

2.   The article states that the Curies decided not to patent their extraction process and that they always published their work so others could share their knowledge with them. Do you believe such sharing of information is good or bad? Should it be required in all fields and among all countries?

    Attitude about sharing information: _____

349

NAME _____

The First Great Woman
Scientist . . . And Much More

_____

_____

_____

3.   If a person or an organization develops a potentially dangerous device, should that development be withheld from the public?

Yes _____   No _____

Reasons for choice: _____

_____

_____

_____

4.   Assuming that you are impressed by the Marie Curie story,
can you determine what your response would be if she had been
working on a book, symphony, or painting rather than on something scientific? Discuss the importance of "humanitarian" contributions to world knowledge.

Definition of a humanitarian contribution: _____

_____

_____

_____

_____

5.   What should be the role of government in supporting research, whether in the natural sciences or the social sciences?
Should people like the Curies be free from financial worry and
be given government support? If you believe they should be given
financial support, what ought their obligation, if any, be to the
government?

NAME _____

The First Great Woman
Scientist . . . And Much More

FOR WRITING

1. If you are impressed by one of Marie Curie's accomplishments, either personal or professional, tell why you made that choice. If you are not impressed by any of her personal or professional accomplishments, tell why you are not.

Impressed by: _____

Reasons: _____

_____

Not impressed by any because: _____

_____

_____

2. "Marie Curie was as successful a human being as she was a scientist." Agree or disagree with this statement, using information from the article to support your position.

Agree _____   Disagree _____

Definition of a successful human being: _____

_____

Reasons for choice: _____

_____

_____

3. Imagine you were given this article to make into a television program. At what points would you approve commercial breaks and why? Would you like to have any parts acted out? Which ones and why? Which photographs or drawings would you order and why?

NAME _____

*The First Great Woman
Scientist . . . And Much More*

Location of commercial breaks:

(Page: ____) _____

(Page: ____) _____

(Page: ____) _____

	Parts to Act	Reasons
(Page: ____)	_____	_____
(Page: ____)	_____	_____
(Page: ____)	_____	_____

	Art to Order	Reasons
	_____	_____
	_____	_____
	_____	_____
	_____	_____
	_____	_____

NAME _____

from *The Wrath of Achilles*
in *The Iliad of Homer*

EXERCISE [*Story on Page 159*]

FOR UNDERSTANDING

1.   How did Achilles make certain that Hector did not get out-

side help before they met in single combat?   _____

_____

2.   How was the outcome of the fight between Hector and

Achilles decided?   _____

3.   Recount the part Athene played in Hector's defeat.

_____

_____

4.   Does Athene act as you would expect of a god or goddess?

Yes ____   No ____   Reasons: _____

_____

_____

5.   One of the characteristics of the poetry and the prose translations of *The Iliad* is the use of similes (use of "like" or "as" to
compare two different things). Quote two such similes from the
passage just read.

a.   _____

b.   _____

6.   Another characteristic of the writing style in *The Iliad* is
that adjectival descriptions of characters are placed next to their

353

NAME _____

from *The Wrath of Achilles*
in *The Iliad of Homer*

names. "Swift-footed Achilles" is an example. Point out three other such descriptions.

a. _____

b. _____

c. _____

7. Using quotations from the text, show how Achilles and Hector felt toward each other.

Achilles to Hector: _____

_____

_____

Hector to Achilles: _____

_____

_____

FOR DISCUSSION

1. Do you think it is fair that Athene, a goddess, should help Achilles win, although Hector had no such special help? Should such encounters as the one described always be balanced? How do you feel about outside help in a modern prize fight, gang war, or national war?

Fair _____ Unfair _____ Both _____

My opinion about outside help: _____

_____

_____

354

NAME _____

from *The Wrath of Achilles*
in *The Iliad of Homer*

Special situation which might change this opinion: _____

_____

_____

2.   After 10 years of war, the best fighter from each side met and decided the outcome for their supporters. How good a method is this to settle other similar group arguments?

Good ____   Bad ____   Undecided ____

Reasons: _____

_____

_____

Effect upon other people involved: _____

_____

_____

3.   Achilles and Hector, in this very brief portion of the rather long *Iliad*, talk only about themselves and their private problems. Does this seem unusual for men who represent great armies? Does this indicate that they are putting personal problems before national ones? Should they not be concerned about larger, more important issues?

Place of personal concerns in relation to other things: _____

_____

_____

_____

4.   How "successful" do you consider Achilles' victory, since

355

NAME _____

from *The Wrath of Achilles*
in *The Iliad of Homer*

he had special help? _____

_____

5.   Is the "how" of winning as important as the victory itself?
Consider this question in relation to family arguments, national
wars, student concerns, the desires of minority groups, and so on.

_____

_____

_____

_____

6.   Draw a parallel between this description of single combat
and the meetings (in television debates, in news conferences,
and so on) of people running for political office.

Achilles and Hector   Politicians

_____   _____

_____   _____

_____   _____

_____   _____

FOR WRITING

1.   Describe what your feelings would be in a situation in which
you won a victory (not necessarily a physical fight) over someone
you considered a real rival. The event could be winning an award,
a job, an election, a following of friends, and so forth.

Event: _____

NAME _____

from *The Wrath of Achilles*
in *The Iliad of Homer*

Time and place: _____

People involved: _____

Situation: _____

_____

_____

Personal reaction: _____

_____

_____

2. Tell about a situation in which you participated or that you witnessed in which one person or group was trying to gain power (physical or otherwise) over another person or group.

The situation: _____

_____

_____

The people involved: _____

_____

_____

The time and place: _____

_____

_____

3. Many people have suggested that settling modern wars in this ancient manner, that is, by a single representative of each

357

NAME _____

from *The Wrath of Achilles*
in *The Iliad of Homer*

warring side meeting with a representative from the opposite side, would be a good idea, because it would avoid enormous bloodshed. Write a theme supporting or rejecting this idea.

Support _____   Reject _____

Consequences of such action: (List.) _____

_____

_____

_____

4.   Retell this story in modern terms (use slang if you wish) for some group that would not be likely to listen to or appreciate its original writing style.

Group: _____

_____

_____

_____

_____

_____

_____

_____

_____

_____

_____

NAME _____

The Real Black Power

EXERCISE [*Article on Page 166*]

FOR UNDERSTANDING

1.   What information concerning Mayor Stokes in the article is about his personal life?

_____

_____

_____

What information is about his public life?

_____

_____

_____

2.   The article ends with a statement that Stokes is expected "to excise [cut out] the civic decay that has retarded Cleveland's progress." What facts about the abilities of Mayor Stokes already presented in the article would lead to that conclusion?

_____

_____

_____

_____

3.   Cite at least six words or phrases that slant the article in order to make readers sympathetic to Mayor Stokes.

a. _____   b. _____

359

NAME _____

The Real Black Power

c. _____   d. _____

e. _____   f. _____

FOR DISCUSSION

1.   How important to such issues as the control of violence, job opportunities, and other current problems is the election of Negroes to such important political positions as mayor, congress-

man, and so on? _____

_____

_____

_____

2.   Do you view the attainments of black people in politics, entertainment, education, and so forth as individual success, tokenism, or group progress?

Field	My Attitude	Reason
_____	_____	_____
_____	_____	_____
_____	_____	_____
_____	_____	_____
_____	_____	_____
_____	_____	_____
_____	_____	_____

NAME _____

The Real Black Power

FOR WRITING

1.   Assume that you are an editor of *Time,* the magazine in which this article appeared, and that you have the opportunity to tell the writer to change or add to his work. Write a memo to the author telling him what you think ought to be added to or removed from the biographical portion of the article about Mayor Stokes. Provide reasons for each suggestion.

Add	Remove	Change
_____	_____	_____
_____	_____	_____
_____	_____	_____
_____	_____	_____

2.   Write a sketch of a person who achieved something you, or he, thought he could not attain. Tell enough about the person to explain how he accomplished what he did.

Person: _____

His achievement: _____

_____

Why I did not think he could do it: _____

_____

How he accomplished it: _____

_____

_____

361

NAME _____

The Real Black Power

ESSAY

NAME _____

from *Fidel Castro Speaks*

EXERCISE [*Article on Page 168*]

FOR UNDERSTANDING

1. The 1959 speech excerpt is almost entirely a series of questions. Why are there no answers to these questions?

_____

_____

2. Many of the words in the 1965 excerpts are the same ones used by other Communist speakers. List at least three of them.

a. _____

b. _____

c. _____

Why do these words not appear in the 1959 speech?

_____

_____

FOR DISCUSSION

1. There are many appealing phrases and ideas in the 1965 speech excerpts: "fighting for a higher type of society," "more just and perfect," people will no longer be sacrificed for money, they will be among the first in the world to achieve these idealistic objectives. Discuss the appeal of what Castro seems to be offering.

NAME _____

from *Fidel Castro Speaks*

_____

_____

2. Studying history, it seems impossible that whole countries could have been fooled by their leaders. Hitler said he was doing one thing when in actuality he was doing another; Castro won support by insisting he was leading his people to freedom from an oppressive regime, whereas, actually he was leading them toward Communism. How can you explain that whole nations could have followed such men? Do you feel that any such dangers exist in this country; that is, that leaders are gaining a following for goals that are not in the best interest of the country?

Explanation: _____

_____

_____

_____

Present dangers: _____

_____

_____

_____

3. The materials you just read are translations of Castro's words. Would you rather read such speeches or read about them? How do you feel about reading interpretations of such speeches? Discuss the difference between a speech and a report of it.

Speeches: _____

_____

Reports of speeches: _____

364

NAME _____

from *Fidel Castro Speaks*

Interpretations of speeches: _____

A Speech

A Report
of a Speech

4. What does it take to be a political success? Discuss the candidate's personal qualities, the extent of professional management, the ability to take a stand on an issue; the necessity to work with varied groups, and so forth.

Definition of a political success: _____

Qualities required: (List.) _____

365

NAME _____

from *Fidel Castro Speaks*

FOR WRITING

1.   Some people believe it is all right <u>not</u> to make your objective known if by openly stating it you could <u>not</u> reach it. Write a theme agreeing or disagreeing with this viewpoint.

Agree _____   Disagree _____   Reasons: (List.) _____

_____

_____

_____

Circumstances under which my ideas might differ:

_____

_____

_____

2.   Both Castro and Mayor Stokes (subject of the previous article) are lawyers, as are many people in high governmental office. Write a theme explaining the kind of preparation (personal and educational) you believe people seeking high elective office should have.

Specific offices: _____

Preparation	Reason for Choice
_____	_____
_____	_____
_____	_____
_____	_____
_____	_____

NAME _____

The Wonderful Dog Suit

EXERCISE [*Story on Page 171*]

FOR UNDERSTANDING

1. Lester is so good in his imitation of a dog that at the end of the story he is mistaken for one. Does he actually *become* a dog? What information earlier in the story shows how capable Lester is of accomplishing what he sets out to do?

a. _____

b. _____

c. _____

d. _____

2. What characteristics are evident in the two families Lester is with?

First Family   Second Family

_____   _____

_____   _____

_____   _____

_____   _____

_____   _____

_____   _____

_____   _____

367

NAME _____

The Wonderful Dog Suit

FOR DISCUSSION

1.   If you have read much fantasy or science fiction, discuss its appeal for you. Why does this type of story attract such large numbers of readers?

My interest in fantasy literature: _____

_____

Reasons for other people's interest: _____

_____

_____

2.   Under what circumstances could someone be "too successful"?

_____

_____

3.   Do you think Lester got what he deserved? Something he didn't deserve? Support your viewpoint.

Deserved   Not Deserved

_____   _____

_____   _____

_____   _____

FOR WRITING

1.   The last paragraph is Mr. Hall's way of bringing this fantasy to a conclusion. Write another ending, either omitting the last

NAME _____

The Wonderful Dog Suit

paragraph or making the last paragraph the beginning of your own new ending.

2.   Pretend that you are a newspaper reporter who has interviewed Lester's mother. Write the story you would submit to your editor.

Description of mother: _____

_____

_____

Questions asked: (List.) _____

_____

_____

_____

_____

ESSAY

_____

_____

_____

_____

_____

_____

_____

NAME _____

The Wonderful Dog Suit

NAME _____

A Bachelor at 16

EXERCISE [*Article on Page 173*]

FOR UNDERSTANDING

1.   List the facts that are stated in order to keep Mr. Zagier from sounding like someone who studies constantly, or who in some other way is "peculiar." _____

_____

_____

2.   What kind of information about Don Zagier do you believe

has been omitted from this article? _____

_____

_____

_____

FOR DISCUSSION

1.   Would you be as impressed with a student of the same age whose degrees were in the humanities or social sciences? Would such a person be as likely to be noted in a national news story? Would you be impressed with someone who started a successful

business at a very early age? _____

_____

_____

_____

NAME _____

A Bachelor at 16

2. Discuss your attitude toward the information that Mr. Zagier's school grades were not always high.

Importance of grades: _____

_____

_____

What grades show: _____

_____

_____

FOR WRITING

1. As someone who has already been in school for a number of years, write a letter to a younger friend or relative telling him what he needs to do in order to succeed in school.

Letter to: _____

Definition of success in school: _____

_____

How to achieve it: _____

_____

_____

_____

2. If you would like to meet Don Zagier, write an imaginary letter to him suggesting such a meeting and giving reasons for your desire to get together. If you would not like to meet Don Zagier, write a letter declining such an invitation.

NAME _____

A Bachelor at 16

Reasons for meeting: _____

_____

_____

_____

Reasons for not meeting: _____

_____

_____

_____

ESSAY

_____

_____

_____

_____

_____

_____

_____

_____

_____

_____

_____

_____

NAME _____

A Bachelor at 16

NAME _____

from *Pygmalion*

EXERCISE [*Play on Page 175*]

FOR UNDERSTANDING

1. What words or stage directions lead you to believe that this play was not written by an American?

(Page: _____) _____

(Page: _____) _____

(Page: _____) _____

(Page: _____) _____

2. How does having Nepommuck present at the party allow Shaw to strengthen the possibility that Professor Higgins may

win his bet? _____

_____

_____

3. What device does Shaw use to keep you in suspense about Eliza's ability to win the bet for Higgins?

_____

_____

_____

4. What does Eliza say that could give herself away?

a. _____

b. _____

375

NAME _____

from *Pygmalion*

FOR DISCUSSION

1.   How important do you think a person's speech is for his success?

Very _____   Partly, or sometimes _____

Not at all _____

Reasons: _____

_____

_____

_____

2.   Discuss the possibility that by changing Eliza Doolittle, as he did, Professor Higgins could do more harm than good.

_____

_____

3.   Were you really hoping that someone would discover who Nepommuck or Eliza really were?

Yes _____   No _____

Reasons for choice: (List.) _____

_____

_____

4.   In Britain, as in the United States and other countries, there are many regional differences in speech because of word choice. For example, "a bag," "a sack," and "a poke" all mean the same thing, but are used in different sections of the country. Note some words special to your own region.

376

NAME _____

from *Pygmalion*

_____   _____

_____   _____

_____   _____

_____   _____

Does special usage seem detrimental to people who move from one part of the country to another?

_____

_____

5. Do differences in pronunciation or dialect cause you to look upon other people in an unfavorable manner?

Yes _____   No _____   Sometimes _____

Reasons: _____

_____

_____

FOR WRITING

1. Sometimes people who speak differently are called "affected" or "uncouth." If you know anyone who speaks differently, that is, with an accent or a dialect, write a paper telling him why he should or should not change his manner of speaking.

Should change _____   Should not change _____

Reasons for choice: _____

_____

377

NAME _____

from *Pygmalion*

_____

_____

2.   Many expressions of speech are common to certain age or interest groups, and are unfamiliar to people outside that group. Write a paper explaining such expressions that you know to a parent, teacher, or other person who would not understand them.

Person writing for: _____

Words or expressions to explain: _____

_____

_____

_____

Should the person learn these? _____

_____

3.   Sometimes it is not only speech, but dress, food preferences, behavior, and so on that makes a person uncomfortable in an unfamiliar group. Write a theme telling an outsider what he would need to know about one of these things in order to be comfortable in your own group of friends.

Subject: _____

How it differs: _____

_____

What stranger should know: _____

_____

_____

_____

378

NAME _____

from *The Pearl*

EXERCISE [*Story on Page 181*]

FOR UNDERSTANDING

1.   The canoe Kino uses is important in this passage. List at least seven things Steinbeck, the author, tells about the canoe.

a. _____   e. _____

b. _____   f. _____

c. _____   g. _____

d. _____

2.   What evidence is there showing that Kino is good at his work?

(Page: ____) _____

(Page: ____) _____

(Page: ____) _____

3.   How does Juana help her husband in his work?

(Page: ____) _____

(Page: ____) _____

4.   Note at least two customs of the people you learned from reading this chapter.

a. (Page: ____) _____

b. (Page: ____) _____

5.   What words or phrases indicate that this is a place in which life usually proceeds smoothly on the surface?

379

NAME _____

from *The Pearl*

_____

_____

_____

What indicates that there may be agitation or unrest beneath the surface?

_____

_____

_____

6. From what you have read in this chapter, what do you think Kino will do with the pearl? Cite passages in this chapter to support your view.

_____

_____

_____

FOR DISCUSSION

1. It is possible that a goal that seems very good may prove to be, when it is reached, either bad or, at least, not desirable. Discuss the reasons for a change of view. Give specific situations as examples.

What makes a result change in value: _____

_____

_____

380

NAME _____

from *The Pearl*

Possible examples: _____

_____

_____

_____

2.   There are some people who would say that Kino and his people are "uncivilized," and should be shown more modern ways. Discuss what makes a man "civilized." What are your feelings about changing a man's way of live?

Definition of civilized: _____

_____

People who differ should _____ should not _____ be

changed because: _____

_____

_____

_____

FOR WRITING

1.   Write a description of a place familiar to you. Choose only a small area and include as many details as possible.

The place: _____

What it looks like: _____

_____

_____

381

NAME _____

from *The Pearl*

Its "atmosphere": _____

_____

_____

_____

_____

2.   Describe in detail how to do something you can do well. Choose something that can be done in a short time, and do not attempt anything as complex as trying to explain how to play football.

What I can do well: _____

Equipment needed: _____

_____

_____

How it is done: _____

_____

_____

_____

3.   Describe a special personal goal you have and tell what you are doing to achieve it.

My goal: _____

Why it is special: _____

_____

NAME _____

from *The Pearl*

How I hope to achieve it: _____

_____

_____

4.   In this chapter Steinbeck explains how a pearl is formed. Write a theme explaining how some other natural object grows.

The object: _____

Its growth pattern: _____

_____

_____

_____

ESSAY

_____

_____

_____

_____

_____

_____

_____

_____

_____

_____

383

NAME _____

from *The Pearl*

NAME _____

Existence

EXERCISE [*Poem on Page 186*]

FOR UNDERSTANDING

1. Summarize the main idea of this poem.

_____

_____

2. How do the words chosen for lines 1, 3, 5, and 7 support the feeling or attitude that is the main idea of the poem?

_____

_____

FOR DISCUSSION

1. Discuss what good it does, if any, to work out your anger, disappointment, or frustration by talking about it, by writing about it, by drawing to express it, or by using the arts as an outlet.

2. Would any other title be suitable for this poem?

Yes _____ No _____ If yes, what? _____

3. What does the author of this poem believe success is? Does it coincide with any of your own beliefs?

Saavedra's idea of success: _____

_____

_____

My own ideas of success: _____

385

NAME _____

Existence

FOR WRITING

1. Can you think of two different lines to conclude the poem? If you can, explain why you made the choice.

New lines: _____

_____

Reason for choice: _____

_____

_____

_____

2. Describe a situation in which you have felt great dissatisfaction. Then tell what you did, or could do, to get out of it.

The situation: _____

Reason for my dissatisfaction: _____

_____

How I got out of it: _____

_____

_____

Result of getting out of it: _____

_____

_____

_____

NAME _____

from *Don Quixote of*
La Mancha

EXERCISE [*Story on Page 187*]

FOR UNDERSTANDING

1.   List at least 12 pieces of advice Don Quixote gives Sancho about his personal behavior.

a. _____   g. _____

b. _____   h. _____

c. _____   i. _____

d. _____   j. _____

e. _____   k. _____

f. _____   l. _____

List at least three pieces of advice Don Quixote gives Sancho about his appearance.

    a. _____

    b. _____

    c. _____

List at least three pieces of advice Don Quixote gives Sancho about how to rule.

    a. _____

    b. _____

    c. _____

2.   Neither Don Quixote nor Sancho Panza are portrayed in a serious manner; Cervantes always manages to make one or the

NAME _____

from *Don Quixote of*
La Mancha

other appear foolish in some way. Which two passages are obviously meant to be humorous?

a. _____

b. _____

3. When Don Quixote tells Sancho not to use too many proverbs, Sancho answers with proverbs. Point out three of them.

a. _____

b. _____

c. _____

FOR DISCUSSION

1. Which piece of Don Quixote's advice do you believe is the
best or most useful you could receive? Which the least useful?

Least   Reason

_____   _____

_____   _____

Best   Reason

_____   _____

_____   _____

2. Don Quixote is often thought of as an old fool. On the basis
of what you have read here, discuss that evaluation of him.

Definition of a fool: _____

_____

388

NAME _____

from *Don Quixote of*
La Mancha

Ways in which he does or does not fit description: _____

_____

_____

My evaluation of Don Quixote: _____

_____

_____

3.   What kind of advice do you personally feel you are most in need of? Who do you think best qualified to give you that advice? (The person you select may be someone you do not know or have no chance of meeting.) What kind of advice do you feel you get too much of?

Advice needed: _____

From whom: _____

What is not needed: _____

Why not needed: _____

_____

4.   Sancho is about to undertake the rule of an "island" when he receives this advice. What advice would you give to people about to begin a job such as president of a club you know, about to lead a community group, or about to take a local, public elective office?

Position   Advice

_____   _____

                                          _____

                                          _____

389

NAME _____

from *Don Quixote of*
La Mancha

_____   _____

    _____

    _____

_____   _____

    _____

    _____

FOR WRITING

1.   Select one piece of Don Quixote's advice you would like to have someone pay attention to. The person could be someone you know or someone you have heard about but have never met. Write a theme explaining why you made this choice.

Advice to: _____

The advice: _____

Reasons for choice: (List.) _____

_____

_____

2.   Some of Don Quixote's advice might be valid today, and some is obviously outdated. Choose what is outdated and modernize it.

Outdated   Modernized Version

_____   _____

_____   _____

NAME _____

from *Don Quixote of
La Mancha*

_____   _____

_____   _____

3.   Choose someone you know and something you would like to have him succeed in. Then write him advice on how to attain that goal.

Person: _____

I would like him to succeed in: _____

Advice: _____

_____

_____

_____

4.   Think of something you wanted to accomplish but did not. Try to analyze why you were unsuccessful.

My goal: _____

What was required to reach it: _____

_____

_____

_____

Why I did not reach it: _____

_____

_____

_____

NAME _____

from *Don Quixote of*
La Mancha

SUGGESTED ACTIVITY

Compare the advice Don Quixote gives Sancho with the advice Polonius gives Laertes in *Hamlet,* Act I Scene 3.

NAME _____

Feiffer cartoon

EXERCISE [*Cartoon on Page 192*]

FOR UNDERSTANDING

1. What is a cliche? _____

_____

Which of the boy's statements are cliches? _____

_____

2. How does the father's changing expression reflect what the

son is reading? _____

_____

_____

3. What is the meaning of the father's line, "I think that's

almost it"? _____

_____

_____

FOR DISCUSSION

1. The boy's composition supposedly is based on what he believes. Do you believe the same things? Do you differ in any way?

      Boy's Beliefs   My Beliefs

_____   _____

393

NAME _____

Feiffer cartoon

_____   _____

_____   _____

_____   _____

_____   _____

2. The father says he and the mother will read the boy's paper before the theme is turned in. How much do you think a parent (or other person) ought to contribute to a student's assigned themes? To other kinds of homework? If something big is at stake, such as passing a course or winning a prize, would your opinion differ?

Extent of another's contributions: _____

_____

Effect of special circumstances: _____

_____

_____

_____

FOR WRITING

1. . The boy in the cartoon is writing on how he believes a person should act in order to advance himself, though his theme has a more general title. Write a theme titled "What I Believe." (It will help if you choose a more specific area, such as how to advance yourself, or about your religious beliefs.

My beliefs about: _____

Note them here: (List.) _____

394

NAME _____

Feiffer cartoon

_____

_____

_____

2.   Have two people write (or dictate to you) themes on the same subject. Compare them. Or, choose one person whose ideas are similar to yours and another whose ideas you know differ from yours, and have them write on the same subject; then compare them.

ESSAY

_____

_____

_____

_____

_____

_____

_____

_____

_____

_____

_____

NAME _____

James Brown Sells His Soul

NAME _____

James Brown Sells His Soul

EXERCISE [*Article on Page 197*]

FOR UNDERSTANDING

1. What is the meaning of the title of this essay?

_____

What play on words does it depend on?

_____

2. List at least seven examples of material evidence of James
Brown's success as chronicled in the article.

a. _____   e. _____

b. _____   f. _____

c. _____   g. _____

d. _____

3. List at least four evidences of success *not* based on material
goods that the article suggests.

a. _____   c. _____

b. _____   d. _____

4. List at least four points of information in the article that
are flattering to James Brown.

a. _____   c. _____

b. _____   d. _____

List at least two points of information that are unflattering to
James Brown.

NAME _____

James Brown Sells His Soul

a. _____

b. _____

Is the author of this article trying to persuade you to form an opinion for or against Brown, or is he trying to be objective and reportorial?

Opinion for _____   Opinion against _____

Objective _____

Reason for choice: _____

_____

_____

FOR DISCUSSION

1.   If you or any of your friends are James Brown fans, how do you, personally, account for his popularity?

_____

_____

_____

2.   Do you think popular entertainers should take part in public affairs or should they try to do nothing more than entertain?

Entertain Only   Take Part

_____   _____

_____   _____

_____   _____

398

NAME _____

James Brown Sells His Soul

_____   _____

3.   Does a person who reaches the top in his chosen career owe anything to people who have helped him achieve his position? Does he "owe something" to some people but not to others?

Owe _____   Does not owe _____

Reasons for choice: _____

_____

_____

FOR WRITING

1.   Write a theme explaining the popularity of someone you know. The person does not need to be anyone widely known or in the public eye.

The person: _____

Evidence of his popularity: _____

_____

_____

Source or reason for the popularity: _____

_____

_____

_____

2.   Tell about a concert, play, or art exhibit you visited recently. Consider and write about how it affected you, rather than about the place itself or what you saw.

NAME _____

James Brown Sells His Soul

The event: _____

The time and place: _____

My impressions: _____

_____

_____

_____

NAME _____

Nehru Speaks
to Mourning Millions

EXERCISE [*Speech on Page* 204]

FOR UNDERSTANDING

1.   Nehru spoke of Gandhi as a "light." What does the word mean when used this way?

_____

2.   List at least four things that Nehru indicates the people should have learned from Gandhi.

a.   _____   c.   _____

b.   _____   d.   _____

3.   For what reason other than paying tribute to the fallen leader does Nehru use this radio message?

_____

4.   Both Gandhi and Nehru were Hindus. Name at least two Hindu customs the speech refers to.

a.   _____

b.   _____

FOR DISCUSSION

1.   What forces must motivate a person to devote his entire life, as Gandhi did, to an ideal which could bring no personal or material gain?

_____

_____

401

NAME _____

Nehru Speaks
to Mourning Millions

2. How effective do you believe nonviolence is in attaining social justice? Think in terms of cases you actually know of, as well as those that are possible.

Cases when it has worked: _____

_____

Cases when it has not worked: _____

_____

My opinion of nonviolence: _____

_____

_____

_____

FOR WRITING

1. Few people decide on one principal goal while young, and devote their entire life to achieving it. However, it is possible at any age to select a goal that seems worth pursuing for the rest of one's life. Choose such a goal and explain your choice.

The goal: _____

Why chosen: _____

_____

_____

Hopes for achievement: _____

_____

NAME _____

*Nehru Speaks
to Mourning Millions*

Result of achievement: _____

_____

_____

2.   Choose a person who has had a strong influence on you and has caused you to change (for better or for worse) in some way. It may be a parent, teacher, friend, employer, and so on. Write a theme on the subject.

The change: _____

Person influencing me: _____

How he exerted influence: _____

_____

_____

Result of change: _____

_____

_____

_____

_____

NAME _____

*Nehru Speaks
to Mourning Millions*

ESSAY

NAME _____

from *I Have a Dream*

EXERCISE *[Speech on Page* 207]

FOR UNDERSTANDING

1.   On the basis of the topics Dr. King mentions, summarize

the dream he had.   _____

_____

_____

2.   How does the song "My country, 'tis of thee . . ." summarize

Dr. King's beliefs?   _____

_____

3.   "Let freedom ring" is the second often-repeated phrase in
this portion of Dr. King's speech. Each location mentioned is a
high geographic spot in the United States. Why are the heights
chosen?

_____

What particular significance can you attach to at least three of
the eight places specifically mentioned?

Location	Significance
Hilltops of New Hampshire:	_____
Mountains of New York:	_____
Alleghenies of Pennsylvania:	_____
Rockies of Colorado:	_____
Peaks of California:	_____

405

NAME _____

from *I Have a Dream*

Stone Mountain of Georgia: _____

Lookout Mountain of Tennessee: _____

Hill and molehill of Mississippi: _____

FOR DISCUSSION

1. What nonpersonal "dream" do you have; that is, of something not for yourself, but for people you either know about or

for a group you belong to? _____

_____

_____

2. Assess the success of Dr. King's dream in the years since he

made this speech. _____

_____

_____

3. Discuss the possibilities for success of large public meetings (such as the one at which this speech was made) in achieving its goals? Compare it to the possibilities for success of individuals working separately or in their own ways.

Large meetings: _____

_____

_____

Individual works: _____

_____

NAME _____

from *I Have a Dream*

FOR WRITING

1.   Do you disagree with or not believe in anything in this speech? If so, tell what it is and why you disagree with or do not believe in it.

Disagree with: _____

Do not believe in: _____

Reasons for choice: _____

_____

_____

2.   State some of your principal goals and explain them.

Goals   Reasons for Choice

_____   _____

_____   _____

_____   _____

_____   _____

407

NAME _____

from *I Have a Dream*

ESSAY

Appendixes

Biographical Notes

MARTIN ABRAMSON   (b. 0000) is a graduate of the Columbia University School of Journalism and has been writing for newspapers and magazines for more than 20 years. He was a correspondent during World War II, and wrote for television. He is the author of *The Real Al Jolson,* coauthor of *A Child of Miracles,* and with Barney Ross wrote the boxer's autobiography *No Man Stands Alone.*

ARNOLD ARNOLD   (b. 1921) came to the United States from his native Germany in the 1930s, and attended art schools and college here. He did designs for advertising agencies and publishers, and now has his own design company. A noted designer of children's play and learning materials, he also writes on the subject of children's play.

RUSSELL BAKER   (b. 1925) has been writing his "Observer" column for *The New York Times* since 1962. He holds a degree from Johns Hopkins University, and worked on the *Baltimore Sun* before joining the Washington Bureau of the *Times.* He is also the author of the books *An American in Washington, No Cause for Panic,* and *All Things Considered.*

MORRIS BISHOP   (b. 1893) received his Ph.D. from Cornell University, and was Professor of Romance Languages there. He is the author of 17 books, a translator and editor of note, and a contributor to many magazines, especially *The New Yorker* and *Horizon.* Although widely known for his light verse, he is also a well-known scholar who has been awarded five honorary doctorate degrees.

FIDEL CASTRO   (b. 1927) became a strongman-ruler of Cuba in 1959. Educated as a lawyer at Havana University, he began active opposition to the Cuban dictator Batista on July 26, 1953 and was soon caught and sentenced to jail. He went into exile after being given amnesty three years later, but returned to land in Cuba with a small force and eventually to overthrow Batista.

411

Appendixes

Castro was awarded a Lenin Peace Prize in 1961, was named Hero of the Soviet Union in 1963, and became First Secretary of the Communist Party of Cuba in 1963.

MIGUEL DE CERVANTES SAAVEDRA   (1547 to 1616) wrote a variety of verse and stories, but his lasting fame rests on the single novel, *Don Quixote.* He had an adventurous youth as member of a cardinal's household in Italy, he fought in the Battle of Lepanto (1571), he was captured by Turkish pirates and held prisoner in Algiers until ransomed, and finally returned to Spain where he held minor government jobs and wrote his masterpiece.

CHIEF BUFFALO CHILD LONG LANCE   (d. 1932) is a chief of the Blood Band of Blackfoot Indians. He was appointed to West Point by President Wilson and was a hero of World War I. The book *Long Lance,* from which the excerpt in this volume was taken, was published in 1928. Chief Buffalo Child Long Lance had never written for publication before.

ROBERT CRICHTON   (b. 1925) was born in Albuquerque, New Mexico. He is a former magazine editor, but now is a full-time writer. He received a B.A. from Harvard. He is the author of *The Rascal and the Road* and of two best-sellers: *The Great Imposter* and *The Secret of Santa Vittoria.*

ROALD DAHL   (b. 1916) has been a free-lance writer since the end of World War II. He was born in South Wales and now lives in England with his wife, the American actress and Academy Award winner Patricia Neal. He has written seven children's books, several books of short stories, and the scripts for James Bond movies. Twice he has been honored by the Mystery Writers of America. His stories often appear in *Playboy, Esquire, Saturday Evening Post, Atlantic Monthly, Harper's,* and so on.

MELVILLE DALTON   (b. 0000) was educated at Ball State Teachers College, and received a Ph.D. in Sociology and Industrial Relations from the University of Chicago. He teaches at the University of California in Los Angeles and acts as consultant to both labor unions and management groups.

WILLIAM S. GILBERT   (1836 to 1911) is best known for his
412

Biographical Notes

words to the music Arthur Sullivan wrote for light operas including *H.M.S. Pinafore, The Mikado, The Pirates of Penzance* and others. Although he was a lawyer, Gilbert is best known for his verse, including two volumes of nonsense poetry, and his satiric songs about snobs and sentimentalists.

OROON K. GHOSH (b. 1917) has written and translated many tales of his native India. He serves his country, presently in London, as an economist and financial expert, and has published books in both fields.

MAX GUNTHER (b. 1927) is a graduate of Princeton University. He worked for *Business Week* and *Time,* but is now a freelance writer whose work often appears in the *Saturday Evening Post, True, Argosy, The Reader's Digest,* and *The New York Times.* He is coauthor of *Split-Level Trap* and the author of *Weekenders.*

DONALD HALL (b. 1928) is Professor of English at the University of Michigan, writer of poetry, fiction, and nonfiction, and in much demand as a speaker. He has written three books of poetry and three books of prose, has edited seven books, has written plays, and has published in most of the leading periodicals. From 1953 to 1962 he was poetry editor of *Paris Review.*

LANGSTON HUGHES (1902 to 1967) emerged as an important literary force in what was called the Harlem Renaissance in the 1920s. Although he was born in Joplin, Missouri, he is best known as a long-time resident of New York, which supplied material for many of his articles and poems. He wrote approximately 30 volumes, including two autobiographies, edited many works (especially collections by Negro authors), and wrote 20 plays.

ALBERT IDELL (1901 to 1958) was a professional wrestler, public accountant, caterer, rancher, and finally a successful businessman whose two loves were travelling and writing. He wrote mystery stories, nine novels (including *Centennial Summer* and *The Corner Stone*), and made a scholarly translation from which an excerpt appears in this book.

MARTIN LUTHER KING, Jr. (1929 to 1968) received the Nobel

413

Appendixes

Peace Prize in 1964. He was educated at Morehouse College, Grozer Theological Seminary, and the University of Pennsylvania. He received a Ph.D. from Boston University and a D.D. from Chicago Theological Seminary. He remained co—pastor of a church in his native Atlanta while president of the Southern Christian Leadership Conference and during his civil rights activities. He was the author of four books: *Stride Toward Freedom, Strength to Love, Why We Can't Wait,* and *Where Do We Go from Here: Chaos or Community?*

ANN LANDERS   (b. 1918) has been writing her advice column since 1955. It is one of the most widely syndicated columns in the world, and in order to handle the more than 30,000 letters that she receives each month, she needs 11 assistants. She was born in Sioux City, Iowa and attended Morningside College there, but she now lives in Chicago.

CHRISTOPHER MARLOWE   (1564 to 1593) wrote some of the most intense and penetrating poetic drama in the English language. He was educated at Cambridge, and achieved great fame with his plays *Tamburlaine, The Jew of Malta,* and *The Tragical History of Dr. Faustus* before being killed in a tavern brawl.

W. SOMERSET MAUGHAM   (1874 to 1965) received a medical degree, but never practiced medicine. Instead, he became a writer and a success with his first novel, *Of Human Bondage.* Although Maugham was born in Paris, he was a British subject and a member of the British Secret Service during World War I, and he did special work for the British Ministry of Information during World War II. He travelled widely and wrote about the many people he met, in the form of fiction. He was honored in the United States and Britain for his prolific work: innumerable books, stories, edited collections, essays, and plays.

SIR THOMAS MORE   (1478 to 1535) was a lawyer, a member of Parliament, and, finally, Lord Chancellor of England under Henry VIII. Because he was unwilling to support the king's break with the Church in Rome, More was beheaded. In 1935 he was elevated to Sainthood in the Catholic church. *Utopia,* his best known work, was written in Latin in 1516.

Biographical Notes

MARIANNE MOORE   (b. 1887) began publishing her poetry in 1915. In 1951 her *Collected Poems* won the Pulitzer Prize, the National Book Award, and the Bollingen Prize. She was born in St. Louis, was graduated from Bryn Mawr College, and has long lived in New York City, where she is known as an animal lover and a baseball fan.

OGDEN NASH   (b. 1902) attended Harvard and worked in the editorial and publicity departments of publishing companies. He has written and edited many books of verse, wrote the lyrics for the show "One Touch of Venus" and for the television program "Art Carney Meets Peter and the Wolf." He is a member of the National Institute of Arts and Letters.

JAWAHARLAL NEHRU   (1889 to 1964) was educated as a lawyer at Cambridge University in England, then returned to his native India and became a protege and closest collaborator of Gandhi in the Indian struggle for self-rule and the nonviolent movement. As India's first Prime Minister, he led his country to neutrality and democratic socialism. He is also the author of several books.

SIR WALTER RALEIGH   (1552 to 1618) is probably best known for his friendship with Queen Elizabeth I, but he was an explorer, soldier, sailor, statesman, poet, and author of a *History of the World,* which was written while he was a prisoner in the Tower of London. He was sentenced to prison by King James I and was released after 13 years to search for gold in the New World, but was arrested again when the expedition failed.

SUSAN RAVEN   (b. 0000) is English and was educated at Cambridge University. She has been a journalist since 1956 and spent seven years on the staff of the *London Sunday Times Colour Magazine* before joining the regular staff of *The Times.* Her first book, on the Romans in North Africa, was published in 1969.

ROBERT REINHOLD   (b. 1942) is a graduate of Johns Hopkins University, where he studied science, and he attended the Columbia School of Journalism. He has written articles for an encyclopedia, was editor-in-chief of his university newspaper, and worked in various jobs on *The New York Times* before join-

Appendixes

ing the news staff of that paper. He specializes in scientific writing.

I. A. RICHARDS   (b. 1893) was born and educated in England, but was Professor of English at Harvard for 20 years, and is now working at the Language Research Institute in Massachusetts. He became known as a semanticist and has been an influential literary critic. He has written plays, has won awards for his poetry, and was elected as a member of the National Institute of Arts and Letters.

EDWIN ARLINGTON ROBINSON   (1869 to 1935) received his start as a poet while a student at Harvard, and had his first success at the turn of the century. From 1905 to 1910 he held a minor government position in New York City, which was given to him because of President Theodore Roosevelt's interest in his work. He wrote three long poems based on the legends of King Arthur, but is best known for his poems about a variety of characters, most of whom lived with illusion and fantasy.

MIKE ROYKO   (b. 1932) has always lived and worked in his native Chicago. He is now a columnist for the *Chicago Daily News,* and is the author of two books, *Up Against It* and *I May Be Wrong But I Doubt It.*

GUADALUPE DE SAAVEDRA   (b. 1936) is the son of Mexican migratory workers. He decided to become a writer after winning second prize in a sixth-grade essay contest. He started to study for the priesthood, held various jobs, was in the Marine Corps, but finally became a writer. After several personal tragedies, he joined the Watts Writer's Workshop (in Los Angeles) in 1966.

WILLIAM SAROYAN   (b. 1908) often celebrates his native California in his many stories. His first success was a book of stories, *The Daring Young Man on the Flying Trapeze,* published in 1934. His novels include *The Human Comedy* and *My Name is Aram;* he has published many collections of short stories, and since 1939 has written at least eight plays, including *The Time of Your Life,* which won the N.Y. Drama Critics' Circle Award and the Pulitzer Prize.

Biographical Notes

GEORGE BERNARD SHAW (1856 to 1950) was an ingenious and witty intellectual critic of his time. He was born in Dublin and lived primarily in Ireland and England. He was a London newspaper critic of music and drama, but is best known as a playwright whose situations were artificial but whose characters were mouthpieces for his social and literary theories. Among his most well-known plays are *Androcles and the Lion, Man and Superman, The Devil's Disciple, Major Barbara, Mrs. Warren's Profession,* and *Pygmalion.*

PERCY BYSSHE SHELLEY (1792 to 1822) was expelled from his studies at Oxford University for writing a pamphlet about atheism. He had great faith in the progress and perfectability of man, and he celebrated these ideas in his romantic and lyric poems. He also wrote the lyrical drama *Prometheus Unbound.*

WALTER STARKIE (b. 1894) is a literary historian, long-time Fellow of Trinity College and director of the Irish National Theater (Abbey). He has taught and lectured on Romance languages in the United States and Europe, has written 11 books, and was awarded the Order of the British Empire for his work in Spain on behalf of the British government. He now lives in Los Angeles, California.

JOHN STEINBECK (b. 1902) was awarded the Nobel Prize for Literature in 1962. He attended Stanford University in his native California and held many odd jobs before becoming a full-time writer. His long list of books include *Of Mice and Men* (also, the play), *The Red Pony, The Grapes of Wrath* (which won the 1939 Pulitzer Prize), *The Pearl* (and the narrative of the motion picture based on it), *The Log from the Sea of Cortez, East of Eden,* and *Travels with Charlie.* His works have been translated into at least 33 languages.

L. B. TAYLOR, JR. (b. 0000) is a native of Daytona Beach, Florida and a graduate of Florida State University. He is an aerospace writer-editor at John F. Kennedy Space Center and a freelance writer whose work has appeared in *Reader's Digest, Parade,* and *Popular Science.* He has dived with Kip Wagner at the wreckage sites of the treasure hunters on the Florida coast.

Appendixes

MARK TWAIN [Samuel Langhorne Clemens] (1835 to 1910) had less than 10 years of schooling, but became one of America's most famous writers. He held many jobs, including that of steamboat pilot on the Mississippi, was a Confederate soldier for a few weeks, and went to Nevada and California as a prospector and journalist. He published sketches and books based on his travels, lectured in the United States and Europe, and is best known for *The Innocents Abroad, The Adventures of Tom Sawyer, The Prince and the Pauper,* and the book considered to be his masterpiece, *The Adventures of Huckleberry Finn.*

HELEN WELLS (b. 0000) was born in Georgia and was graduated from George Washington University. She has been society editor of the *Miami Herald* since 1953.

LEONARD WIBBERLEY (b. 1915) attended schools in Ireland and England. Except for the years during World War II, he has always worked in publishing or journalism. Since 1952 he has had several books published each year, under his own name and under various pseudonyms.

MEL ZIEGLER (b. 1945) earned a B.A. from Pennsylvania State University, where he was an editor of the college newspaper, and an M.A. from Columbia University. He has worked on newspapers in California and has written for magazines in New York. He now writes for *Tropic* magazine in Miami.

MIKHAIL ZOSCHENKO (1895 to 1958) was a Czarist officer during World War I, joined the Red army in 1917, and is now known as the chief Russian humorist of the Revolutionary period. His best works are short stories written in a breezy, colloquial style. The Party became suspicious of him about 1930; he seemed to "go back into line," but in 1946 the government attacked him again, and he fell into disgrace. After expulsion from the Writers' Union in that year, his name disappeared from magazines and textbooks on the history of modern literature inside the Soviet Union. He wrote again briefly after Stalin's death and before his own soon afterwards. His stories are collected in eight books, but he also wrote plays and an autobiography.

Using Films

As a statement in a nonprint media, films have a growing influence on thought, manners, customs, attitudes, and certainly on the development of personal values. Thus, a film may be used in the same way as the material in this book.

A film may be viewed in many ways: by concentrating on the acting, the movie-making techniques, the script, the setting, the music—or by just getting the "feel" of it. The criterion used in making the following selected list was the relevancy of each to a concept of success.

There are many film distributors and no special claim is made for the three listed here as sources. In fact, the same film is often available from several distributors. Many distributors maintain offices in various parts of the country in order to facilitate shipments. The eastern offices of the three sources in the following list are:

Audio Film Center
34 MacQueston Parkway South
Mt. Vernon, N.Y. 10550

Brandon Films
200 West 57th Street
New York, N.Y. 10019

Contemporary Films, Inc.
267 West 25th Street
New York, N.Y. 10001

This list is necessarily a partial one, for every month many new films are released for rental. Also, anyone examining a film catalog can readily add to the list by exercising his own judgment about the meaning of success and how it may be illustrated.

419

Appendixes

SHORT FILMS

TITLE	DESCRIPTION	TIME	SOURCE
THE ADVENTURES OF *	color; animation	10 min	Brandon

Shows the life of * as a child and as an adult overcome by dullness until awakened by a child who makes him see the world anew. Music by Benny Carter and Lionel Hampton.

TITLE	DESCRIPTION	TIME	SOURCE
THE DAISY	color; animation	6 min	Brandon

A daisy refuses to yield to destruction despite an arsenal of weapons. Bulgaria; 1965.

TITLE	DESCRIPTION	TIME	SOURCE
DAY OF THE PAINTER	color	14 min	Brandon

Spoof of how a modern work of art is created. 1960.

TITLE	DESCRIPTION	TIME	SOURCE
HAPPY ANNIVERSARY	black and white	12 min	Audio

A husband's hilariously frustrated attempts to reach home in time for an anniversary dinner. France; 1963.

TITLE	DESCRIPTION	TIME	SOURCE
L'OISEAU (THE BIRD)	color; animation	9 min	Contemporary

A clockwork bird becomes bored in his gilded cage, falls asleep, and dreams of liberty in a world of other birds. France; 1966.

TITLE	DESCRIPTION	TIME	SOURCE
AN OSCAR FOR SIGNOR ROSSI	color; animation	12 min	Audio

Comedy of an amateur photographer who accidentally wins a film festival award. Italy.

Using Films

THE PUSHER   black and white   17 min   Brandon

Satirical biography of a man who pushes himself upward through life
until he is replaced by the newly aggressive brother he had pushed
aside since childhood. Yugoslavia; 1962.

SONG OF THE   color; puppet   18 min   Audio
PRAIRIE   animation

A standard western complete with villain and chase sequence; the hero
gets the girl. Czechoslovakia; 1951.

THE STRING BEAN   color; black   17 min   Contemporary
(LE HARICOT)   and white

Story of an old woman who cultivates a potted string bean plant in order
to give meaning to her drab existence. France; 1964.

THE TOP   color; animation   8 min   Contemporary

Bright new look at the attainment of material success; 1965.

UNICORN IN THE   color; animation   9 min   Contemporary
GARDEN

Film of the well-known story by Thurber incorporating the familiar
"battle of the sexes;" U.S.A.; 1962.

THE VIOLINIST   color; animation   7 min   Brandon

A spoof on the saying that an artist must suffer to create great music.
Voices by Carl Reiner; U.S.A.; 1959.

THE WALL   color; animation   4 min   Contemporary

A devastating and cynical comment on those who use other people.
Yugoslavia; 1965.

421

Appendixes

FULL LENGTH FILMS

| ALL THE KING'S MEN | 109 min | Contemporary; Audio |

Broderick Crawford, Joanne Dru, John Ireland, Mercedes McCambridge. Prize-winning film chronicling the rise of a farm boy to governor. From the novel. 1949.

| BORN YESTERDAY | 103 min | Audio |

Judy Holliday, William Holden, Broderick Crawford. A beautiful but dumb blond is transformed into an intelligent young woman by a political writer hired by her junk-dealer boyfriend. From the play. 1950.

| THE BRAVE BULLS | 108 min | Audio |

Mel Ferrer, Anthony Quinn, Miroslava. After being gored by a bull and experiencing great fear, a famous matador overcomes his fear of death and of life; 1951.

| THE CHAMPION | 99 min | Audio |

Kirk Douglas, Arthur Kennedy, Marilyn Maxwell, Ruth Roman. A fighter relentlessly driving his way to the top wrecks other people without regard for them; 1949.

| THE CORN IS GREEN | 114 min | Audio |

Bette Davis, John Dall, Joan Lorring, Mildred Dunnock, Nigel Bruce. A teacher in a Welsh mining town devotes herself to training a promising student, but the boy almost loses his chance to escape being a miner; 1945.

| CITIZEN KANE | 119 min | Audio |

Orson Welles, Joseph Cotten, Everett Sloane, Agnes Moorehead, Dorothy Comingore. Chronicles the rise of a farm boy whose desire for power and possession takes him to the head of a giant newspaper chain; 1940.

Using Films

HIGH NOON   87 min

Gary Cooper, Grace Kelly, Thomas Mitchell, Katy Jurado, Lloyd Bridges. Prize-winning film of a small town sheriff's devotion to duty; 1952.

I LIKE MONEY

Peter Sellers, Nadia Gray. Comedy of a simple schoolteacher who finds a quick way of becoming a ruthless millionaire. 1962.

THE INSPECTOR   102 min   Audio
GENERAL

Danny Kaye, Walter Slezak, Elsa Lancaster. From Gogol's short story. An illiterate carnival worker is mistaken for the Czar's Inspector General, and he plays the role to the hilt; 1949.

THE LAST ANGRY   100 min   Audio
MAN

Paul Muni, David Wayne, Betsy Palmer, Luther Adler. The last of an "old breed" of doctors passes his principles on to younger people; 1959.

THE LAST   121 min   Contemporary
HURRAH

Spencer Tracy, Jeffrey Hunter, Donald Crisp, Dianne Foster, Pat O'Brien. Story of a northern mayor's diminishing control over his party machinery. From the novel; 1958.

LILIES OF THE   97 min   Audio
FIELD

Sidney Poitier, Lilia Skala, Lisa Mann. A young itinerant finds himself helping a group of nuns build their church; 1963.

THE MOUSE THAT   85 min   Audio
ROARED

Peter Sellers, Jean Seberg. Sellers appears in a triple role in this comedy about how the world's smallest army wages war on the United States — and wins; 1959.

Appendixes

OUR MAN IN   112 min   Contemporary
HAVANA

Alex Guinness, Noel Coward, Burl Ives, Ernie Kovacs, Ralph Richard-
son, Maureen O'Hara. Comedy of a vacuum cleaner salesman who
dupes the British secret service. 1960.

THE PRISONER   91 min   Audio

Alec Guinness, Jack Hawkins. A battle of strong wills and brilliant
minds between an interrogator and a cardinal, and former resistance
leader, charged with treason; 1956.

A RAISIN IN THE   128 min   Contemporary
SUN

Sidney Poitier, Claudia McNeil, Ruby Dee. From the play. A closely knit
family begins to fulfill its aspirations. 1961.

TREASURE OF   102 min   Audio
SIERRA MADRE

Humphrey Bogart, Walter Huston, Tim Holt, Bruce Bennett. Three
down-and-out Americans follow their greed on a gold hunt to Mexico,
but are disintegrated by their distrust of each other. 1948.

Index

A Bachelor at 16, 173
ABRAMSON, MARTIN, 31
Academy of Sciences Chooses 50 Members and 10 Associates, 144
"*. . . and of course you all remember . . . ,*" (cartoon), 117
Anne Marie and Steven, 43
ARNOLD, ARNOLD, 195
A Sure Way to Succeed, 113
As U.S. Speeds up the Space Race, 66

Bernal Diaz Chronicles, The, from, 70
BISHOP, MORRIS, 51
Boy with Balloon, (cartoon), 30
Businessman Who Can't Fail, (cartoon), 18

Cleopatra's Joke on Marc Anthony: 40 B.C., 116
CRICHTON, ROBERT, 24

DAHL, ROALD, 121
DALTON, MELVILLE, 140
Davy, the Dicer, 120
Day the Mouse Roared, The, (advertisement), 180
DE CERVANTES SAAVEDRA, MIGUEL, 187
DE SAAVEDRA, GUADALUPE, 186
Don Quixote of LaMancha, from, 187
Dream Variation, 196

Ego Trap, The, 104
Eight Days to Foreclosure and Family Strikes Silver, 39
18-Foot Leap Wins Frog-Jumping Title, 111
Elopement, (cartoon), 112
Existence, 186
Explainers, The, from, 192

FEIFFER, JULES, 192
Fidel Castro Speaks, from, 168
First Great Woman Scientist . . . And Much More, The, 146
$500,000 Thaws Peggy's Icy Outlook, 10

GERBERG, MORT, (cartoonist), 43
GHOSH, OROON, (trans.), 48
Ghost Horse, The, 96
GILBERT, WILLIAM S., 22
Grandmother, 62, Runs 100 Miles for a T-Shirt, 94
Guernica, 165
Guernica (studies for), 163, 164
GUNTHER, MAX, 4

HALL, DONALD, 174
Harry, 11
Historic Voices from Space, 67
HOFF, SID, (cartoonist), 57
How a U.S. Astronaut "Walked" from Hawaii to Florida in 20 Minutes, 68
How Plays Shape Up on the Great White Way, 63
How Savitri Retrieved Her Husband from Death, 45
How We Feel about Our Money, 4
HUGHES, LANGSTON, 196

"I Have a Dream," from, 207
I May, I Might, I Must, 209
IDELL, ALBERT, (trans.), 70
If at First You Don't Succeed . . . Skip It, 41
Iliad of Homer, The, from, 159

James Brown Sells His Soul, 197
Japanese Child Eats Nails After Viewing Stunt on TV, 143

425

Kindly Unhitch That Star,
    Buddy, 93
KING, MARTIN LUTHER, JR.,
    86, 207

LANDERS, ANN, 194
LONG LANCE, CHIEF BUFFALO
    CHILD, 96

Making Park Promise Good, 85
Man on Globe, (cartoon), 40
MARLOWE, CHRISTOPHER, 114
MAUGHAM, W. SOMERSET, 133
MAULDIN, BILL, 206
Men Who Manage, from, 140
Midrash, The, from, 113
MILLER, WARREN, (cartoonist), 30
Miniver Cheevy, 118
MONAS, SIDNEY, (trans.), 58
Montage of Success Stories, 9
Moon Cooperated for Greene's
    Party, 381
MOORE, MARIANNE, 209
MORDILLO, (cartoonist), 112
MORE, SIR THOMAS, 120
"Most successful suit sale . . .,"
    (cartoon), 57
Mouse That Roared, The, from, 80

NASH, OGDEN, 93
Nehru, Jawaharlal, 204
Nehru Speaks to Mourning
    Millions, 204
Notorious Jumping Frog of
    Calaveras County, The, 105
Nymph's Reply to the Shepherd,
    The, 115

"Odd thing about assassins, The,"
    (cartoon), 206
Overshoe, The, 58
Ozymandias, 50
Ozymandias Revisited, 51

Passionate Shepherd to His Love,
    The, 114
Peanuts Cartoon, 92
Pearl, The, from, 181

Personal Rolls-Royce, The,
    (advertisement), 36
PICASSO, PABLO, 163, 165
Pieces of Eight, from, 75
Plutarch, from, 116
Policeman in Brooklyn Lassoes
    Zebra in Bay, 95
Pygmalion, from, 175

RALEIGH, SIR WALTER, 115
RAVEN, SUSAN, 146
Real Black Power, The, 166
REINHOLD, ROBERT, 61
Richard Cory, 49
RICHARDS, I. A. (trans.), 159
Richest of the American Rich, 34
ROBINSON, EDWIN ARLINGTON,
    49, 118
Robot at M.I.T. Builds Towers Out
    of Toy Blocks, 61
Rodrigues, Charles, (cartoonist), 117
ROYKO, MIKE, 41
Ruler of the Queen's Navee, The, 22

SAROYAN, WILLIAM, 11
SCHECTER, LEONARD, 104
SCHULZ, CHARLES,
    (cartoonist), 92
SEMPE, JEAN-JACQUES,
    (cartoonist), 18
SHAFER, BURR, (cartoonist), 84
SHAW, GEORGE BERNARD, 175
SHELLEY, PERCY BYSSHE, 50
SIGMUND, PAUL E., (trans.), 168
STARKIE, WALTER, (trans.), 187
STEINBECK, JOHN, 181
Strength in 77 Seconds,
    (advertisement), 35
Success is Something You Can't
    Leave a Son, (advertisement),
    191
Success Rushed Up to Pat Palmer,
    31

Tactical Missiles: A Report from
    General Dynamics, 64
TAYLOR, L. B., JR., 75
Tongue Twisters, 195
TWAIN, MARK, 105

Index 427

Underwater Bonanza, from, 75

Verger, The, 133

Way Up to Heaven, The, 121
Wonderful Dog Suit, The, 171
Wrath of Achilles, The, from, 159
WAGNER, KIP, 75
WELLS, HELEN, 38
When She Lost Pounds . . . , 194

Where Do We Go From Here: Chaos or Community?, from, 86
Where We Are Going, from, 86
WIBBERLEY, LEONARD, 80

You Got to Be a Hero, 24

ZIEGLER, MEL, 197
ZOSHCHENKO, MIKHAIL, 58